PRAISE FOR
THERE'LL BE PEACE WHEN YOU ARE DONE

"*Supernatural* has often been seen as a quote-unquote little show in the larger scheme of premium networks and a peak TV era that has expanded to more than 500 scripted shows alone. In a way, that descriptor is perfect for this show, though, because like its characters, it has been quietly doing important work—unknowingly to many, but life-changing for the special group whose lives have been directly touched by Dean and Sam Winchester and their friends. Using stories from those who worked on the show, including Jensen Ackles, Jared Padalecki, and Davy Perez, as well as those extended #SPNFamily members who have been touched and inspired by the show, *There'll Be Peace When You Are Done* poignantly and poetically captures the bigger legacy of *Supernatural*. For 40-odd minutes a week, it was about hunting, but, as this volume of unabashedly honest and open essays proves, for 24/7, 365 it has been about saving people."

—Danielle Turchiano, senior features editor at *Variety*

"*Supernatural* represents an extraordinarily special moment in pop culture history and in this moving, thoughtful and beautifully curated collection, Lynn Zubernis has perfectly captured being a part of such a wild—and inimitable—ride. The Winchesters' greatest accomplishment (outside of saving the world a few times) is definitely the #SPNFamily, and the beating heart of the fandom and the good works it has inspired live in the pages of *There'll Be Peace When You Are Done*. I can't think of a better tribute or testament to a show that has meant so much to so many than this wonderful book."

—Courtney Summers, *New York Times* bestselling author of *Sadie*

THERE'LL BE PEACE
WHEN YOU ARE DONE

ALSO BY LYNN S. ZUBERNIS

Family Don't End with Blood
Cast and Fans on How Supernatural Has Changed Lives

Supernatural Psychology: Roads Less Traveled

Fan Phenomena: Supernatural

Fangasm: Supernatural Fangirls

Fandom at the Crossroads
Celebration, Shame, and Fan/Producer Relationships

Fan Culture: Theory/Practice

Case Conceptualization and Effective Interventions for Counselors

THERE'LL BE PEACE WHEN YOU ARE DONE

ACTORS AND FANS CELEBRATE
THE LEGACY OF *SUPERNATURAL*

Edited by Lynn S. Zubernis

An Imprint of BenBella Books, Inc.
Dallas, TX

Smart Pop is an imprint of BenBella Books, Inc.
10440 N. Central Expressway
Suite 800
Dallas, TX 75231
www.benbellabooks.com
Send feedback to feedback@benbellabooks.com

BenBella is a federally registered trademark.

Printed in the United States of America
10 9 8 7 6 5 4 3 2 1

Library of Congress Cataloging-in-Publication Data is available upon request.
ISBN 9781950665327 (print)
ISBN 9781950665488 (ebook)

Editing by Joe Rhatigan and Leah Wilson
Copyediting by Karen Levy
Proofreading by Jenny Bridges and James Fraleigh
Text design and composition by Aaron Edmiston
Cover design by Sarah Avinger
Cover illustration by Christine Griffin
Printed by Lake Book Manufacturing

Distributed to the trade by Two Rivers Distribution, an Ingram brand
www.tworiversdistribution.com

Special discounts for bulk sales are available.
Please contact bulkorders@benbellabooks.com.

To the SPNFamily

CONTENTS

INTRODUCTION

SPNFamily Forever

LYNN S. ZUBERNIS

There are certain experiences that happen in our lives that we will never forget. Psychology even has a term for the memory created by this kind of experience: a *flashbulb memory*. When something happens that shakes our world especially profoundly, the brain encodes that moment differently, and more vividly, than it does our everyday memories.

Back in the day, a flashbulb was a cube that sat on top of your camera and went off to illuminate a scene you were capturing with a photo, freezing it in time forever (it's now just a light on your smartphone). Our brain, when it records a flashbulb memory, does something similar: it freezes the important, often upsetting moment in time forever. The sights, the sounds, the smells, and the emotions of that moment are all preserved deeply. The memory doesn't fade like other memories, or lose its emotional intensity. Instead, it remains as clear and vivid as if it happened yesterday. We remember the clothes we were wearing, or exactly what we were doing or thinking, or who we were talking to. We remember our initial shock and then the moment when our emotions kicked in.

Most often, flashbulb memories are about world-changing events like September 11 or shocking personal news. But they can also be things you wouldn't expect. Sometimes, something is so important to you that the news of its impending loss hits hard enough to freeze the moment in time. I think that's what happened to me on Friday afternoon, March 22, 2019, the moment I found out that *Supernatural* would end after its fifteenth season. That might seem like an odd thing to be preserved forever as a flashbulb memory, and it's certainly not equivalent to world-changing events, but that's not how our brains work. When something is important, it's important. And for many people, myself included, this little television show that lasted for fifteen seasons is personally and emotionally important.

After the news of the show's cancellation, many fans were confronted with family, friends, and coworkers who didn't quite understand that importance—who said something like, "It's a television show, for godsakes, get a grip!" Probably those loved ones meant well, but when you're grieving, that lack of understanding is like salt in the wound. There's a psychological term for that too, in fact—*disenfranchised grief*. It can be hard to find room to express our feelings when others don't recognize the loss as valid. How do you explain that, for most of us, *Supernatural* is a lot more than a television show? How do you describe the ways in which *Supernatural* has changed all of our lives and gotten us through some of our toughest times? It's difficult for anyone outside the SPNFamily to understand what we've gained from this show and how hard that is to lose.

The actors and fans who wrote chapters in this book share their own emotional stories of what *Supernatural* has given to each of them. They take us along on their personal journey with *Supernatural*, writing about how it changed their lives and what they'll take with them as the show comes to an end. The importance of the show differs for everyone. For some fans, the connection they feel to one or more of *Supernatural's* vividly written and acted fictional characters has been pivotal. We all figure out who we are by "trying on" aspects of others' identities, a process psychologists know as *attribute substitution*. Maybe you admire your great-aunt Sally's gregarious way of interacting with literally everyone she encounters on the street, but find that quickly exhausts you and decide to model your socialization routine after great-uncle Joe's introversion. Maybe you aspire to be a leader like Dean Winchester or to "always keep fighting" like Sam Winchester, and that keeps you going when things are tough. Maybe you see some aspect of yourself in Castiel and decide that if he can keep on trying, you can too. Maybe it's Charlie, or Jody, or Donna, or Billie. Maybe it's Bobby, or Kevin, or Ketch. The point is, we don't know who we want to be until we see who others are—we don't even know what it's *possible* for us to be until we see it in someone else.

This idea, which is part and parcel of human development, is the reason why so many people talk about the need for representation in media. Books and films and television shows are where we find the exemplars of how to be human. As a species, we evolved to write our own life stories by absorbing the narratives of our culture and then making them our own. When we connect strongly with a particular story and that story's characters, it impacts the course of our own development.

When *Supernatural* premiered fifteen years ago, the media landscape was different. There were fewer female characters for fans to emulate and fewer characters of any gender who were not straight and cis and white and young and able. Fans turned to fan fiction, creating stories where women also saved the day and characters weren't all straight and men did talk about their feelings, and all sorts of stereotypes about race and gender and disability were turned on their heads. Fans longed to see the diversity that existed in their own communities and penned it themselves as they waited for media to catch up.

Over the years, *Supernatural* (along with television as a whole) evolved. Female characters who weren't just on-screen to be love interests or eye candy, who had backstories and personalities and emotional arcs and relationships, began to appear—and talk to each other about something other than men! There were women who were both strong and vulnerable, successful and not, emotional and rational. The male characters on the show evolved too, with more characters breaking the straight white male stereotype. Even the Winchesters' mantra of "no chick flick moments" evolved, as the brothers learned to be vulnerable and talk to each other. Both male and female characters on the show were gay and lesbian and bisexual and persons of color and deaf and blind and using a wheelchair and older than their twenties and all sorts of other things that we humans are. The show itself began to reflect its own fandom a little more accurately, and in the diversity of those characters, many fans found that elusive thing called representation in their favorite show.

But it's not just identifying with favorite characters and witnessing their journeys over the years that has had an impact on fans. The relationships we've made as a result of the show and the fandom have changed our lives in countless ways. The value of making the world better is an integral part of our community, and the charity work fans have taken on together, and with members of *Supernatural*'s cast, has also been life affirming for many people. People have found friends, confidants, travel partners, even soul mates. The ways in which *Supernatural* and the SPNFamily have changed all of our lives are the reason saying goodbye is so hard. But sharing our memories and hanging on to all the good we've taken from this show eases the loss a little. That's why we all wrote this book.

In each chapter, people share their perspectives on what made this little show on the CW so special. Cast members who played memorable characters on the show write about how their character or the fandom's response to that character impacted their lives and their own development. The characters they played are diverse in many ways: they are straight and queer, women and men of color from different backgrounds, hearing and deaf. The actors are equally diverse, and they write with emotion about their own struggles with representation and identity and self-acceptance, within the intense atmosphere of a business that makes those struggles even more difficult. Like the cast, the fans whose stories appear here are also diverse, and they write with great candor about how the characters on the show have inspired and changed them, and how the community of fans has done the same. Reading their stories, it's clear why *Supernatural* ending is something significant and memorable.

As we all come to terms with the show's ending, fortunately there's a lot of support within the fandom community, in all its various forms. In fact, that's one of the reasons that *Supernatural* is so important in the first place: the supportive community that was inspired by the show. Yes, fans are incredibly sad to be losing Sam and Dean and Castiel, the fictional characters who mean so much to us. But the show is more than that. *Supernatural* created a family over these past fifteen years. It's where many fans found their best friends, their support systems, the people who finally "got" them. It's where they felt like they belonged, maybe for the first time. The SPNFamily is the community that allowed them to get sober, change careers, leave a cult, keep living.

Perhaps unlike shows that run for a year or two, *Supernatural*, after fifteen years, has changed not only its fans. *Supernatural* and the SPNFamily have also changed the lives of its cast and crew and writers in equally powerful ways. They too have channeled the support of the SPNFamily to take risks, be vulnerable, and reach out and connect with fans in life-changing ways. The reciprocal relationship that has developed over fifteen years between the *Supernatural* actors and fans is unique and powerful. After interacting with fans both face to face and online for all these years, the actors have forged connections that allow them an unprecedented level of understanding and a degree of genuineness that is rare in the media industry. It's not just the fandom who considers us all "SPNFamily."

The respect and understanding that the actors have for the fandom was obvious on that day in March when the news of the show's cancellation broke. It says something about Jared, Jensen, and Misha that they insisted on telling their longtime crew first. Many had been with the show since the beginning and were truly family at that point. Then they recorded a video message for the fans so we could find out directly from them that the fifteenth season would be the last. Although all three were clearly struggling with their own emotions, they wanted their fans to hear it from them. It's the same reason they wrote chapters for this book and for *Family Don't End with Blood* in their own words: because this is too important to telegraph through someone else.

Jensen and Jared tear up at their last Comic-Con panel.

It's a testament to *Supernatural*'s impact that the news of its ending brought such an outpouring of love and gratitude, on every social media platform and on every mainstream media outlet. Actors who guested even once or twice on the show sent messages of respect and support. The British Columbia film industry itself weighed in, with gratitude for what the show has done for that industry and for Vancouver, including huge financial benefits and providing a talented and hardworking crew with jobs they could not only count on for fifteen years, but also love. Journalists from many of the publications that cover fan-favorite shows shared their own stories of how *Supernatural* impacted them, from inspiring them to enter the field to the joy of being able to write about something they're passionate about.

Fans reached out to other fans, offering a safe place to talk, a shoulder to cry on, whatever support might help. Then, as fans embarked on the inevitable process of grieving, they began to look back with gratitude on what *Supernatural* has given each of us and to celebrate the legacy of this remarkable show. The hashtag #SPNGaveMe sprang up on Twitter, and fans started sharing all those life-changing things that *Supernatural* brought to their lives. I saw many posts from fans of other shows who had never even seen an episode of *Supernatural*, but who, as fellow fans, understood the depth of this loss and reached out with sympathy. As always, fandom took care of each other.

I did my own looking back and my own assessment of what #SPNGaveMe and why this show is so special to me. I've published six books about the show that trace my own journey with *Supernatural* and how the show and the characters have inspired me and changed me, but I don't think I'll ever have enough words to truly describe the profound impact that this little television series has had on my life. I found my voice—and myself—through this show and this fandom. I changed jobs, started writing, learned to speak up. I've realized that I can be criticized and not fall apart, and that criticism can be helpful once I'm able to listen. I've gone from being the painfully shy girl who failed geography class because I never spoke, to doing panels at San Diego Comic-Con and actually enjoying it. I had never traveled by myself until *Supernatural*, and now I have navigated airports and train stations and bus stations all over the world—because seeing my SPNFamily was totally worth the anxiety attacks! The show's mantra of "Always Keep Fighting" has been my mantra too, and it's kept me moving forward just like Sam and Dean and Cas.

I am, quite literally, a different person than I was in 2005 when this little show began.

When I first heard the show was ending, I was volunteering at the Project Fancare table at Lexington Comic-Con, surrounded by copies of *Family Don't End with Blood* and fellow fans. Project Fancare is a nonprofit that gives fans a forum to talk openly about how television and film and books and all sorts of fandoms have helped them get through tough times, and why that's a good thing. I had just finished talking to a woman who stopped by to tell me what *Family Don't End with Blood* and *Supernatural* have meant to her.

As the woman walked away, my friend Kim leaned over and said softly in my ear, "You need to take a break. Take your phone and go to the bathroom and watch the video that Jensen just posted."

That's all she said, but instantly I knew. I knew from the genuine emotion in her voice, and the concern for me that I could hear there. I knew because there's a part of me that had been waiting for that news and anticipating it and knew it was coming sooner rather than later. My stomach instantly fell and my brain kicked into survival mode, blocking all my emotions and making me feel oddly calm even though intellectually I knew I wasn't. I can vividly see the table in front of me, the books spread out there, and the woman walking away. She was wearing one of the first Represent "Always Keep Fighting" T-shirts and she had bright red hair and a bag with the protection symbol on it. I can see it like it's a photo frozen in time—as bright as if lit by a flashbulb—and I can hear Kim's voice and her words like she just finished talking, even though it's now many months later.

I stood in the alcove by the bathroom in the giant convention center and pulled out my phone and found the video—and as soon as I saw their faces, before they even started speaking, there was no doubt in my mind. Jared, Jensen, and Misha are extraordinary in how open they have been with their fans, and I could see all the emotion they were struggling to contain before I ever hit play to listen to the message. I am forever grateful that I got to hear it from them.

As *Supernatural* comes to an end, we are all trying to find a way to cope with its loss. Not everyone will understand how people can grieve for a television show or for fictional characters who don't exist or for friends you've never met in person, but the grief is real because the loss is real.

There's research about how we get the same emotional satisfaction from spending an evening with our favorite fictional characters as we do from having dinner with family or close friends. Fictional characters play a role in inspiring us and fictional stories are a way of making sense of (and even rewriting) our own life stories. Sam and Dean and Castiel and the other characters we love have been, and always will be, an important part of our real lives. Friendship can transcend the physical realm, and online communities can be amazing sources of support. All of that is real, and all of that is healthy.

There will be many things I'll miss going forward. I'll miss the anticipation that we all shared as we awaited a brand-new episode after days of devouring tidbits of information and video previews and tantalizing speculation about what might happen and how our heroes would deal with it. I'll miss a fandom community so active and vibrant that I could check Twitter at any time of the day or night and find new posts from fandom friends or check Instagram or Tumblr and find new photos and art and videos about my favorite show. I'll miss the sheer immediacy of this SPNFamily and the all-encompassing nature of a fandom that has new content to pore over every single day. I am so very grateful for so many years of that.

This book is a celebration of the show and not a goodbye. What *Supernatural* and the SPNFamily have given us cannot be erased or taken away, even though the show itself is no longer in production. Sam and Dean and Cas and Jody and Donna and Charlie and Bobby and all the other characters we fell in love with will live on, not only in reruns on TNT, but also in the countless ways they've inspired us in our real lives. That decision you made to "always keep fighting," because that's what *Supernatural* taught you, sent your life in a different direction, and you're still here now because of that. Nobody can take that away from you. We are all different people than we were on that day we first saw the Impala roar across our screen. That change is permanent. This show did that.

Some things will change going forward, but not everything. I have no doubt that the SPNFamily will live on. We may not gather together to dissect the latest episode or argue amongst ourselves about which way canon "should" go, but we will have fifteen seasons of rich and nuanced and fascinating adventures to keep watching and keep talking about. As with any fandom, a lot of what my SPNFamily friends and I talk about on a daily basis doesn't even have anything to do with *Supernatural*. We talk about family stresses, job challenges, kid questions, politics, that awesome thing we found at Target—whatever! They are the people I can reach out to for support, no matter what the problem. Fandom friends become forever friends, and the friendship is all the richer for that amazing show that brought us together. Ten years from now a bunch of us will say, hey, let's all watch the pilot, or "The French Mistake," or "All Hell Breaks Loose," or the finale. And no matter where we are in life and who we've gone on to become, we'll all pause and be reminded of all the ways that *Supernatural* changed our lives. Maybe we'll get a little teary and reach for the tissues, and maybe we'll share some hugs as we dab at our eyes, either virtual or in person. Because we'll always have this show in common, and we'll always "get it." Nobody can ever take that away.

Because family really don't end with blood. And those of us who have been part of the SPNFamily, whose lives have been changed for the better by this show, are now a little more able to "carry on."

The Winchesters, and Castiel, and all our favorite characters from *Supernatural* have inspired us with their fifteen-year journey and have earned the rewards they never sought in the fictional universe. It's what we hope for them every time we sing along to Kansas at the top of our lungs—that "there'll be peace when you are done."

#SPNFamilyForever

A FAMILY AFFAIR

JARED PADALECKI

When I think about the legacy of *Supernatural*, I feel like the relationships I've been able to build because of this show are what I'll take with me. I've met a couple of my best friends. I met my wife in season 4 and now we have three kids. There's also the relationship with the SPNFamily. The show and the SPNFamily have grown organically, and it's made this into something that's way beyond what any other television show has done. It's always been a family affair, with us as actors a cog in the wheel, too. We wouldn't exist without the fandom, and they wouldn't exist without the show. So it has felt like a communal thing, almost like how Sam and Dean say to each other, "Hey, good job, good job back at you, okay, let's get to work." It's made our work more important; it's given our work more value.

One of the reasons why *Supernatural* has lasted so long is that the fans forgive us, accept us, and love us. They keep watching even when we falter, and they bolster us back up to where we were. We fight for them; they fight for us. It has always felt like a reciprocal situation.

I don't think any of us who make the show care about awards. This is the accolade: having people who actually care about the story and about each other and who have literally raised millions of dollars for charities over the past fifteen years. There was a point a few years ago when the Powerball got to a couple billion dollars, and Jensen and I both bought lottery tickets. We had a funny conversation in one of our trailers the night of the lottery draw. We were like, "Hey, if you win tonight, are you coming to work tomorrow?" We both looked at each other and said, "Absolutely!" It wasn't for the money. It wasn't for the prestige, the fame, or the awards. It was for our family of fans. I was committed to seeing Sam Winchester's story play out and doing whatever I could to make that happen.

I'm very proud of what we've done and of the story that we got to tell. Sam Winchester has inspired me, just like he's inspired many fans. Sam is a character who thinks about things differently. From the start, Dean was written as the let's-go-in-guns-blazing one, and Sam was the let's-think-about-this character, carrying a lot of the weight of the moral and ethical burden of decision making. Do you drink demon blood and hulk out so you can save people? Is it worth letting one person die if it's going to save twenty people? Sam is thoughtful, whereas I tend to be more impulsive like Dean in some ways. But Sam has changed me and helped me be more thoughtful about those things. I think most of us, like Sam, probably do struggle to forgive ourselves sometimes. But I feel like Sam's actions have been kind and sacrificial and loyal, and I have always wanted him to keep fighting—for his brother, for his family, to save people. I value that about him. The way the Winchesters have faced insurmountable odds inspires me and hopefully others to keep on working as hard as we can.

I feel sad about the show ending, but I *want* to feel sad about it ending. I don't want to feel relieved. I don't want to feel like it's time and I'm relieved to be done with it. I want it to be how I felt about Harry Potter—*you're still alive, J.K., write some more!* Even though it's hard, I want the show to end with me wanting more.

So what is the legacy of this show? It's the relationships. The relationships that fans have made, the relationships the cast and crew have made, and the relationships that we have with the fandom. I'm so grateful for the family that's been built because of the show. There are other shows that are bigger and more famous, but they don't have something like the SPNFamily. They didn't create something extraordinary like that over the last fifteen years. Someone asked me recently what it's going to be like saying goodbye to Sam Winchester. And my honest answer was that I can't say goodbye to him. Sam Winchester will forever be a part of my life. I'll always love Sam, and he'll be a part of me forever. And I hope for the fandom that has spent 327 hours watching our 327 episodes that he will always be a part of them too. That the part of them that felt this way because of *Supernatural* will be a part of them forever.

DREAM A LITTLE DREAM OF ME

AMY HUTTON

FADE IN:
SYDNEY, AUSTRALIA, JANUARY 2006
INTERIOR LOUNGE ROOM:
A young woman sits on her sofa, alone, watching television.

On-screen a scene plays out of a mother and father saying goodnight to a baby called Sam. In the father's arms is a young boy. His name is Dean.

FLASH-FORWARD 14 YEARS
SYDNEY, AUSTRALIA, JANUARY 2020
The same woman sits on her sofa watching television. She's a little older now, and her hair is a whole lot redder. She leans forward, captivated. The children she met in 2006 are now men. The baby called Sam

stands over 6 feet, 4 inches tall. The young boy called Dean is not far behind him. The woman sighs wistfully, every word they speak nestling in a new place in her heart. They have become her constant, her touchstone, her home.

From an outsider's view, it appears not much has changed in those fourteen years. The woman still sits alone, still watching the same TV show. But what is not seen is the throng of people right there beside her. Thousands of voices speaking a language she understands completely. Across Australia, across the globe, sharing in her experience. People who have become friends. People with whom she's traveled the world. People who have given her strength, who have helped her grow, who have helped forge in her a love and acceptance of herself, who have lifted her up and encouraged her to chase her dreams, to be brave, to trust in being the truest version of herself.

As she sits all these years later, unconditionally in love, the light bounces off her face, making her tear-filled eyes glisten. She feels connected in a way she never dreamed existed. Emotional tendrils reach out across the planet, in touch with a thousand other beating hearts.

Okay, okay, it's a bit dramatic, but it's none the less true. Who would have guessed, back on that night in January 2006, that watching a new TV show would eventually help shape my life?

In 2006, I was working in my first big management-style job: a creative manager in charge of a promotions team for television. It was a good job. It was a *great* job. Cool and a lot of fun. But along with the fun came a decent amount of responsibility. I was in charge of creative for the first ever pay-per-view movie service in Australia, and there were a lot of eyeballs watching what I was doing. Looking back on those days, I now understand that part of me was acting out a role. That's not to say I wasn't good at the job (I was) and I loved it and the people I worked with. But it was like I was wearing someone else on my outsides. Someone who didn't quite gel with my insides. Around me, my friends were getting married, having kids, doing *adult* types of things. I wasn't doing any of that, and I felt kind of out of sync. So, I played along as best as I could, being what I thought a grown-up needed to be, trying to look like the right person in the big job, going to the big meetings with the big bosses, complete with smart skirts and sensible tops. But I knew, deep down, I didn't feel like *me*.

I don't know why I decided I needed to be that person—that person who felt they had to change themselves in some way in order to fit in and be accepted. No one ever outwardly told me to do that or gave me that direction. But over the years, I guess I just drifted into it. I guess I simply went along with what I thought everyone else expected me to be.

It wasn't always like that. When I was younger, I was the rebel. I was the kid at school forever in trouble for breaking the uniform rules. The one with the wrong colored tights, wearing the tie and blazer long since banned. The one who dressed in winklepicker shoes to go to the sports carnival, and head-to-toe black. The one wearing crazy eyeliner and earrings as big as her head. I went to pubs when I shouldn't, dated boys in garage bands, wore bright red lipstick and sprayed color in my hair. For a girl who lived by the beach, I definitely stood out, if only for my purposeful lack of a tan. While my peers were enjoying a day in the surf, I was probably scribbling in my school journal or being ridiculously thrilled about tackling an essay assignment on *Macbeth*. I was reading plays for kicks and tinkering with some short story that just popped into my head. I can't remember a time when I wasn't jotting something down in a notebook. I can't remember a time when I didn't love words. It wasn't like I was trying to stand out; I wasn't even trying to be different. I was just being me. At seventeen, somehow, I was being my authentic self without even knowing it.

That seemed to get harder as I got older. I found myself being sucked into the expectations of what we strangely call *the real world* (as if there's any other kind). Without realizing it, I was bending and conforming to become who I thought I was supposed to be, who I thought people wanted me to be. I was so busy trying to make sure I was the right person for the people around me that I forgot who the right person was for *me*.

This makes me sound like Zoolander or something, gazing wide-eyed into a puddle, asking, "Who am I?" But looking back at that time, I don't feel I was like that. I feel like I've always known who I am. I just think that I allowed that sense of self to take a back seat and get muddied by my preconception of others' expectations, and by my own pliancy. My loss of self is all on me, and I'm acutely aware of it.

But all that began to change when I started watching *Supernatural*.

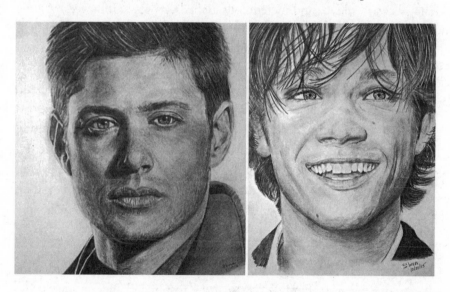

So often media can be a powerful, negative force in how it influences people. As a woman, I'm continually bombarded by messages that don't necessarily ring of positivity for *me*, even if positivity is what they claim to be promoting. All these images and conversations representing every-thing I'm not, and reinforcing the notion that, apparently, I'm doing life wrong. I'm not a wife or mother. I'm not a size 6 with bouncy hair. I'm pretty much none of the things I see as being the media's construct of a woman. So, who am I if I'm not the things the world is forever telling me I should be?

I sometimes find myself thinking about my place as a woman who doesn't follow society's traditional gender-assigned role. Intellectually, I know women have come a long way toward gender equality, and I have reaped the benefits of the courageous women who stood up and fought for a world where the law says I cannot be discriminated against because of my sex. But when the first question out of someone's mouth when they meet me is to ask me if I'm married and have children, it feels like society is still playing catchup.

I'm not going to lie: there've been times when I've struggled with and avoided situations where I knew that I'd be faced with that eternal "Are you married?" conversation that plagues women of a certain age. The awkward silence and incredulous arched eyebrows, followed by some misplaced pity when I say no, is sometimes too exhausting to shoulder. I've definitely turned down invitations, I've definitely been made to feel less than, and sometimes, if I'm feeling particularly wobbly, I've definitely questioned my value as a woman who has chosen a nontraditional path. And boy, does that make me mad at myself! I'm smart and a decent human who's not ashamed of who I am. I am not disappointed in my life. I dig my life—it's full of love, family, friendship, adventure, and independence. My need for that independence, my wanderlust and my urge for freedom, is part of what makes me who I am, and I genuinely like who I am, even if sometimes I still stumble a little bit. It's the life I chose, and it fits my soul, and I shouldn't be made to apologize for that. I mean, screw destiny right in the face, right?

It took me a while to get to that place, where I can quote Dean Winchester and mean it. Finding *Supernatural* inspired change in me slowly; it wasn't an overnight thing. I didn't suddenly dye my hair and get fifty tattoos. But something in the story of those brothers and the family they built up around them stood out to me. Something in their love, their devotion, and their fight for their own identities. Something in the way they lived their lives, their determination to live them as best they could regardless of the circumstances, connected with me on such a deep-down level that it lit a light inside me bright enough to guide me on a journey that would, over the course of more than a decade, totally shift my perspective and alter my entire life.

It's kind of wild to think that a TV show can affect an individual so entirely. Hell, not just affect them, but help them reconnect with not only who they are, but who they want to be and what they want to stand for.

I sometimes wonder what would have happened if I hadn't tuned in to watch *Supernatural* on that fateful Monday night all those years ago. I often wonder who I would have become without the influence of *Supernatural* and this profoundly individual adventure. Would I have eventually found my way around to be the same person I am now? Would I have still been brave enough or passionate enough to completely upend my life, as I decided to do in 2018? Because it was *Supernatural* that inspired that too.

Loving something as much as I love *Supernatural* made me want to talk about it, share my enthusiasm, share my experiences, share my connection.

After penning ridiculously long comments on my friends' blogs that were dedicated to the show, I was encouraged to start my own. So, in April 2010, for *Supernatural*'s 100th episode, I did just that. At first, I simply wrote episode reviews, but it wasn't long before I ventured into fan fiction, then convention reports. Then, at some point along the way, I started writing a book. Suddenly, every spare moment I had, I was writing. I was doing this thing that I'd loved all my life, and yet somehow in the mists of time and obligations, had forgotten all about. It was a revelation, remembering my excitement for words. I found the experience incredibly liberating, and inevitably, incredibly exhausting. As I juggled my day job with its ever-increasing stress levels and responsibility, I was writing all night and all weekend. I was getting up in the wee hours of the morning to ensure I got a jump on the day, making sure the article I was working on was uploaded before I trundled off to my *real* work. During my (rare) lunch breaks, I would polish the fan fiction I'd come up with the night before or read the chapter of my book I'd been working on until 3 a.m. that morning, editing, making notes. Then, as soon as I got home, I'd start writing again. I was existing on a few hours' sleep, and I started to burn myself out in the process. Between work and my passion, I wasn't giving my mind that much-needed downtime. In the end, something had to give, and of course, it had to be the writing. The thing I loved the most, the thing that made me feel the most like me.

I didn't even notice at first that I had completely stopped writing. First the book fell to the wayside, because that was the hardest, then it was the fan fiction, and then the blogging, and eventually it was writing altogether. I didn't even notice, until I looked around and realized all I did was work, think about work, and usually, rant about work. I was no longer doing the thing that gave me so much joy, because I seemed to only have space for the thing that was feeding my mortgage. "Hey," I thought. "That's life." But should it be?

I remember Jared Padalecki saying that he used to live by the mantra "life is short," but now he lives by "life is long." When I heard him say that, something clicked for me, because life is long, if we're lucky, and we should all be endeavoring to do something that's important to us and makes us happy, because we could be doing it for a helluva long time, and we only get one shot.

It took a while for me to get up the courage to make the changes to my life I knew I needed to make. That *Supernatural* inspired me to make. I wanted to do something that made my spirit soar again, I wanted to do something that reflected how I wanted to move forward with my life, something that felt like me, something that made me happy. In my heart, I knew writing was that thing. Whenever I was doing it, I felt such exhilaration, such joy. I wanted so badly to finish the book that I truly had faith in. It had become a dream of mine. I had several failed starts, I'd get back into the discipline, but then I'd have a long, fraying week at work and, boom, I'd stop writing again. I just couldn't seem to muster the consistent creative mental energy for the level of commitment I needed. When it came to that energy, I gave it at the office. Quite literally.

In the end, I knew the only way it was going to happen was if my dream of writing became my priority. If I truly wanted to write, I was just going to have to *write*. So, one day, in the spring of 2018, after floating the idea with my family and a few close friends, I decided to do it. Follow through on that idea that had been percolating, tickling the corners of my brain for a while. Trust in myself, take a deep breath, and go for it. So, I chucked it all in. Sold my apartment, quit my job, moved back into my family home, and decided to concentrate on becoming a writer full time. Sound crazy? Maybe. Sound easy? It absolutely wasn't. It was one of the hardest things I've ever done. It was terrifying and nerve-racking, and most of the time I felt like I was about to throw up in my mouth. Years of associating my self-worth with my career was a tricky thing to put down. I was tossing it all away. Everything I'd worked for. Stability, security, respect, I walked away from all of it. But I knew it was the right move. I knew it in my gut. As frightening as it was, I never had a doubt. This was about being me. This was about reclaiming and starting my life.

I'm pretty sure I would never have gotten to *this* place if it hadn't been for *Supernatural* and all that came with it. If it hadn't been for Sam and Dean and the lessons they taught me—their continual fight for themselves and each other.

One of the many reasons I'm so drawn to Sam and Dean Winchester is because of how they choose to live their lives, and how unapologetic they are about it. They've both fought a long, tough, internal battle to

discover who they are and where they fit in a world where they're not only different, but often invisible. That's something I relate to profoundly. They fight so hard to never lose their sense of self, even when faced with situations that threaten to completely strip away their identity. They never compromise if it's something they truly believe in. They keep moving forward, trusting in themselves, in each other, and in what they value, regardless of what any given day throws at them. No matter what they're faced with, they continue to choose the life they've learned to embrace and love. I feel like their search for peace in their own skins mirrors mine. I feel like we've been on our epic journeys together.

When, during *Supernatural*'s landmark 300th episode in 2019, Dean said that he was good with who he is and good with who Sam is, it was not only a cathartic moment for the characters, but it was also a cathartic moment for me. If I hadn't been bawling my eyes out at the time, I would have fist-pumped the air. It was such an incredibly positive message to come out of that man's mouth, a man who has hated himself for most of the time we've known him. I was so proud of Dean (who I feel an emotional bond with that's sometimes a tad overwhelming), and upon reflection of that moment, I realized I was also so proud of me, because at this point I'm good with who I am too. Owning and, more importantly, liking who you are, and what you stand for, is important in this world, and is a valuable lesson for all of us to take to heart. Be confident in who you are, be proud of what you've achieved, and be comfortable in your skin. This is what Sam and Dean Winchester have taught me, and what I've slowly been able to embrace in my own life over the past fifteen years of watching this show—just like Dean. This is why I will be eternally grateful for the gift that is the Winchesters and *Supernatural*.

As we get older, we're bombarded with messages that tell us to forgo pleasure for duty. We're told to be careful, not to risk our livelihoods or our futures. To keep our dreams realistic. Our individuality can be stymied as we follow society's "rules." We can end up feeling shame or guilt over doing the things we enjoy, because they might be viewed as selfish, or childish, or a waste of time. It's a big reason I kept quiet about my passion for *Supernatural* in the early days, because I knew that people might think it was weird, that I was weird. Apparently, at the time, I still cared about that. Now when people question my devotion to a TV show in a less-than-positive way, I say, "Hey, some people collect stamps." If that's what blows your hair back, who am I to judge? Who is anyone to judge? If you dig it, do it. It took me a long time to understand that. It took me a long time to own my happiness.

A good pal of mine once said to me that though I always seemed happy, now I seem like I'm who I'm supposed to be. It made me laugh. I said, "Yeah, I feel like that too." She asked what had changed. I said, "Well you know what, as buckets of crazy as this might sound to you, it was *Supernatural* and everything that's come along with it." The brothers, the story, the cast, the crew, the fans, the friends, the conventions, the love and acceptance. It was seeing actors release long-desired albums, bloggers become showrunners, and other fans putting their art on the line. It's given me the courage to take risks. Big ones. It's given me the desire to learn, to do good in this world, and to be a better and more accepting person. It's changed my internal and external gaze and expanded my horizons. It's helped redefine who I am. I have a community where I feel wholly represented and uniquely embraced, like a wave of people have my back: the SPNFamily, who always encourage me in absolutely everything I do; the cast, who embolden me; my friends; and, of course, my amazing family, who supported my decision to flip my life 100 percent and are so very proud of me for taking a great big leap of faith. All of this has helped form me into a person that I understand (mostly), and that I've grown to love. It helped me reach for and follow my dream. I'm writing full time, every single day. And that book I was telling you about? Guess what? I finished it.

I'm in the driver's seat of my own life now; I'm no longer riding shotgun.

And to think, it all started with a couple of boys on a TV show.

HOW CAN I HELP YOU SAY GOODBYE?

Disability, Loss, and Grief in the Fandom

VICKIE ANN MCCOY

As I sit and reflect on fifteen years of *Supernatural* and the community it created, the same question echoes over and over: How can I help you say goodbye? I believe that Lynn Zubernis is doing just that by creating this love letter to all who will grieve this loss. I have been given the task of voicing my thoughts regarding what this show has meant to a community of persons with disabilities. And while I would not be so arrogant as to suggest that my single voice speaks for all persons with disabilities, it does represent my experience and that of several others who have found a home in the online community that was constructed around *Supernatural*.

Persons with disabilities have long found comfort and community in online chat rooms, forums, and social media groups. We enjoy the experience of communicating with others around shared passions, without intrusive questions and lingering stares. It is freeing to be anonymous.

It is empowering to be known for our ideas, words, poetry, stories, and artwork instead of for our limitations.

Over the years, my life changed after I sustained a head trauma in a car accident and later received several chronic health diagnoses. There were many losses of function, and a sense of loss of self, as I struggled to accept my new normal. As I am not a digital native, the idea of finding community online evolved slowly over the years as technology changed and provided ever-expanding opportunities to connect with others who experienced challenge and loss. My early interactions were with others who enjoyed entering contests and sweepstakes (or "Sweepers," as we are called), many of whom were/are persons living with disabilities who used their computers (then laptops, then tablets, now phones . . . someday cyborg interfaces?) to connect with the sweeping opportunities and then with each other.

The first time I found out about conventions where we could all meet in person, I was intrigued and terrified . . . as if someone had just broken the fourth wall. The role I played in my secret online life had just been acknowledged and exposed as real, which meant that the relationships were real as well. What an awesome realization that was. That experience led to greater comfort in immersing myself in the online world surrounding *Buffy the Vampire Slayer*, a community that saw me through many difficult years and was my gateway to pop culture fandoms, fan fiction, cosplay, and finding my voice as a woman standing at the intersection of an already complex identity, which now included disability. Combining my personal story with my professional experiences in disability rehabilitation has helped me understand that, in essence, online fandoms save lives and provide a sense of belonging and acceptance to persons who might not otherwise have access to communities of like-minded supportive individuals.

So, with so many fandoms in our reach, why is *Supernatural* different? My inner child is stomping her foot and declaring, "Because it just is!" Yet, I know I need to say more than that. I've been wanting to try to explain it for years, so I offer the following thoughts and observations in an attempt to tie it all together, for myself as much as for you.

What was more empowering than Bobby Singer in a wheelchair, still badass and still himself? He was not a different Bobby, but the same

Bobby we knew and loved, who just used a wheelchair for mobility and struggled to understand the sense of loss associated with his new normal. Some members of the community were concerned that once Bobby was portrayed as a paraplegic, his role as a father figure would lose strength as he struggled with depression and feelings of uselessness. In all fairness, this is somewhat true, yet many of us appreciate that adaptation to disability often comes with negative emotions, initial feelings of anger and uselessness, and fervent wishes to return to a time before the limitations. Quite frankly, *Supernatural* does not sugarcoat the painful aspects of life, so I am appreciative that viewers saw the raw grief that often accompanies loss of function. And while there are plenty of critical voices that question the decision to reestablish Bobby's mobility, I believe that many of us watch *Supernatural* (and other fictional adventures) because we are strengthened by the escape from our permanent limitations, and an immersion into a world where dead is not really dead and loss is not permanent.

As we watched Bobby Singer face his physical limitations, we also watched Dean Winchester struggle for psychological healing after trauma, and we also saw Sam Winchester battle his addiction. *Supernatural* did not avoid the topic of mastering life with a disability. For many of us who are used to the discomfort of watching television and seeing our life "othered" (Hallmark Channel, anyone?), the brutal honesty of *Supernatural* is refreshing. We recognize ourselves in Bobby's anger as he faces obstacles in his determination to remain a hunter. We understand Dean's suffering as he returns to a world that does not honor his heroism or the trauma and sacrifice that has changed him forever. We feel Sam's insatiable craving for the very substance that can destroy him. We see all of this poignantly magnified in an episode where the trio faces a staircase. Sam with his invisible disability is able to take the stairs with ease. Dean, with his somewhat hidden disability, struggles but manages his way to the top. Bobby sits at the bottom in frustrated rage at the impossibility of the task. This scene caused some divide in the online community, sparking debate about "real" disability and "mild" disability. Ultimately, however, it became a source of healing as we all dialogued to understand that differing challenges provide differing experiences, but we all unite over the experiencing of real-life othering that is soothed by the unity of *Supernatural* fandom sameness.

Moving the discussion from characters to actors, the community is strengthened by Jared Padalecki's candid disclosures about his anxiety. As we watched his growing success as an actor, we were also watching him use space in the fandom as a safe environment to be open and honest about his longtime battle with anxiety. When Jared proclaims, "This is who I am," we are all given space and freedom to say, "This is who we are." Of course, we are also free to remain anonymous if we prefer. That is the beautiful intersection between disability and online communities, a place where we can honor our personal comfort levels with self-disclosure. We can begin to type the words, delete them, try again, hit send or delete, or just close the window, letting our words sit in ambiguity in a text box. Like the LGBTQI+ online community, we have learned that when online, coming out is a choice. Those of us with invisible (or at least less obvious) disabilities are familiar with the privilege (burden?) of the self-disclosure process, but for those with visible disabilities, the online experience provides a new opportunity to choose when or whether to share this aspect of our identity.

Though choices differ, when Jared Padalecki speaks about anxiety, it is an easier opening of space to find a way to say, "me too." And if that is not

enough of a gift, he also gives us the opportunity for reciprocity when he welcomes support from the fandom as a source of comfort and empowerment in his journey. The cyclical nature of this relationship changes what it means to be a fan and validates the human existence of those of us on the other side of the screen. We are not watching from afar, but are engaged in an experience that is part of our intersectional identity.

The announcement that *Supernatural* would end with the fifteenth season was not unexpected, yet it created a wave of anticipatory grief that washed over the fandom. Even those of us with progressive disabilities, who have learned to anticipate and roll with the losses, were somehow caught off guard. We may always know that more bad news is around the corner, but until we have to turn that corner, we hold out hope.

My friends, we are at the corner. It is time to find a way to say good-bye to the thrill of new episodes and acknowledge that the road is longer behind us than in front of us. In my humble opinion, I think that those of us who are at the intersection of advancing age and progressing disability might have a few ideas to loan to the community at large. We have learned how to simultaneously say goodbye and hold on tightly.

In my work training the next generation of counselors, I often teach them about stages of life. The students often enjoy discussing the stages of childhood and adolescence, but the mood in the room grows somber as we discuss the final stages of life. The discomfort of discussing endings becomes palpable. Why can't the good stuff go on forever? Why does life have to end? Why must we lose our strength and energy? (And why must *Supernatural* end?) I offer that the joys of life are more intense because we understand that they are not permanent. If I've learned one thing from my obsession with vampire novels and all things supernatural (and yes, that's a lowercase *s*, but it is certainly inclusive of the capital *S* show we are here to discuss), it is that immortality can create bored, restless, self-absorbed creatures who long for our humanity. We, as humans, feel all the feels and embrace the spectrum of emotion because we value the lack of permanence. Thus, my advice for all of us is to focus on the ride itself instead of the ending. It is not generally a good idea to wait in line at an amusement park for hours to ride a four-minute thrill and then spend the ride mourning its brevity. Let's not be that elderly relative who keeps reminding everyone on Christmas Day that it will all be over tomorrow. Let's just throw our hands in the air, tear off the wrapping paper, and enjoy the moment.

There is also a concept from life as a college professor that I want to borrow and use here. In his 1982 book *The Life Cycle Completed*, Erik Erikson labeled our last stage of life "Ego Integrity vs. Despair," meaning that during this time, we look back and contemplate our accomplishments, wondering if we have led a successful life. We try to accept our one and only life cycle as something that had to be. We are looking for our life to have been a meaningful whole. If we cannot find that sense of value for our life, we run the risk of becoming dissatisfied with life and developing a sense of despair that may lead to depression and hopelessness.

I think that many of us with difficult diagnoses and disabilities visit this stage earlier in life, seeking wisdom that will enable us to look back with a sense of closure and completeness, and also help us accept the inevitability of death without as much fear. Perhaps we can view this final stage of our fifteen-year life in the *Supernatural* fandom as a time to look back on the experience as a whole and embrace it as an experience that just had to be. Personally, I have learned that the process of looking back and smiling at the memories is a powerful balm for grief that helps me resolve loss and face endings with a sense of integrity rather than despair. I've learned to find strength in sifting through boxes of photos of loved ones who have died, to find meaning in getting together with old school friends to talk about days when we were young and strong and able-bodied, or to find familiar escape in bingeing seasons of *Buffy the Vampire Slayer* or rereading *The Black Dagger Brotherhood* novels.

So, this is how I suggest we say goodbye to *Supernatural*. Let's go back to the beginning and rewatch it all. Let's continue the conversations and keep the fandom alive. Let's continue to support each other and follow the future endeavors of all who created *Supernatural* for us, and with us. Let's refuse to dwell on endings, but instead embrace this as a new phase of the fandom. No matter how much life changes or how much I hate loss, I find comfort in knowing that I am the same girl who ran on the boardwalk every morning in the predawn haze. I am still a descendent of the Boyd sisters from Opelika, Alabama. I am still twenty-five years into my relationship with the BTVS fandom. And in many ways, I am just beginning a reflective stage where I examine in greater depth my journey with *Supernatural*. I think it will be a journey that ends with integrity and appreciation.

CARRY ON, EILEEN

SHOSHANNAH STERN

American Sign Language is my first language. I use it pretty much all the time. Even when I'm not, the fact that it's my native language is still pretty obvious because of my accent; a lot of people think I'm from Norway. It's oddly specific, I know.

One time, I decided to just go with it. Someone asked, "Are you from Norway?" and I said, "Yeah, sure, I'm Norwegian." Then they started speaking what seemed like fluent Norwegian.

That didn't really work out.

But to be completely forthright, I've never liked talking about my accent. Which is probably because, for a very long time, I never liked having one. I've always been a perfectionist about certain things. I don't like doing things if I don't feel like I'm good at them, and to this day, I still can't express myself as easily when I speak as I can when I write or sign. In fact, during my college years, I stopped speaking completely. I'd speak to my extended family in the privacy of our home or to complete strangers when I was really drunk. And that was about it. But after college, I decided to do this totally, completely crazy thing: become an actor. And what I like about acting is that often, it's about doing things that scare you. So I started speaking again. Even though I was asked almost right away about my accent.

For a while, it went better than I had ever thought possible. During this time, I thought maybe my fear about my accent was unfounded—that it was all in my head. And then one day, while filming a show, I was asked if I could make my accent less strong, or even maybe make it go away completely. I didn't think I had anything to lose by trying, so I did. I didn't know that by trying, I would enter into one of the most intense low points I've ever been at in my life. No matter how

many speech therapists I went to, every time I tried to say "New Jersey" I couldn't isolate the "z" sound that shouldn't even be in that fucking word because, *hello*, there's no "z" in Jersey! I was still saying it wrong.

And then a weird thing happened—my voice actually got worse, to the point where my accent became a monster. It became so big and so ugly that I spent days hating it, and wishing that I didn't have it. I fixated on it. It obscured everything else in my life.

One day I was stuck in traffic because someone got naked and was running around and screaming in the middle of the street. The police tried to calm him down, but he kept beating up as many cars as he possibly could. When he ran by me yelling, I thought to myself, "I bet *he* doesn't have an accent." And then the police tackled him. I like to think he woke up the next day and turned his life around, and he's living his best life now.

But in that moment, I caught myself. The monster I was fighting wasn't my accent. It was *me*. I was giving it all its power. But even as I recognized that, I still couldn't quite understand where all that power was coming from. So I picked up a book, and something jumped off the page at me, and it has stayed with me since. Whenever you hear or see (because believe it or not, sign languages have all kinds of accents too) an accent, it means the person who has it learned your language because they want to communicate with you. They want to reach out to you, and they're willing to put a lot of effort into doing that. That message might be the only reason why I ended up making a grudging sort of peace with my accent—because I (mostly) love people. I'm curious about them. I want to communicate with as many of them as I can. Except when I really, really need my coffee. Coffee first. Then communication. Unless, of course, I need to communicate my need for coffee.

The thing is, my native language is one that not many people outside of my community know. Even inside my community, many, maybe even most, people don't have access to it on a daily basis. That's why I never take any sort of communication for granted. When you use a minority language, you recognize the value of it more. And beyond that, you recognize that it's a part of who you are. For example, ASL is what I like to call a pretty blunt language. In English, there are different definitions for a single word. You can say one thing and mean many things. In ASL, there is a different sign for every definition. There are different signs for "run," depending on whether you're going for a run, if the water is running, or if there's a run in your pantyhose. You always have to say exactly what you mean. Maybe that's why, even when I communicate in English, I don't really know how to *not* say what I mean. It often gets me in trouble. In fact, I know that what I'm about to say *right now* might get me in some.

Eileen died. And that sucks.

Actually, it was devastating. But to accurately explain why, I have to start not at the beginning, but before the beginning, so I can give you a full illustration of where I was in my life when Eileen came to me. I'd just given birth to my daughter, Mayim. It was an equally beautiful and surprising moment. Before her, I'd never been a patient person. I'd always wished that I could be. I'd see other people with their kids, and they'd have this sort of beatific calm, even when their kid was lying on the floor in the middle of the aisle screaming with snot flying out of their nose. I'd think, "Shit. That is never, ever, going to be me." I was the type that would hammer the horn and flip people off in traffic. And I live in Los Angeles. Everywhere you go, it's traffic all day, every day. (It only seems glamorous on the outside. You also think you'll get used to traffic. You don't.) So if you're not blessed with the gift of patience, then you basically flip people off all day, every day.

But after I gave birth, I caught my younger brother talking about me. This was maybe the second time he'd met my daughter. I was going to put Mayim down when I caught him telling our parents, "Wow. Shoshannah is so patient with Mayim." I stopped on the stairs, thinking, what the fuck did he just say? And I realized to my shock that he was right. Somehow, in that short span of time, I had become extremely, even extraordinarily, patient. Just when I let that sink in, my brother added, "Do you think she's . . . okay?"

It was a strange time, even beyond suddenly being bestowed with the patience of a saint, which I, surprisingly, still have. Motherhood, then and now, has been one of the most fulfilling things I've ever done. But that fits into the narrative people expect. So it's a relief that I can say that, and have it be true. What people don't expect, and often don't talk about, is that being a new mother is also an exceedingly vulnerable time. It's a time that requires recalibration. It's as if you've been taken apart, and you now have to put yourself back together again. It allows you to see all the complicated little nuts and bolts that come together to make you who you are. I was prepared for the recalibration of my body, because it had, well, supported an actual life, and because I had a rather complicated birth. But what I hadn't expected was that I would also have to recalibrate my heart and my mind.

I loved Mayim in a way I had never dreamed I could love anything. But that love was accompanied by a sort of guilt I had also never felt before. I felt guilty for loving the same things I loved before she came along . . . for wanting the same things. The message I was getting from the world around me was a mindfuck. People would ask me if I was still going to act, if I was still going to live in LA, if I was still going to teach. (I taught culture and translation at a university for years, right up until I sold the Sundance series I co-created, *This Close*.) And by answering yes to all those questions, it felt as if I were somehow violating a contract I hadn't known I signed. It was as if being a mother meant that all the rest should have changed. That I, as a person, should have changed.

For some of my friends, that did happen. One of my best friends, who I met when we did a television show together, had her son four days after I had Mayim. After she had her son, and then her daughter, she slowly realized she had absolutely no desire to return to acting. Zero. Her life felt full, fuller even, without it. She didn't need any of it anymore. I told her I thought that it was wonderful, and I meant it.

Motherhood is a different journey for everyone. You have to figure out yours as you're traveling it, not before. For some people, it transforms them. For me, it was less of a transformation and more of a ground-breaking. I felt like it had opened up layers to me that I didn't know I had. If anything, I felt like I had become more myself, that there was suddenly more to me than there had been before. Everything I had felt before Mayim, I felt more vitally. Now that I had this new human being depending on me, literally looking up to me, I knew that I wanted—no, I *needed*—to prove to her that her mother could do . . . **it**.

It wasn't anything that could be seen or touched. **It** was a feeling, a want, a need for something that I couldn't yet see. **It** had always been there, before Mayim, but it was Mayim who helped me finally put it into words. Now that she's older (three at the time I'm writing this), she likes to look at pictures that were taken before she was born, from my wedding or from when I was playing soccer as a child. She always looks at them very intently, and then she'll ask, "Where was I?" It's a strange concept to explain to anyone, much less a very small human. At first I tried telling her, "Well, you weren't here yet." But she'd always nod and say, "Yes . . . but then where was I?" And so I ended up telling her, and still tell her . . . the truth. That she was a star in the sky.

But that complex feeling I could so clearly see and feel her struggling with was something I found a strange sort of solidarity with—she wasn't here until . . . she was. And now that she's here, it seems very strange, even ridiculous, that there was a time when she wasn't. It's so obvious and so right that she is here now, that to think that there was a time when she wasn't here seems bizarre, even wrong.

It felt exactly like that.

Here's the thing. Ever since I was old enough to notice, I've known that the world doesn't always see me as I see myself. A nice way to describe that position would be to say that it's humbling, but sometimes there really isn't anything nice about it at all. For me, being creative has always given me somewhere to put **it**. It's not just that I want to do what I do, but I *need* to do it. I've gone years on end, several times in my career, without working—not just because I wasn't booking auditions, but because I couldn't get in the door to be seen in the first place. And sometimes when I did, they were for characters framed by people who live their lives differently than me. Because of that, I was expected to see my life the same way they did—as one less than theirs, focused on and filled with that loss and devoid of something essential. Sometimes I'd get sent characters that were tragic, tormented, even victimized, by what they couldn't hear. I'd think, "Fuck this bullshit."

But later, usually in the middle of the night, I'd think, "Should I feel the way these characters do? Is it possible I'm delusional? Could this be like that time I convinced myself that my accent was no longer an issue? Am I just setting myself up for failure for thinking things can be different?" But every time I really considered that, **it** would surface. And **it** always won.

It meant that instead of waiting for the world to supply me with a space that felt like my own, I would have to create that space, that **it** for myself. Just like Mayim made her own place in this world, after being a star in the sky. So I did. And **it** became *This Close*.

But doing anything means that at first you try to do it, and you're not very good at it. So that's what I did. I tried. I wrote a bunch of things with my writing partner, Josh Feldman, who is also deaf. The first thing we wrote together was about a private investigator who was deaf and lived in San Francisco, close to where I grew up in the Bay Area. I think her first case was about a missing cat. Like I said, not great. In hindsight, I think we were trying to write what we thought people wanted to see and not the story we wanted to tell. Also, to be fair, there were a lot of shows like that on television at the time. We moved on from that one, thankfully, and wrote the first iteration of *This Close*, called *Fridays*. It was about two best friends, Kate, a deaf woman, and Michael, a hearing gay man. It was loosely based on our real-life friendship.

With this idea, we went a little bit further than we previously had. At one point, we had a production company show interest in developing it, but then they pulled out. They said they didn't understand why the character of Kate was deaf. They said there had to be a reason why she was, and we weren't providing one.

But that was the point! *I* don't know why I'm deaf. I just am. None of us knows why we are the way we are, why we came into this life in the body that we did. We're all just trying to figure it out the best we can.

So Josh and I did the mature thing. We went to happy hour to drown our sorrows. Surprisingly, that sorrow never came. Instead, we became bizarrely and completely invigorated. By the time we ordered our second round, we decided that instead of trying to explain it to them, or to anybody else, we would just have to show them. And if we wanted to show them, we would just have to do it ourselves. Even though we didn't really know what we were doing.

And since we were going to do it ourselves, why not just go balls to the wall and make both characters deaf? I knew that if we didn't do it, nobody else would. When I first ran that by Josh, he said, "Wow. But who's going to play Michael?" He had absolutely no intention of acting, only writing. But I didn't think I would ever write, other than in secret, so it made sense that we were pushing each other in opposite directions, right out of our respective comfort zones.

So, we shot the extremely amateur pilot of *Fridays* in an extremely beige apartment that belonged to our friend. (It wasn't her fault it was beige. She was renting.) We shot it in one day for $250 out of our pockets. The next day, my little family and I moved to New York for a job I was doing. While I was there, we put *Fridays* up on YouTube.

For the job I was doing in New York, one day, I had to do this very difficult interview. I don't know what made that one particularly painful. It was like so many others I've had to do in my life, and ones that I have done since. But on that day, it was agonizing. It's not that the questions were new. I still get them all the time. It's that they're questions I have never known the answers to.

What's it like not being able to hear? I don't know. I was born this way. I don't know any different. *What sort of challenges have you overcome?* Answering stupid fucking questions like that one, maybe?

But I get it. People who live outside of my experience want to be inspired. They want to see my being deaf as an actual obstacle. I scale that wall, I grovel through the green goo (I'm clearly thinking of *Double Dare* here) on my hands and knees in slow motion and then . . . I'm up and over and away and I'm free.

Only I haven't actually overcome anything, and I'm not going to. I'm deaf. I've always been deaf. I'm always going to be deaf.

This might be a good time to share that I am aware of the cochlear implant and I have no interest in getting it. A lot of people, sometimes even strangers, feel it's helpful to suggest I get one, so I thought I might beat you to the punch. There's no drama behind that decision for me. I'm simply not a viable candidate for it. I decided to be evaluated for one when I was twenty, out of sheer curiosity. It's possible that with changing technology, I might be a candidate now. But the thing is, even if I were a candidate and I decided to get one, I would still be a deaf person with a cochlear implant. Once the external device is off (and it's supposed to come off), the person is still deaf. That's because there is no cure. And I don't want a cure. Being deaf is a part of who I am. It's part of what makes me . . . me. I wouldn't be who I am today if I weren't deaf. I don't know who or what I would be. Maybe I'd be something more, maybe I'd be something less, but what I know for sure is that I'd be completely different.

On that day in New York City, these questions forced me right back into the very space I was fighting to get out of. The space they saw me being in, rather than the space I was actually in. It was the space opposite of **it**.

Maybe it was especially painful because I was trying to make *Fridays*. I was trying to convince myself that once it was out there, it would take on a life of its own. It'd be alive, it'd be here, and there would be no going back. Much like life was with my daughter, who was five months old at the time. But on that day, walking in the cold to catch my train home to my baby, I thought . . . maybe I had been all wrong. Maybe **it** couldn't happen. Maybe it was better that I go back to whatever space the world would allow me, even if I didn't feel as if that space were truly mine. Maybe I was a complete and total moron for thinking things could ever be different. Maybe things couldn't, and wouldn't, change.

And then, my phone vibrated.

It was an email from my manager asking me if I'd be interested in doing the television show *Supernatural*. No audition. No script. Just, "Hi, are you available to play a hunter on the show?" There wasn't even a character name for this hunter at first. So when I first looked at this email, I thought they wanted me to play someone named Hunter on the show. I was like, *Wait, who's Hunter? Am I supposed to be familiar with this character? Is this Hunter person like Ruby (who, coincidentally, I had auditioned for years before) who comes back in different forms?* Of course, when I read the email more carefully, asked questions, and things came to be, I learned that the character was going to be a hunter who was deaf, she would hopefully be recurring, she might possibly be a love interest for Sam—

Okay. I know some of you are probably throwing tomatoes at my head right about now. If I'm being completely honest, which is basically always, I'm still not sure if it makes sense for Sam to have a love interest with the way his life is, so I get it. But it wasn't like it was a choice I personally made. That was in the character description they sent to me from the beginning. *Okay?*

. . . And her name was going to be Eileen. And because of Robbie Thompson, who had created her for me, she turned out to be a fully realized character who wasn't defined by her deafness, but she didn't try to hide it either. She was just like **it**. She *was* **it**. And the timing was something I could not get past. It was like a burning bush. I had asked the universe for a sign, and they sent me Eileen.

She was evidence that this crazy thing I was doing just might work. She was proof that there was mainstream interest in characters who were deaf, past them just being deaf. And from that point on, Eileen, and *Supernatural*, became strangely interwoven with *This Close*. I shot "Into the Mystic," my first episode as Eileen, while I was writing the second iteration of the show, which at that point had become a webseries we sold to Super Deluxe. (The VP of development had somehow stumbled across our beige pilot on YouTube and so we redeveloped it with them.) It was called *The Chances*, and it premiered at the Sundance Film Festival that year.

Exactly a year after that festival premiere, I sat down at the premiere dinner of the television show on Sundance Now that the webseries had become, now called *This Close*. The premiere of the show had also taken place at the Sundance Film Festival, which was a very full and uncanny circle. I was feeling a lot of feelings that night. To distract myself, I asked the general manager of Sundance Now at what moment they decided they wanted the show when they first saw it the year before. He told me it was when Kate shits her pants.

Now, Kate never actually does that. At least she hasn't yet. But she *did* pee her pants in the very first scene of the first episode of the webseries— the exact same scene I had written in my trailer while shooting "Into the Mystic."

After they saw Kate pee her pants, the network executives at Sundance Now asked us to pitch the show to them. I said that was fine, but we would have to do that within the week because I had to go shoot, once again, *Supernatural*. So we pitched the show and then I immediately flew to Vancouver to do "The British Invasion," my second episode as Eileen. By the time we shot "There's Something About Mary," my third episode, I knew we were going to make *This Close* a television show.

And in that third episode, Eileen died.

I had seen it coming. There was just something about the way her second episode was written, particularly the stuff between her and Sam. I remember thinking, after reading the scene where Sam hugs Eileen at the end of the episode, "Yeah, okay, she's going to get dead." I mean that scene was great, but where do you go from there? I felt like there were only two possibilities. Either they get it on, or she dies. The second way seemed more logical for *Supernatural*. I think I even told Jared that at some point while we were shooting that second episode. I don't remember what he said in response. In any case, I was nervous about getting the script for Eileen's third episode.

So when I actually saw the script for "There's Something About Mary" and saw her death on the page, I cried. (And I was in the middle of Trader Joe's, so it wasn't a very good look.) But after I had that ugly public cry, I thought, *At least that's done and out of my system*.

Only it wasn't. I actually went through a period of grieving. I kept waking up in the middle of the night feeling as if someone had died. I'd feel a heavy sort of physical sadness before I could process it logically and tell myself, "Body, it's just Eileen. She's not real." But it kept happening, so I decided to talk to my sister about it. She's my best friend and a profoundly brilliant artist who has always had this amazing ability of helping me articulate my feelings. I am not always very good at doing that. I said to her, "I keep feeling as if someone real died, and I don't know why." And she said, "Because Eileen was real to you. And thank God for that."

Right after she said that, something clicked. I realized that Eileen was so strong and brave that from the time I first heard (no pun intended) about her, I had unconsciously drawn strength from her. That day on the street in New York City, I had been about to let fear govern me. I had been about to give up. But Eileen wasn't someone who allowed fear to govern her or any of the choices she made. Without her, I was afraid that I'd become governed by fear again. I remember when I told my husband that my gut feeling had been right and Eileen was going to die, he said, "Well, she can't. Just don't do it. Say no." I laughed. He was joking. Kind of.

But I did actually consider doing that. For a heartbeat. And I said to myself, *No. I'm going to do this. I am going to fly to Vancouver to die.* Because any time I get the chance to work, as difficult as that job may be, it's still a victory. When I get material that's difficult for me to swallow, I give it my very best. And if my best isn't enough, then maybe what's difficult about it is beyond my reach. My hope is that if the material disturbs me, it's meant to disturb, so it will also disturb others. Perhaps then a necessary dialogue will be born out of it. That's the only way change happens. And when Eileen died, that dialogue happened, even in the world of *Supernatural*, when death isn't always final. People said that in Eileen's death, she was marginalized and silenced, killed by a hellhound she couldn't hear. They said it was especially brutal because she came from a community that is already often marginalized and silenced, both because of the language they use and because they don't rely on their sense of hearing. And I had never ever seen that discussed like that, out in the open in the mainstream.

That's the way change happens.

Every single one of us lives our life always looking out from behind the same two eyes. We can try to imagine what the world looks like through other people's eyes, but no matter how vivid our imaginations are, we are bound by our own experiences. We're limited to our own perception. I think the most compelling stories take you out from behind your own two eyes and allow you to look at things through a different sort of lens. Until that happens, I don't think anyone can ever realize what their own personal lens is. But the conversation I saw after "There's Something About Mary" was exciting and interesting, and most importantly, it looked at Eileen's death through her own two eyes, even though that wasn't the same lens the rest of the show was shown through.

And the fact was, in my life, Eileen died around the same time *This Close* was born. I hadn't told anyone on the show about it other than my interpreter, because she had asked what I was writing during my first episode. I ran a few lines by her, and she laughed so hard I let myself think, probably for the first time, that maybe I'm on to something here.

The timing of Eileen's death and the birth of *This Close* wasn't planned. Meaning, I never asked to be written off the show. I wouldn't—and to be honest, couldn't—do that. Doing the show and that character was so fun and meaningful that I would have been happy to do the show for as long as they'd have me. And I had no reason, contract wise, to ask to be written off. Recurring characters like Eileen usually have pretty flexible contracts. If you have a scheduling conflict, you say you can't do the episode they're asking you to do, and then you hope they'll bring you back for another episode when you're available. But these are just the logistics. The fact is, there's a reason why death happens. It happens in order to make room for something new. For something else. I believe Eileen's death made room for the value of her life. And her death taught me a lesson about my own life.

Eileen was strong. And then she died alone in that forest because she couldn't hear the invisible monster that was attacking her. But here's the thing: whether we like it or not, we are technically *always* alone. We are *always* inside our own heads, and that's where the most vicious monster of all lives. Nobody can hear or see this monster, except for you.

We all do the best we can in this strange thing called life. Sometimes our best just isn't good enough, and that's when the monster comes out. It makes us think the most monstrous things possible . . . things that we'd physically attack people for saying to someone else. Yet, we allow this monster to say them to us. The monster knows all our weak spots, the vulnerable places in our armor. It has a very long memory. It's especially good at hoarding painful times and then slowly pulling them up one by one and throwing them at us at full force. It magnifies these times to the point where they're all that we see, and we feel like they're all that there is. It makes me wonder where I'd be really, if, somehow, I wasn't born into my body, into the skin that I'm in. Maybe it would be someplace better. Somewhere easier. And that's really fucking lonely. But owning that loneliness, talking about it, that's how Eileen lived, and that's how I made *This Close*. Through making that show, I discovered that everyone feels that way, no matter who or what they are. Everyone has their own monster.

In retrospect, I think that's why I always wanted *This Close* to look gritty. I love movies. I always have. I love the experience of going to movie theaters and sitting down and watching something totally fucking epic—well, when they're captioned and when the captions actually work, which is rarely, but that's another story. That beautiful veneer of gloss? It costs a lot of money. It *is* money. It's top-of-the-line lighting and cameras and makeup and hair and . . . stuff. But think about what gloss actually does. When there's gloss on a wooden table, you can't feel the texture of the actual wood. There are no bumps, no imperfections, no ripples. All you feel is the gloss. It separates you. Sometimes when there's too much of it, as a by-product, it's more difficult for me to lose myself in it and forget I'm watching a movie. I feel like I'm watching a spectacle instead. And spectacles are awesome. There's a time and place for them. But I don't think anyone's actual life is a constant spectacle. I don't think life has that kind of gloss on it every day. And that's what it's about. It's about feeling it all. The smooth parts, the imperfect parts, and yes, even the monstrous parts.

So, yes, they killed Eileen. And I hated that they did. I wanted to erase her death and keep what came before, the good, strong, flawed, human parts of her. Just like I once wanted to erase my accent, but keep everything else that made me, me. It doesn't work that way. Eileen's death was a part of her story, whether I like it or not. I am in this body, whether I like it or not. My body has strength, and it has weakness. It has an accent. It has limitations. If I allow the monster to focus on the limitations, the good parts fade away. But the opposite is true, too. If you try to erase what you don't like and keep only the good, easy parts, then you lose all of it. There's nothing that's completely good. There's nothing that's completely easy. We can't take away what we don't like about ourselves or erase what we don't like about our story. Trying to do so might be the very definition of being wayward.

Because just like we all have a monster, we all have an **it**. I'm not sure we can have one without the other. Maybe they're one and the same. Our monster makes us weak, but then it also makes us strong. You can let it eat you alive, or you can make that monster your bitch and make it work for you and help you make your own personal **it**, whatever **it** means to you. The monster belongs to you. It is yours. It is you.

Eileen died. But before that, she was here. She lived.

You are here. You are alive. You are enough. You are Wayward.

Besides, it turns out that nothing stays dead on *Supernatural*. Including Eileen.

HE HAD ME AT "YOU HURT?"

How a Single-Episode Character Wouldn't Let Me Go

TEDRA ASHLEY-WANNEMUEHLER

"**Y**ou hurt?" came a voice from above.

Someone offered Dean a hand. He accepted the help and was pulled from the ground, from the spot where he had almost died, yet again, if not for this stranger saving his life. It didn't take long for those of us watching the episode to learn the stranger's identity.

It was César, hunting partner of Jesse, pursuing the same bizarre monsters (bizarre even by *Supernatural* standards) Sam and Dean were—monsters that emerged, cicada-like, every twenty-seven years to occupy the bodies of their victims and reproduce before killing their hosts and going back underground.

When they were kids, one of these creatures took Jesse's older brother Matty, never to be seen again. Jesse had been seeking revenge ever since, and having joined forces with César, they were closing in on their prey.

I learned a bit more about César and Jesse soon after that initial intro-duction as they sat around a table in a bar with Sam and Dean:

DEAN: Ah, you guys fight just like brothers [chuckles], almost as bad
     as us.
CÉSAR: Well, [pause], it's more like an old married couple.
DEAN: [laughs] That's . . . [looks to César]
César gives Dean a knowing look. Dean turns to Jesse.
DEAN: [with realization] Oh, so . . . [points back and forth from Jesse
     to César]
CÉSAR: Yeah.
DEAN: Okay, that's . . .
*César puts his beer bottle on the table and looks at Dean, while Jesse
     remains silent.*
DEAN: What's it like, settling down with a hunter?
CÉSAR: Smelly, dirty. [turns to Jesse] Twice the worrying about
     getting ganked.
Sam smiles understandingly and looks away.

So normal. I loved César immediately because he was so normal. He was not a stereotype. His sexuality was part of his DNA, not his defining attribute. He was gay, like me, and the fact that he was a man made him no less relatable. He was so honest, and for a hunter, so open. He takes a risk telling Dean that he and Jesse are a couple, yet Sam and Dean take it in stride immediately.

For a single-episode character, César stuck with me. I loved César's instant chemistry with the Winchesters and his obvious love for his part-ner. I connected with him in the way he showed his love, both through his sacrifices for his partner and in his drive to help Jesse get what he needed. It struck me that I have loved people who, like Jesse, endured a past they never deserved. I have desperately wished I could erase the pain of those experiences, and in that way, I've experienced things from César's point of view. I am also lucky enough to have a wife who has sacrificed her own ambitions for my unique career more times than I can count over our twenty-seven years together. In that way, like Jesse, I've been on the receiving end of someone else's sacrifice. I could relate to both characters.

At the start of this episode, a young Jesse confides in his trusted older brother about a kiss at school with another boy. Matty warns him to be careful, but he is nothing but supportive. This scene was extremely touching to me because I remember being young, and gay, and feeling like I was the only girl who had ever loved another girl. Some of the best "firsts" in my life were with someone of the same sex, and I instinctively knew that I needed to keep my excitement over these early relationships to myself. At fifteen, I had no one else to confide in. It was isolating when my other female friends chatted away about first boyfriends and first dates while I felt it was safer for me to keep quiet. By nineteen, I had found another teenager (another gay woman) who understood. Finding that one person I could share my experiences with was completely freeing.

Writer Nancy Won chose to show that Matty accepts Jesse the way he is, and he even has plans to move with him to a safer place where a gay kid might not be harassed as badly as he would have been in their hometown. This struck me as a truly unconditional love between brothers. I remember thinking how wonderful it was that Jesse had a protector and that he was going to have it easier than most gay kids have it in real life. The fact that Matty was gone soon after Jesse confided in him was devastating and made Jesse's quest for revenge believable to me. His support system had been stripped away. I was worried for him. I understood the importance of having that one person you could confide in, and the thought of losing that, at that age, was heartbreaking.

As I grew up, I saw very few depictions of nonstereotypical female characters on TV, let alone gay characters. The gay characters I remember in movies or TV shows were usually there for comic relief. They were silly or, worse, they were criminal deviants or the deserving victims of a crime they had obviously brought upon themselves through their own actions. I never related to these characters and, perhaps for that reason, combined with the fact that I wasn't aware that I knew any gay adults, I did not consider myself gay for many years. What I saw in the media regarding gay people was often sad and ugly. What I experienced in my own life was the exact opposite. For me, love with another woman was love on a level I never thought possible. It was fundamentally different from my early relationships with guys. It was soul-expanding and beautiful and just *right*.

Since loving someone in secret was nothing new to me, perhaps it's not surprising that I watched and loved *Supernatural* in isolation for the first five years from 2005 to 2010. I was embarrassed that I, a grown adult with a full life, an amazing wife, and a job I love, could feel so passionately about characters on a TV show. I didn't want to admit I loved something that was deemed so silly and superficial by society in general, but society's disapproval was also nothing new, so I kept right on loving *Supernatural* and the story of Sam and Dean's unbreakable connection as they went about saving the world. The writing in those early years made me care deeply about these characters, and it was something I couldn't quit, no matter what society thought.

Around 2010, I bumped around the net until I stumbled across the *Supernatural Fan Wiki*. This was a comparatively old, disorganized site originally founded by a teenager and cobbled together by a series of fan administrators over the years. Nevertheless, here I'd found a place where other fans were talking about episodes . . . about the plot . . . about more than how hot Jared and Jensen were . . . and the fans on the site were even using decent grammar in their discussions! I created an account for myself. I started commenting. Little did I know the ways in which my life would change when I tentatively created that first wiki username.

During the course of those episode discussions with other fans, I found Nikki, Gisa, Karen, and Katie, four women who, for this only child, are the sisters I never had. They are incredibly smart, articulate, caring, and devoted friends who went from being strangers on the wiki to being people I message daily. The things I've been able to do with this group and the incredible support they've given me have gone beyond my wildest expectations. This group of friends, who would not be in my life at all if not for *Supernatural*, has changed who I am, and they've taken me places I never thought I'd go.

Our friendship led to annual meet-ups on a convention weekend with our group of five that went from, "I'll just do this once" to "I will do this every year come hell or high water." For several in this group, meeting at a convention requires cross-country flights and long drives, but all of us make it a priority because our friendship has become a priority.

At conventions we discuss the show in depth. We calm each other's nerves before photo ops. We eat pie. So. Much. Pie. We laugh until we cry. Early on, when the offerings in the vendor's room didn't live up to our expectations, we started making gifts for each other that were better and more meaningful than those we could buy. We watched the costume contests and ultimately entered with a group costume. We built a *Supernatural*-style motel room with my wife Suzanne contributing her carpentry skills, complete with retro wallpaper, a green couch, a sunburst clock, and a star-shaped room divider, taking second place in Minneapolis in 2017 and first in Chicago the next year. (Two people were seated to make up the couch with an arm in each armrest, another supported the wall, and everyone else was pressed into service as stagehands moving everything on and offstage quickly.) This loner actually worked with a group.

When a businessman in a three-piece suit shared an elevator with me during the Chicago con in 2014, he asked in a hushed tone, "Have you *SEEN* the people here?!" Apparently he was not used to a rainbow sea of flannel punctuated by the occasional set of devil horns and massive black angel wings. I knew with confidence that I was telling him the truth when I replied, "Actually, I'm one of those people."

At our first shared convention, I felt I had found my tribe. These women are family. Those feelings only intensified over the years as our bond grew and led to some truly incredible experiences that expanded my world and nudged me in unexpected new directions. My love for the show led to a crazy seven-hour drive from central Illinois to Lawrence, Kansas, with Nikki to visit and photograph Mary, a replica Impala owned by Marcus and Megan Woodard. They had Mary restored down to the last detail, from the glossy black paint to the plastic soldiers in the ashtray, the Legos in the vents, and the carved initials on the back deck. They filled the trunk with a completely accurate weapons cache inside a hidden weapons box until their car resembled Dean's Baby as closely as possible.

Marcus and Megan spent years taking Mary to conventions and using those appearances to raise $7,000 for local Kansas charities, including the Kansas City Anti-Violence Project, an organization that helps LGBTQ victims of bullying. All in all, by partnering with other charities, they used Mary to raise a staggering total of $45,000 for a variety of worthy causes. When Nikki and I set out to meet a stranger who owned a '67 Impala, I never thought I would find a straight man who was such a tireless supporter of gay rights. I started to feel that allies outnumbered bigots, at least within the *Supernatural* Family. Marcus spent hours with us, even though he was mere days away from moving halfway across the country and had plenty of other things he could have been doing. I was touched by his selflessness, how generous he was with his time, and his dedication to making sure we, these strangers he had just met, got all the photos we wanted, no matter how long it took.

Nikki and I braved wearing flannel in 93-degree heat and enlisted Marcus's help in taking photos with Mary, aiming to recreate some stills from the show. This was something I had wanted to do for several years while I looked for an Impala owner willing to go along, and something I never actually would have done before meeting Nikki and my other SPN sisters. Before that trip, I had been afraid someone would think a photo shoot with a car was a silly waste of time. It was a challenge to explain to family at home why we were going so far to visit a car that we were not going to buy . . . just visit. The photos and the entire trip were most definitely not a waste of time.

While in Kansas, I never expected to attend a Sunday service at the Stull Methodist Church. Instead of snooping around the Stull cemetery—I had read that the church was not crazy about that for fear of vandalism—I thought, why not meet the real people who lived there? But church? Me? No thanks. Nikki, a regular churchgoer, basically told this atheist "just come on" and we went. The Stull congregation was extremely welcoming. There was not a portal to hell in sight and nothing burst into flames when this nonbeliever stepped into the sanctuary. Making even a temporary connection with the people who lived there was more rewarding than I ever thought it could be. I would never have had this experience without Nikki, and I would never have met Nikki without *Supernatural*. Nikki is the kind of friend who will go to the ends of the earth for me. She is endlessly supportive and encouraging. I don't think any friend has made me laugh harder. I don't think anyone has a bigger heart.

Another friendship forged on the wiki led to a flight to Austin to meet up with Gisa. Gisa is my complete opposite in many ways. She is always on the move, in charge, and incredibly outgoing. She pushes me and encourages me and is my ceaseless cheerleader in every endeavor. If not for *Supernatural* bringing us together, I likely would never have approached her, and now I can't imagine my life without her.

One goal that Gisa and I had in Austin was to visit the Family Business Beer Company in its third month in operation. We sat on the large porch with our second (perhaps third) awesome beer as the moon rose over a peaceful grove of live oaks swaying in the spring breeze. This place I'd never been to before felt as comfortable to me as if I were a regular. We also checked out the cozy San Jac Saloon, relaxing with a drink at the end of a day spent exploring Austin.

We spent a few golden late afternoon hours roaring around the back roads of Texas in Renegade, another fan replica Impala owned by Lisa

Diamont. Lisa cranked the classic rock, revved the engine, and we flew down the two-lane blacktop with the windows down, resulting in the most worth-it bad hair day in history. The engine growled, the road stretched out in front of us, and it was amazing to see everything from Sam and Dean's perspective. We also got a lot of envious stares at stoplights. We continued what was fast becoming a bit of a tradition when we parked the car and Lisa helped us take photos recreating some of our favorite scenes and promo shots. Lisa was completely on board with the plan and already had several locations in mind when we arrived. She did all of this after a long day at her job as a teacher. The amazing generosity and enthusiasm of fellow fans never fails to make me smile. In fact, I don't think I stopped smiling during our entire time with Lisa and Renegade. Taking the photos this time, I no longer worried about what anyone else might think.

The wiki connection also led to Karen, a veterinarian, an editor, and a veritable SPN encyclopedia. Karen is one of the kindest people I know, the type of person who will leave her phone on next to her bed all night, halfway across the country, in case I need a vet on call at 3 a.m. when my cat is recovering from surgery. This is just another example of fans putting others before themselves. Karen's work ethic and devoted friendship led to both of us becoming more involved with the wiki, where we are now co-admins.

Through my friendship with Nikki, I was introduced to smart, observant, wickedly funny Katie. Mutual love for those who create *Supernatural* pushed me and Katie, both natural, dedicated introverts, to get up the nerve to talk to the actors we admired so much at conventions, encouraging each other through each attempt. Katie, though quiet, always has my back and is enthusiastically willing to try any crazy thing I suggest. Photo op test shots? She's there. Rainbow slinky races down the hotel stairs at 1 a.m. (okay, that was her idea)? She's there. Can I buy another photo op (FYI, the answer is usually "no")? She's there to remind me of what's really important and save me from myself.

As my comfort level increased, I suddenly had the desire to host open house events in our hotel room at the cons, inviting complete strangers in to appreciate *Supernatural*-themed art and eat pie. That out-of-character gesture was rewarded when I saw new friends who had met at one of our open houses—people who had bravely come to the convention alone—spending the rest of the convention weekend together. I had previously never wanted to talk to strangers, let alone help facilitate strangers talking to each other. I have an easier time talking to any stranger now, and I credit some of that to my amazing *Supernatural* sisters.

Over the years, these friendships have become an intrinsic part of my life. We support each other's business ventures, gladly take middle-of-the-night texts when someone has a family member in the hospital, and our group is a place where we can, and do, say anything.

Speaking of business ventures, *Supernatural* started to seep into my work. I'm a professional custom bookbinder who does commissioned work for people all over the world. I spend most of my time creating bindings to other's specifications, and that is rewarding in its own way, but *Supernatural* gave me new ideas I wanted to try, so I started doing bindings of *Supernatural*-themed books. Sometimes they were for myself, sometimes they were gifts for friends, and eventually, some were special orders placed by other fans. The designs I wanted to create required materials and techniques I had not tried before, materials like bullet casings. Where in the world does one find bullet casings? I found a source for them, and the desire to incorporate these elements into my work meant inventing new techniques for crafting book covers. After more than two decades as a bookbinder, I felt new inspiration and attempted designs that pushed my skills to the limit.

The hammered silver jewelry I was making as a side business started to take a decidedly *Supernatural* turn as it morphed into designs inspired by the shapes of old motel signs—the kind I'd seen in Jerry Wanek's amazing sets.

First, I made silver cuff bracelets for my group of convention friends that included a piece of steel from the body of a '67 Impala. The group loved them, and I loved the idea of using part of an actual vintage car in my metalwork. That experiment with the cuff bracelets made me want to collect more materials, and that necessitated learning how to dismantle a car body with an angle grinder. I had to get over my fear of intimidating power tools in order to obtain what I needed to complete the designs I was sketching.

(left) Custom rebinding of Family Don't End with Blood *with the* Supernatural *Family tree reimagined as a target with Jared and Jensen at the center and the names of other actors and fans who contributed chapters to the book radiating out like ripples on the water. Goatskin leather, binder's board, real bullet casings courtesy of @zerbehunter, hot foil stamping. (right) Custom blank book with the Impala, raised, on the cover. Pigskin and goatskin leather, carved board, various colors of goatskin leather inlay, hot foil stamping.*

I ended up scouring vintage car salvage yards across South Dakota, accompanied by my ever-patient wife Suzanne, in search of specific colors of vintage body steel to use in my jewelry. The evolution of my jewelry designs compelled me to walk into the salvage yard offices, overseen by men who could easily have been Bobby's clone, ignore their confused looks, and describe what I was searching for. After a short conversation about why this lone woman had walked up their long dirt road (on the occasions when Suzanne stayed with our truck), they were always extremely helpful. It was getting easier to speak up for myself. It felt empowering.

The amazing connections I can attribute to *Supernatural* reach outside the world of the wiki and conventions. I had limited experience selling my jewelry at art fairs until my current art fair partner, Lydia, approached me when she saw a photo of Jared and Jensen on my iPad start-up screen when we happened to be selling at the same show in 2016. What began with, "You like *Supernatural?*" has turned into partnering at twenty-two art sales and counting, with plans for future collaborations.

(left) Forged sterling silver pendant inspired by retro motel sign
shapes and featuring steel from a '61 Plymouth Valiant.
(center) Sterling silver "road" cuff with raised Impala cornering light cage.
(right) Forged sterling silver motel pendant featuring steel from a '67 Impala.

I began to realize that taking a chance, no matter what the outcome, was its own reward. Sometimes it's a failure, but sometimes it's a spectacular success, as it was when I risked reaching out and opening up to my four SPN sisters. I can be myself with them. We love the show with equal intensity and we have come to love each other as well. Perhaps because we each started out loving *Supernatural* alone, the fact that we can now love it together has led to an extremely rare feeling of openness and honesty in our group. The fact that I'm the only one in the group who's gay? No big deal. Not any kind of deal, actually. We live in different parts of the country, and we have very different backgrounds, families, religious beliefs, and careers, but there is something about loving *Supernatural* that means we have many of the same core values of loyalty, persistence, depth of feeling, and dedication to family and friends.

It's not only the connection with other fans that has made me feel like a part of something larger than myself. It's also the willingness of the actors to connect with the fans that I believe sets the *Supernatural* Family apart and contributes to the feel of a vast, varied, caring, and accepting fandom.

I started following actor Hugo Ateo on Twitter soon after he played César on "The Chitters" episode. On October 11, 2018, he posted:

Hugo Ateo
@HugoAteo

I always assume everyone knows but someone politely pointed out that I have not mentioned it here, so... on Coming Out Day, I am not coming out, just confirming thaT YES, I am a proud, happy gay man. Wouldn't change it for anything! #HappyToBeMe #proud #LGBTQIA #loveislove #BeYou

10:58 AM - 11 Oct 2018

I had no idea. I guess I hadn't thought about it much. Straight people play gay roles all the time and vice versa. I replied to that effect, and then he replied:

Hugo Ateo
@HugoAteo

Replying to @waywrdaughter67

That's the first gay character I've been allowed to play in 25 years. When I audition for a gay role I'm often deemed "not believable as gay" 😖 which of course means "not stereotypical enough". Hopefully times are changing. #diversity #AllFlavors #NoToStereotypes

12:31 PM - 11 Oct 2018

Wait, *WHAT*?! How crazy is it that a man who is actually gay was deemed "not believable as gay" by other casting directors? Yet *Supernatural* chose him to play a complex character who also happens to be gay. I'm extremely proud of the choices made by this show that I love. I hope this small but vital step shows some kind of evolution in the way gay characters are portrayed in the entertainment industry.

Sexuality is personal. It is truly no one else's business, but as long as prejudice exists, I feel it is important for those who might harbor some bigotry to know that gay people aren't outsiders. We are your neighbors and coworkers and family members. We are people you meet and interact with every day. *Supernatural* approached this gay character in this way, as a person who is valuable and trusted and loved. There are gay members in almost every family. The *Supernatural* Family chooses to recognize that fact, not make a big deal out of it, and give us characters who feel extremely real because they have a depth that goes far beyond a stereotype.

There is a great scene in "The Chitters" where César and Dean are talking while driving in the Impala about how revenge never really solves anything, but when someone is out for revenge, you can't talk them out of it. Dean talks to César like he's known him for years. There's some level of instant comfort there between the characters, and that's how I felt about César: instantly comfortable. This is also one of the very few times on the show that Sam and Dean consider partnering with another pair of hunters. They both seem to trust César and Jesse immediately, unlike any other single-episode characters I can recall. Perhaps the way César and Jesse are so honest with Sam and Dean about the nature of their relationship, and how important this hunt is for them, allows for the same sort of trust in return.

Hugo Ateo played César as incredibly capable, loving, and understated. Normal. When César smiles near the end of the episode, talking excitedly about his plans to retire with Jesse (played by Lee Rumohr) to New Mexico and raise horses, I could feel the happiness there. I wanted the best for them. I also REALLY wanted them to become regular characters. I wanted more. I still hope for many more complex and capable gay characters like César on future shows.

Of course, I also fell in love with Charlie (played by Felicia Day) several years earlier for some of the same reasons. She was another "oh, by the way, she's gay" character, where that part of her life was a footnote to her other prominent traits of brains, compassion, self-doubt, and determination. I love Dean, but I never wanted to be Lisa. I always wanted to be Charlie, who became Dean's best friend and the sister he never had.

I loved Charlie so much that I jumped at the chance to meet Charlie's creator, writer Robbie Thompson, at a DePaul University symposium in 2015, where he was the keynote speaker. I mean, come on, a college symposium weekend entirely focused on *Supernatural*? How awesome is that?! Robbie Thompson created Charlie with a subtle complexity that had more time to play out over multiple episodes. I loved that she could be supremely confident in some areas (leading a cosplay army) and completely terrified in others (breaking into the headquarters of leviathan Dick Roman). This made her believable to me. When I briefly discussed Charlie with Robbie Thompson, he said he put a great deal of thought into making sure that being gay was not her primary feature. Sam and Dean loved Charlie like family and the fact that she was gay posed no barrier between them in any way. As with César, the writers of *Supernatural* made her anything but a stereotype. They took the time to craft her as a fully realized character, which resulted in unforgettable, creative, and touching episodes like "Pac Man Fever," which is still one of my all-time favorites. Robbie Thompson said he fought like hell for her character to continue, even though the decision was ultimately made by others to kill her off, a loss which still hurts, even now.

Making the trip to speak to Robbie Thompson is one of the ways in which my love for these characters has pushed me to do things I would never have had the nerve to do before. It sounds crazy, even to me, but *Supernatural* has made me more fearless. More aware. More open. I'm not the same person I was in 2005.

I have been lucky as a gay woman. For the most part, I have had extremely supportive friends and family members. I have never experienced the horrible things that many gay people have had to endure in order to survive. Perhaps that's why I connected with César's normalcy and Charlie's almost-incidental sexuality. In Charlie, the writers of *Supernatural* gave us a fascinating character who always had the best of intentions and always worked to be stronger than her fear. In César, they gave us a character who earned our love and respect through his actions, the way we should all earn it.

I was not looking for validation or acceptance when I watched Dean break into Sam's Stanford apartment on September 13, 2005. I was simply tuning in to a new show whose promo, with the image of a woman burning on the ceiling, was unforgettable and extremely compelling. I didn't think I wanted approval from anyone. It turns out I did want it and somehow found it in a TV show, of all places, and in an extended family of actors and fans. The relationships I've built within the *Supernatural* Family and the incredible acts of generosity, charity, and kindness I've witnessed in this fandom give me hope that love will ultimately win out over hate. The creative and emotional back roads the show has led me down leave me excited for the next essential, soul-expanding experience I never knew I needed.

I am different now, and I am better.

Validation, it turns out, feels very good.

Chicago convention, 2014
My shirt reads, "Sam and Dean Winchester—Keeping
gay girls just a little bit straight since 2005."
This is a risk I never would have taken before—a funny shirt photo op.
Would Jared and Jensen get it? Was it even appropriate? I should not
have worried. Jared chuckled and Jensen outright laughed and stopped
the photo line, enlisting Jared to snap a picture of us with Jensen's phone
to send to a family member he thought would get a kick out of my shirt.
I felt nothing but acceptance. When the two leads set such a welcoming,
caring, accepting example, it's no wonder that this fandom has felt that
support and used it to evolve into a fundraising powerhouse as well as
an international web of crucial friendships and incredible creativity.

HUNTER HUSBANDS

LEE RUMOHR

I have only filmed one episode of *Supernatural*, but the experience had an impact on me, and from what I understand, it also had an impact on the fans. The episode "The Chitters," directed by Eduardo Sánchez, focused on my character, Jesse, his search for the brother he lost as a child and the healing that has eluded him, and his relationship with his partner, César (played by Hugo Ateo). When Hugo and I were on set the very first day, and even during the audition in the room, Eduardo was very nice, and while it might be kind of a cliché to say, he was easy to work with. He gave us free range to do whatever we wanted, which goes along with his personality. Aside from his intimidating tallness, he's a quiet, gentle dude. Of course, being tall is not uncommon on that set!

Supernatural opened some doors for me professionally, and it definitely attracted some new fans, which is wonderful. I was able to understand how some of the fans were feeling about the episode and my character when they reached out to me personally, which was really nice—and I was able to contact every single person who reached out. I'm not a big celebrity, so I was able to do that. It meant a lot to me that I was able to participate in an episode that had such an impact on a lot of people's lives, and I hope to take on more roles that speak on important issues.

But being a part of *Supernatural*, just being on the set, was over-whelming at first. At that point, I'd been an actor for more than twenty years, and I'd been on numerous sets, but you don't get that initial feeling of overwhelming love and welcoming on too many sets. It's hard to form a family-based level of trust and respect on episodic television because things change so fast that it's often difficult to form those bonds. *Supernatural* was at that time eleven seasons in, and you got a good sense of trust on that set. They allowed you to be you. Everybody is just normal, and they appreciate the next person beside them, whoever that is. And amaz-ingly, there wasn't this feeling of hierarchy, of somebody trying to take the next step on the ladder. Everybody was equal, and that was really nice to see and feel and hear.

Jared and Jensen are two strong moving forces on that show. I think, as leads on a TV show, they take the weight on their shoulders for every-one else. They are the faces of the show. And those two guys really are like brothers. I had some great conversations with them, some heart-to-hearts. They told me that they lean on each other. If one of them is feeling off that day and/or week for whatever reason, the other one kicks in and helps out. When you're on set, you see that and you feel it. You can't have a successful show without that, but they also treat the crew with equal respect. They don't think they're better than anybody else, and that trickles all the way through the whole show. Everybody is the same. It's very nice to feel that, and I was truly blessed to have that experience. They've formed a big family bond there.

As a guest actor, the challenge was to make sure that I gained the trust of all of them, not just the actors but also the crew and the network, so that they could feel confident that their choice in picking me for this character was the right one. I hope they were able to get that from me; it felt like they did. Eduardo allowed Hugo and me to experiment and go with the flow. He trusted us. When you're a guest star on a long-running show, you do get nervous. At least I do, because I want to impress them. I felt like I needed to pick up my game to a degree, to be on their level of professionalism. I have to know my character, and the last thing I'd want to do is screw up my lines. I know it's normal for actors to mess up, especially with the amount of dialogue that I had. Two of the many scenes I had were four minutes long—so I felt the pressure.

The first scene we shot was the one inside the caves, where all the bodies were and where my character's brother's body was found. I don't know if it was strategically planned that they wanted to get the hardest scene done first, but I'm glad that was the first scene up for me, because it got the most challenging emotional scene out of the way. I think it allowed me to get the most difficult part of the episode for my character done, and I also got to show them that they cast the right person for this part—that I had this. From there, I could breathe a little more.

I know a lot of people reacted strongly to that emotional scene. I think that with episodic television, as opposed to movies, it can be hard for actors to find a connection with their characters in such a short amount of time, because it's such a quick take. And you can tell when someone is not connecting and not truly emotionally feeling it. I had to go to a place that I didn't really want to for that scene. My actual brother is still alive, and he means a lot to me. I had to pretend that he was dead; that's something you just have to do sometimes as an actor. I purposely didn't leave the scene, I stayed there while they changed camera lenses or angles or filmed close-ups and so on. I stayed there for the whole scene because I needed to remain in the zone, and they allowed me to be in there. I said, "I've got to stay here," and they were like, "Do what you need to do." It is a team, a total team effort.

I don't know that much about the overall chemistry and relationships on the show and the characters, but I do know *Supernatural* has had a strong impact on many people. I think a lot of people have committed their lives to this show because they can somehow relate. It's about family, about love. I wish I had time to watch it from beginning to end like the true fans have. Those fans are amazing, whether they binge-watched or have been watching from day one, waiting until the next week to watch the next episode. Either way, that's commitment. And *Supernatural* has allowed fans to have a relationship with the actors outside of the show, which is part of the legacy. Whether it's Comic-Cons or conventions or whatever, they have allowed fans to meet them in person and get signatures and photos and make memories. After just one week on the show, I felt a little bit of what it's like to be part of that family. As an empath, sometimes I feel too much and get overwhelmed with emotion. If someone is hurting, I feel it. So I can totally see how the end of this show is going to feel like, *OMG now what am I going to do?*

That's why I'm very happy to contribute to this book. It's almost like another chapter for people and something else for fans to hold on to and read and imagine and sink their teeth into. We all need something to believe in, to inspire us, to pick us up. This show has been that and more for so many people.

I admit I do wish that Hugo and I had played a bigger part on the show, and that our characters were more influential in helping the guys out. Our characters did get to retire instead of dying, which a lot of fans were happy about and satisfied with, but they also were sad that Jesse and César didn't get to come back. We had a good week on the show and made an impact, but deep down I wish we were part of it for longer because it was such a great show to work on. I dreamt a few times that they brought us back and we helped the Winchesters retire. There was a nice parallel between our characters and Sam and Dean, one a hard shell on the outside and soft inside and the other the opposite, and the dream reflected that parallel. I dreamt that Sam and Dean showed up and said, "We need your help. How do we get out of this? How do we retire?" And when I woke up, it felt so real that I had a headache. I was both sweaty and disappointed that it was just a dream. It's too bad, because I know that a lot of people were wanting a *Hunter Husbands* spinoff!

And that brings me to the most important thing about being on *Supernatural*: the relationship Hugo and I got to depict.

When I auditioned for the role, I had no idea that Jesse was gay. The writers didn't telegraph that Jesse and César were classified as "different" by our society. Because really, our characters weren't, and we didn't play it that way. They were everyday people. The writing allowed us just to be human, something you don't always see in the way gay characters are written, and that was really nice. I think Hugo and I had a conversation on the very first day while waiting to film the first scene, during which we pieced it together. I'm not sure which one of us said it first: "I think we're a couple." That didn't change my approach at all. I played Jesse the way I'd play anyone else—without trying to change the relationship dynamic or language to match a specific perception of how a gay person would act. How does a gay person *act* anyway?

It's unfortunate that being gay is still such a topic of speculation and judgment, a lot of which I think is fear based. I'm glad the network, the show, the writers, and Jared and Jensen didn't focus so much on that, because it's a secondary plotline outside of what the episode is really about (which is Jesse and his revenge for what happened to his brother twenty-seven years ago). I think the writers did a phenomenal job keeping it as real as possible, of not making the story solely about the characters' sexuality. And the network did a great job with how they introduced our two characters.

The casting of Hugo and me together couldn't have been any more perfect. When I met Hugo, we just hit it off. It's one of those things—obviously, there's a reason why certain people come into your life. Some relationships are just meant to be. When you know, you know.

I know that there was a lot of appreciation and gratitude from the gay and lesbian community for bringing in Jesse and César. Unfortunately, there was some negative feedback too, but overall the love and positivity for these two characters overpowered the negativity. I'm glad that in the episode they made Hugo and my characters' love so matter-of-fact. It was Hugo supporting Jesse, as any loving person in a relationship would do. I think we can all understand that.

Before passing judgment, my dad always said, "Lee, you always seek to understand."

And that goes a long way.

NOT A DEMON— BUT A SUPERHERO!

HUGO ATEO

Moving to Canada, thereby leaving my telenovela career in Mexico behind, was one of the riskiest, but ultimately most rewarding decisions of my life. Adapting to a new country with a very different culture was a big challenge, but I embraced the adventure gleefully, completely unaware of how big the challenge would end up being. At the time, I had a substantial résumé, which helped open doors to many big-profile auditions. I had great training and a lot of experience, but I didn't realize how different it would be to act in English. My lack of proficiency and my thick accent made me a bad match for many roles.

One particular audition stands out in my memory. When I read the invitation to audition for a show called *Supernatural*, I thought I was perfect for the role. "Castiel is a demon. He is charming, intelligent, but" if I remember the description correctly "somewhat morally flexible. He is helping someone come back from hell to be reunited with his family." It was a really fun audition to go to, and only in hindsight did I realize how this may have been the biggest audition I didn't land.

Not often talked about, but pivotal to the trajectory of an actor's career, is the long list of roles that we really, really want, but never have the chance to perform. I knew another chance would come to audition for this show, and I knew that if I kept working hard I would be ready for it. Years passed and the audition I hoped for wasn't forthcoming; yet, as I followed the growth of *Supernatural* into the phenomenon it has become, I never let go of my desire to get a juicy part on the show.

Life happened and I moved away from Vancouver—first to London, then to Greece—before the beauty of Vancouver and its career opportunities called me back. At long last, I was invited to audition for a character on *Supernatural* named César Cuevas. The audition called for just two brief scenes, but it seemed like a substantial role. I was thrilled to get the callback, even more so when I met Eduardo Sánchez, the director of the episode for which I would be cast. I was greeted personally by him and he took quite some time to work directly with me to understand the role and his directorial intentions. It was then that I first learned that the character of Jesse, whom I had assumed was my brother, was actually my husband.

I hadn't been auditioning for a supernatural creature, a demon, or a ghost.

César was a man committed to helping his partner, the love of his life, face the demons that had crippled him in his childhood. César was a badass fighter, prepared to risk his own life to defend his beloved in the hopes of one day living a life of peace and togetherness in love.

So, I had not landed the role of a supernatural creature, a demon, or a ghost; instead, it was a gay superhero! I couldn't have been happier that this role was mine!

Throughout my acting career, I was often denied the chance to play gay characters because "I was not believable as gay." Strangely, actually being gay (or being an actor) was not considered qualification enough to play a gay character. It was the appearance of being gay that was often considered more relevant than one's ability to act convincingly and develop a full-fledged character. If you were thin and slight, with a high-pitched voice and angular features, you were more likely to be cast for gay roles.

As a gay man, it was frustrating to be told that I was not believable as gay. Of course, this was code for "We would like to continue dealing in stereotypes." You can imagine my surprise when I was suddenly offered the opportunity to play a gay character who defied all stereotypes: César lives in the woods, and he is not glamorous or effeminate or identifiable at all by the characteristics of a stereotypically gay man. However, he does happen to be in love with another man.

At the time of my audition, I was heavier than usual and not particularly fit. In truth, I looked more like a tubby, middle-aged man, a regular no-frills Joe, than a gym-going self-obsessed man-child, which is another gay stereotype we often see. While being gay is a characteristic of both César and Jesse, it is just one aspect of their lives and not a defining one. There are many other traits that better identify who they are: pained, caring, brave, complex, insecure, angry, and tender. And they are determined to change their circumstances so they can live together and love each other in peace. They just happen to be human beings who are gay.

When I met Lee Rumohr, the actor who played my character's husband, Jesse, I found out that he wasn't gay. Despite myself, I have to admit that this made me a little nervous. At first, I debated disclosing to him that I'm gay, fearful of a straight man's reaction to a gay actor playing his husband. But it only took a few minutes of chatting with Lee for my fears to evaporate completely. He was open-minded, sweet, relaxed, and intelligent. And, just as I was, he was inspired by the deep love our characters felt for each other. I was so happy at how easy it was for us both to find a total sense of comfort with one another and develop a genuine rapport, a connection that we share to this day.

The incredibly good luck that got me cast for this role continued on set. Both Lee and I were greeted by a warm and friendly cast and crew. The vibe on set was happy and relaxed, and we felt supported and welcome. When we met Jared and Jensen, they were so at ease and appreciative of everybody's contributions. It felt like more than just a television set. It felt like we were spending time with a very happy family. (Years later, I had the same experience on the set of *Siren*.) It is amazing how important the role of the lead is when it comes to setting the tone of the entire company. Eduardo Sánchez's careful, insightful, and very trusting direction made my experience all the more enjoyable and fulfilling. The entire process was an incredibly positive experience for me and one of the most memorable of my career to this day.

Although I knew we were creating something special during filming, I was unsure how the *Supernatural* fandom would react to our characters. I had the impression that, being a family-oriented show, there might be some pushback because our characters were gay, so I was very happy to learn that when the episode aired it had touched a lot of people.

There is something very powerful about seeing yourself represented on-screen, not as a cliché, but as a relevant, believable, worthwhile human being. I believe that is what many of the fans appreciated about the episode. It is what touched me about it.

I had never engaged much with social media before working on *Supernatural*, but after the episode aired, Lee called to tell me that people were asking about me through his Twitter account. He convinced me to sign up. The morning after I did, I already had more than a thousand followers, which was a bit of a shock for an actor who hadn't previously bothered with social media. I soon abandoned Twitter (I really didn't get it) and switched to Instagram, which suited my personality better. Thus began the adventure of interacting directly with the audience, which was brand-new to me. I now have a diverse group of people with whom I interact, some from my soap opera days, some who follow my current work. And definitely, some of my most passionate followers are *Supernatural* fans. I am happy that I now get to interact directly with my new friends and family.

I am grateful to have been a part of the cultural phenomenon known as *Supernatural*, a show that evolved with the times throughout its many seasons. I am very fortunate to have been a part of such a groundbreaking episode. While I never did get to play the scary demon that I had dreamed of, the role I ended up playing was so much more meaningful and impactful that it was worth waiting all those years!

HOLLYWOOD IS WOKE

ANDREA DREPAUL

Andrea Drepaul here. You may know me as Melanie, the sassy were-wolf villainess from season 14. When Lynn, the editor of this volume, asked me if I was interested in writing a chapter on diversity and inclusivity for this book, I was ecstatic. We human beings are so deeply connected in ways that I am still trying to grasp. (Let me know if you have the secret, will ya?) And yet, there are still things that we let separate us. To understand why diversity and inclusivity are important to me, as well as to our larger society, let's first take a deeper look at the world in which I grew up.

I was born in Brantford, Ontario (home of Wayne Gretzky), to immigrant parents from Guyana and Portugal, making me first-generation Canadian. My parents were both factory workers, and somewhere along that journey they decided to move our family to the small town of Ingersoll, Ontario (aka the black hole . . . or how I felt about it for a long time). Ingersoll was a predominantly Caucasian community. At that time, our family was one of two ethnic families living in that community, the other being African Canadian. Our family was different, there was no denying that. In such a rural place, it was my experience that the general population had never seen a Guyanese person or understood the differences between Caribbean and African cultures. People knew where Portugal

was, but if we are being honest,
Guyana is not a very well-known
country in South America.

I don't ever recall being
taught about slavery or inden-
tured workers in South America
in history class. If we as human
beings take the time to understand our history and culture, it
becomes a tool for understanding
ourselves more deeply. Imagine
what it was like to live in a community where you never saw anyone who looked like you. Maybe
for some of you reading this, it
was your reality also. For a large
part of my life, I spent most of my time trying to blend in. This was an
adopted strategy from my father and was viewed as critical to our survival.
From his perspective, the best way to live a decent life was to fly under the
radar, make no waves, do your job, and be quiet.

This conditioning was ingrained in me. I never stopped to question it
with my adult mind until much later in my life; I wanted so desperately
to be accepted, and looking different wasn't safe. Because of this, I was a
victim of severe bullying. School kids would tease me and call me horrible
names every day. Coming home crying was a regular thing for me. Those
experiences traumatized me in a deep way . . . in ways that would take me
ten years of therapy to crack just the tip of the iceberg of what I taught
myself about who I was. What I learned back then—or rather, my core
subconscious beliefs—was that it was not safe to stand out or be different.
People who stand out are ridiculed and shamed and put back down into
"their" place. Don't make noise, be quiet, and don't be too smart, or it
will make others feel bad. Try to fit in, smile, be happy, don't talk about
how you really feel, and whatever you do, *under any circumstance, do not
out any of the kids who did anything to you.* (Side note: To the kids who
called me names and stuck my face in the dirt and made me eat leaves

and twigs—you are the reason I fight for equality, justice, diversity, and inclusion.)

Growing up in a small town gives you few options in terms of entertainment, so watching films and television became my place to really see the larger world. I began to shift and imagine what this world could possibly look like outside of the confines of my hometown. It lit a fire in me. I wanted to get the heck out of that place and see the world. My beliefs started shifting. I was no longer limiting myself as to who or what I could be. I wanted more. I wanted to be more, to do more. Television changed me.

Back then, the rise of diversity in television had started with the success of *The Cosby Show, A Different World,* and *The Fresh Prince of Bel Air.* I loved these shows because I saw people who somewhat resembled me. I was also learning about other cultures and history. I found that exciting. I think Hollywood really shaped my world; it was where I learned things that I never knew about. It made me want to get outside the box and go have those experiences myself.

DING, DING, DING . . . Cue major defining moment: Shohreh Aghdashloo in *House of Sand and Fog.* Boom. It was like my eyes lit up and my heart opened wide. This was the first time I felt like I saw a woman on TV who really looked like me. She is Iranian, but her hair, skin tone, and the shape of her face—I distinctly remember feeling like, "Hey that woman looks like me!!!!" It didn't matter to me that she wasn't exactly the same, because what I saw was a woman who resembled me, who had a place, a place where she belonged. Then it happened . . . my brain exploded. Wait a minute, if she can do it, why can't I?

Ladies and gentlemen, this is where I learned the true meaning of limitless possibilities. Not in a classroom, not even out in the "real" world, but from a box inside my living room. This is the power of television and film, the positive aspect where you can learn to adopt a new vision of yourself. For me, I could no longer remain in those old core beliefs, bound by the limitations of others trying to keep me down and keep me playing it safe in the world.

Wow, right?! You would think this would have been the best thing in the world. Well, let's just say my mother didn't think it was so great when

I told her, "Hey, Ma, I'm going to finish my degree and then become an actor!!!" (That's another story, for another book perhaps?) I became the first woman in my family to attend college and graduate with an honors degree. In 2003, I moved to Toronto, a city that boasted a complexity of ethnic diversity and was brimming with culture. It's the food mecca of the world, in my opinion. Living in Toronto was one of the greatest joys of my life. I felt accepted, and I saw a beautiful melting pot of culture and diversity unlike anything I had seen before. I felt I could shine there in film and television.

When I got started in this business, there was a multitude of ethnic actors who were on the audition circuit. The industry was very complex back then and not so open to diverse performers trying to make lifelong careers performing in lead roles. Diverse actors were limited in which roles we could book and which shows we could work on. This was dependent on many different marketing variables, as well as the content that was being produced at the time. It became very evident to me that if I wanted to have a career, I would have to be willing to take some jobs that didn't make me feel so good about doing them. I remember auditioning for roles of characters that didn't even have names and were implied to be "bad" people. A large majority of the plotlines of the characters I auditioned for were centered around being a mole, a terrorist, or a killer. Examples: "Terrorist #1," "Muslim girl," "Assassin."

Ethnic actors weren't being given the opportunities to play lead characters because of the way we looked and because we didn't have nearly enough lead experience to book a show—a catch-22. How could we get to be a lead player if we were not given the same opportunities as non-diverse performers? This was our version of a glass ceiling, and artists didn't speak publicly about it, mostly out of fear that we wouldn't work again or would be judged negatively. Even now as I am writing these words, I think of the possible backlash that could come about. Ethnic performers did what was called for; we became better, we studied, we went to classes, we started making our own projects, we took on secondary jobs to pay bills. We trained, and we prepared ourselves for when Hollywood would wake up and see this division. The road from then to now has been paved with a lot of blood, sweat, and tears.

Now, in 2020, the landscape of film and television has become increasingly more diverse and inclusive. We can see the rise of fabulous female directors being given the opportunity to direct films and television series, and more ethnic actors being given the opportunity to play leads on screen than ever before. There is recognition from Hollywood that the scales were, in fact, not in balance. For a long time, women and minorities in the film and television industry struggled to pay bills, own houses, and provide a reasonable level of care for their families. But that is finally—slowly—changing.

Hollywood has a deep impact on society and effectively shapes what is acceptable, normal, and embraced in our belief systems. It's the same logic as telling your children they can be anything—but if they never "see" it in the real world or on screen, how can they truly believe it's possible? For me, this is why representation is so important. There is a domino effect happening right now. People are waking from this "slumber" to realize what is actually possible, and Hollywood is steering that ship.

The process is a complex one. Where does this movement leave the individuals who are of "mixed race" or are not easily identifiable as African American, East Indian, or Latin? The "not enough" syndrome also exists, as some diverse performers are not being given the opportunity to work because they are "not Black enough," "not Indian enough," "not Asian enough," etc. This is where the work still needs to be done in the industry. If an individual is diverse, they are diverse. If a person identifies as LGTBQ, they are that. There is no such thing as not being "enough." That enough-ness stems from a hypervigilance to be as politically correct as possible in a time where every move is being scrutinized. Nobody should feel like they need to do a DNA test to prove their ancestry. But the change that has happened so far is hopeful. I commend and applaud the changes that have been made to even the playing field and represent a more real world. With every year that passes, there is a new focus and new ways to illustrate the larger world at hand.

Take, for example, the film *Crazy Rich Asians*. (I'm obsessed with this film.) In fact, everyone should watch it, not only because it is hysterical and a good rom-com but also because of its attention to detail in telling the stories of the subcultures within the Asian community. It's not just a film for Asians—it's a film for all human beings. And it's a remarkable example of what can be accomplished when Hollywood gets it right. The greatest joy I received from that film was watching it in a theater filled with Asians. Watching them laugh and cry brought me a deep sense of joy and happiness and connectedness, knowing that they could watch people who looked like them fall in love and get their hearts broken. They were validated as human beings through the actors on screen and, by extension, Hollywood. The film was a success because it resonated with the deep human desire to be accepted and loved. And that is something every human being on this planet craves and deserves; it is our birthright. When we make films and television shows that are filled with characters from all walks of life, male or female, LGTBQ, or with disabilities, we are sending a strong message that says, "You are enough. We validate your existence. You matter. You are of value."

This can only lead us to be better human beings. This can help us teach the next generation to be limitless and to have an expansive vision of what they can become or do in this world. These lessons cross gender, race, disability, and religious affiliation. When Hollywood seeks to expand our beliefs, raise awareness, and teach us how to be limitless humans, we can see the ripple effect that trickles down into our psyches.

I know this to be true because it happened to me.

If it happened to me, then it must be happening for others. The key here is to actually become aware of how deeply we are being impacted by what we watch on television or on the big screen. The diversity and inclusivity movement has allowed me to become introspective of the deeper parts of myself and really analyze who I want to be and what I can contribute to the larger world. Seeing "myself" on the screen when I was young essentially gave me some inner permission to shine, and if you look closely, you can see examples of that everywhere. For example, Freddie Highmore in *The Good Doctor* plays a surgeon with autism. He's breaking society's perception of what is possible. Yes, perhaps there will be a certain number of people who think that would never happen in the "real" world. Whether it could or couldn't isn't actually up to us as a collective to decide. Somewhere, someone with autism is seeing himself or herself on TV doing what they love to do and succeeding at it—instant core belief expansion. That individual now knows at some level that becoming more is *possible for them.*

This is what my role as Melanie in *Supernatural* felt like for me. Becoming *more* was possible.

Prior to booking this role, I hadn't worked in fourteen months. I was drained and exhausted. I had just gone through a deep transformation of self and was coming out of a dark place into the light, so to speak. For me, this role was "divinely timed," as I was just beginning to really stand in my authentic self. The journey of Melanie and of me as a human were symbiotic. Melanie is a character who could transform literally into something else. And at the same time, I was transforming inside and changing too.

In our society, there is an immense amount of value placed on our physical appearance: the color of our skin, our weight, the clothes we wear, and so on. We are deeply conditioned to this valuing from a very early age. At its core, those who are victims of racism have deep worthiness issues. We don't always see our own value. The gift of this role is that it allowed me to see my real inner value. I was able to see for the first time that I was not chosen for the color of my skin—I was chosen because of who I am. As a result, I became "more," not because I wasn't enough already but because I had made a choice to grow and be more than that. I am grateful to casting, the producers, the episode's director, Richard Speight, Jr., and the whole cast for embracing me and deeply reflecting back to me what my true value is.

That is the power of diversity and inclusivity. There is an awakening happening. Hollywood is becoming woke. We as a society can choose to embrace that change and take joy in knowing that we are part of this evolving awareness. Our future generations will reap the rewards as they expand their beliefs of what is possible.

BEEN HERE ALL ALONG

EMERSON LOPEZ ODANGO

When I first watched "Weekend at Bobby's," what struck me the most about this monster-of-the-week episode was that it featured a Japanese monster—an *ōkami*. In the six seasons of *Supernatural* that had aired by then, this was the first time I noticed that there was a narrative focus on someone—or something—from my side of the Pacific Ocean. After following a bunch of white dudes traveling across the continental United States all these years, this was intriguing. Season 6, even more so than the ones before, brought to our attention that there really are other monsters out there in the world beyond the places that had already been shown to us in *Supernatural*.

Many of us already know that intimately well. I grew up in the United States listening to my elders' stories about their lives in the Philippines and their encounters with the *aswang*, the vampire-like witches that feed on the unborn or the dead, or the *sigbin*, the monster that appears as a large white dog knocking on your door. They tell these stories as truth, as lived experiences. As a child, I took comfort in knowing that those monsters were not here now, because they roamed the Philippines, and my family and I were in the United States. My parents would usually tell stories of the distant past when they were children, when they had to look out for the mermaid-like *siyokoy* when they played in rivers. I doubt any Filipino parent in America has told their child to watch out for such things when swimming at the beach; we were more concerned with jellyfish and stomach cramps. As a kid, I reminded myself of the fact that we were swimming in the Atlantic Ocean, half a world away from the Pacific waters that seeped into the places where *siyokoy* would roam. There was comfort in knowing that however hair-raising my elders' stories were, those monsters weren't here now.

And then, when I was 18, I read *American Gods* by Neil Gaiman.

And then I started watching *Supernatural*.

My world has not been the same since.

By the time "Weekend at Bobby's" aired in 2010, I'd had a couple of years to sit with the truth bombs from *American Gods*. The deities and monsters from the Old Countries were here with us in the new land—well, "new" to us as immigrants over the span of America's lifetime—because we feed them, call out to them, hide from them, and remember them. They were part of the balance of new hopes and old fears. *Supernatural* had woven that narrative thread into the larger show mythology, both prior to "Weekend at Bobby's" (e.g., Hold Nickar in "A Very Supernatural Christmas" in season 3 and all the gods present in "Hammer of the Gods" in season 5) as well as after (e.g., Prometheus in "Remember the Titans" in season 8). Thus, by the time I watched "Weekend at Bobby's," I didn't think it was entirely unexpected that our protagonists would fight a Japanese monster that is rarely seen outside of Japan. Maybe the *ōkami* have always roamed the American Midwest, and it just so happened that Bobby and Rufus crossed paths with one—and finished the job with a woodchipper.

That episode, however, was the start of a flood of questions for me. How does *Supernatural* present the Other (i.e., anyone or anything deemed by the majority as "different")? It was interesting that the monster of the week was from a place and culture far away from Wisconsin—but what does "interesting" mean here? Was the *ōkami* a tokenized occurrence? But hasn't *Supernatural* been doing this all along? Is this TV status quo for serialized shows featuring the X-of-the-week-along-with-overarching-mythology pattern? These questions made me rethink what I had watched before, and framed what I watched later.

"Wendigo" from season 1, for example, was an episode that I took at face value when I watched it in 2005. "Cool," I thought. "Here is a monster from the Native American world, which is not usually seen on TV." As a budding linguist interested in cultural anthropology, I was fascinated to hear Dean talk about Anasazi symbols for protection and Sam talk about the Cree language etymology of *wendigo*. In only the second episode of the series, we established that our boys would be dealing with more than just ghosts—they would be going head-to-head with monsters from various cultures that have walked this landscape longer than we can imagine.

Fast-forward to 2019, when "Don't Go in the Woods" from season 14 aired. In a season full of stand-out episodes—"Prophet and Loss" and "Lebanon" are at the top of my list—this one stood out because of its contrast to "Wendigo," in that in this later episode, the Native world takes center stage in nuanced ways. The story is about a father—Sheriff Mason Romero (masterfully played by Native actor Adam Beach)—and his son Tom, and how ghosts of the past catch up with the next generations. These are themes we've seen for years with Dean, Sam, and their father John, and heightened especially in season 14 with Dean, Sam, and Cas raising Lucifer's son, Jack. What struck me the most was that this episode was crafted in a way that allowed the Native story to exist on its own, unlike in the earlier episode "Wendigo," yet with thematic ties to the larger *Supernatural* mythology: A father trying to protect his son by lying to him, which ultimately could result in dire consequences. A son going through the challenges of navigating the world of divorced parents, as well as the spectrum of the worlds within and outside of his tribe. A man's memory of childhood monster stories coming back to harm his own child.

"Don't Go in the Woods" was one of the most impactful *Supernatural* chapters regarding the show's construction of modern Indigeneity. Yes, the tokenization is still there, especially given that this was a monster-of-the-week episode. I also wonder about the creative choice to focus on a *kohonta*, which appears to be a concept created for this episode as opposed to being based on a specific Native belief, and the fact that Sheriff Romero's tribe is not identified by name. I would like to think that this suppression (erasure?) of specific Native identity allowed for the father-son dynamic to take center stage. To that end, it did. However, we also see the complexity of modern Indigenous life, where the "exotic" aspects of an unnamed tribe's past have direct impacts on the "mundane" problems of a divorced father scolding his angst-ridden teenage son for not studying.

We have seen Native story lines, characters (and Native actors cast as those characters), words, and symbols appear from time to time on *Supernatural*. "Don't Go in the Woods" went a long way to show us that the monsters we fight—whether they are supernatural cursed cannibals or the small-yet-accreted decisions we make to deceive those we love for their protection—are common to us all. More importantly, though, we need to see that being Native is mundane and exceptional at the same time. *I* needed to see it, because as a Filipino who hasn't seen Dean fight an *aswang* (yet!) or heard Sam pronounce some Tagalog words as part of his research (yet!), I nonetheless see myself in the journeys that *Supernatural* has taken us on, most especially in the growth of how the Native story gets to tell itself. These stories have legs, because they have walked miles and miles for generations, and they have many places to go yet.

That intersection of the mundane/exceptional/supernatural took a similar turn with "Into the Mystic" in season 11. My initial draw to that episode was that there was another *American Gods*–like angle of a monster of the Old Country finding its way to the New World. After eleven years, of course the Winchesters would tangle with a banshee! What was surprising was meeting the kick-ass deaf hunter, Eileen Leahy. Again, as a linguist, my eye/ear was attuned to how American Sign Language (ASL) would be featured throughout the episode. Oh yes, we all remember that embarrassing—yet supremely awesome—scene of Sam doing his best to sign "thank you" to Eileen, and being schooled in the most chill way possible. A deaf hunter? Why not?! How cool! Again, as with "Wendigo," I remember enjoying the episode at face value. It brought in new "exotic" elements, such as seeing ASL dialogue, which didn't have a precedent on *Supernatural* (or most other shows, for that matter).

But with a show that has fifteen years of stories to tell, I was compelled to reread certain chapters to gain deeper understandings of that fictitious world, and thus our own real world. This rereading of *Supernatural* happened a few months ago, during my first semester back at graduate school. After finishing my PhD in linguistics and working in the educational nonprofit sector for a few years, I knew that my passion lay in helping people through language, and I started my journey in speech-language pathology. I co-facilitated an event in which we brought students and faculty together to talk about how we see populations, topics, and ideas connected to our professional practice represented in our favorite popular media, such as TV and movies.

One of our faculty members shared the trailer for *Still Alice* (the 2014 movie about early-onset Alzheimer's disease) because she works with adult communities. I reflected to the group that it was important to discuss such examples because neurodegenerative diseases do not only affect people we consider elderly; they can affect those who are relatively young and healthy. I then summarized for them the *Supernatural* episode "Regarding Dean" from season 12, in which we see Dean essentially go through acute and rapid dementia. I can't imagine what Jensen Ackles had to channel in order to go through that heartbreaking mirror scene. How is it possible for someone like Dean Winchester to be defeated by dementia? How could Sam watch his brother fade away like that? And how could *Supernatural* throw us such a sucker punch of a plot thread even after twelve years?

Reflecting on those scenes made me realize that the representation of people with disabilities—the intentional *crafting* of those stories—has been long running on *Supernatural*. Throughout season 5, I had never thought about Bobby being a person with a disability after he was injured at the start of that season. It was "easy" for me, as someone who has never used a wheelchair, to focus only on Bobby as the badass hunter, just without his ability to walk. In retrospect, I see that the very fact that he is in a wheelchair is a crucial element in his character development. It is not "Bobby (in a wheelchair)." Being in a wheelchair is a part of who Bobby is, and how he grows; his disability shouldn't be ignored. I'm sure there was someone out there who watched season 5 Bobby and thought, "That's me!"

At my school event, I also reflected on how Castiel is portrayed in many ways like a person who has challenges with pragmatics and social cues, which is something relatable to many fans. In various on-screen moments, his challenges are couched in humor (e.g., "I don't understand that reference"). In real life, people who have friends and family members who are considered, for example, on the autism spectrum sometimes share similar anecdotes. Many fans can relate to Castiel's experience, or Abed on *Community*, or many others because art does imitate life to some degree. Castiel's entire character arc of his developing humanity provides glimpses into the real challenges of others in our communities, while also making it clear that Castiel is a hero. *Supernatural* has helped me reflect more deeply about my professional service to others in ways I never could have predicted when I first watched the pilot that night on September 13, 2005.

It has been difficult preparing for the end of *Supernatural* for many reasons—the foremost being that we do not want to say goodbye to this wild car ride in the Impala. There are so many more stories to tell, so many more monsters to encounter and defeat, so many more voices with something to say (or sign) in their own words. I take comfort knowing that I can be a part of sharing those words: geeking out with classmates, imagining worlds with cousins in which our Filipino monsters and heroes take the stage, or starting conversations about topics like dementia because I can play a clip about Dean that says more than a thousand words.

Supernatural has given us a fifteen-year foundation to continue fighting against the monsters[1]—whether corporeal bullies or intangible repressions of our identities, from the Old World or in our emerging landscapes—and to do so in the armor of our own design.

———————————————

Emerson would like to thank Judia Griner for the crucial feedback.

———————

1. Oh, and of course there's my own head canon in which Dean and Sam had probably stopped by some Filipino *turo-turo* restaurant to get food (Dean's favorite is the *adobong baboy*) during a long road trip and somehow they encountered an *aswang* and Sam did some research in which he pronounced *aswang* perfectly and Dean chopped off the *aswang's* head right before its long, undulating tongue was about to attack an innocent victim. It took place in, let's say, season 13 when they road-tripped it to San Francisco. Totally happened, *totoo ang lahat.*

OUT OF THE FRIDGE AND INTO THE FIRE

JESSICA MASON

'm a huge fan of *Supernatural*. I'm also a proud feminist. To some people, these things aren't compatible.

I hate it when people tell me I can't be a feminist and like *Supernatural*. For one thing, it's not very progressive to tell people what they can or should like, but more than that, the oft-repeated assumption that *Supernatural* is horrible to women is just factually untrue. At least . . . it is now. No series that runs for fifteen seasons will have a perfect record with anything, but the really interesting thing to me about *Supernatural* is how its treatment of women and feminist narratives has changed and evolved over a decade and a half.

Through four showrunners and dozens of writers, *Supernatural* has run the gamut when it comes to female representation, and since I have you here for a whole chapter, I'm going to tell you how my favorite show has moved from tired, boring tropes that *were* indeed reductive and sexist to fostering a narrative that allows women to be more than crutches or plot points. There were some stumbles along the way, but just like the story of the Winchesters, there are attempts at redemption. And in the end, I'll be able to explain why I don't just love this show despite being a feminist, but I love it *as* a feminist.

AND FOR WHAT? NARRATIVE SYMMETRY?

There's a famous—or, more accurately, infamous—trope called the "woman in the refrigerator." It is a term coined by comic writer Gail Simone referring to an incident in the Green Lantern comic where the hero returns home to find his girlfriend murdered and her mutilated body shoved into, yes, a refrigerator. In short, it refers to the needless and gratuitous death of a woman that serves only to advance a hero's angst and story.

Supernatural, the series, begins with not one, but two serious incidents of "fridging" with the symmetrical deaths of Mary Winchester and Jessica Moore. These deaths are problematic, there's no getting past that. In the pilot, neither blonde has much character (though obviously this changes for one of them, and we'll get there) and their deaths serve only to motivate our heroes.

But it also highlights how complex and vexing the women in refrigerators trope is . . . because these deaths work *well* to propel the narrative.

It's a cliché, yes, but it's still well done and entertaining, which is the case with a lot of stories that are bad as feminism, but good as entertainment. Jessica's death is genuinely shocking to the viewer. It hooks you and makes you want to see where the series will go. And neither her death nor Mary's is written off easily.

Later on in the series, in "The Monster at the End of This Book," the authors of Mary's death, via their mouthpiece, Chuck, lampshade this egregious suffering for Sam specifically by noting that it was only for the sake of narrative symmetry. It's the kind of meta, knowing commentary that makes *Supernatural* so good as a show. More so than almost any other program, it comments and reconstructs itself and sometimes owns up to its mistakes. But, I'm getting ahead of myself.

The women in the refrigerator that start the show are a sad portent for how women function in the first season. While most of the female characters Sam and Dean encounter are interesting, complex people (Missouri Mosley, Cassie Robinson, Sarah Blake), they pretty much are only there for a few episodes to serve the Winchester story. But again, that's not necessarily a sexist issue. Sam and Dean are the main characters who happen to be men, and all the characters they meet in the early seasons are there solely to propel their story because, well, they're protagonists. One standout who has her own story and survives a long time is Meg, a complex female whose reveal as a demon is, in my mind, the tipping point of the series from fun to "oh my god, I need to see the next episode."

Even so, I think someone, maybe the network, maybe a writer, was aware that the show wasn't doing great by way of women, and season 2 introduced Jo and Ellen Harvelle, two characters who remain extremely popular in fandom to this day because they stand on their own and were powerful characters who happened to be female, but weren't defined by their femininity. Ellen and Jo worked because they fit well into the world the show was beginning to establish, and their introduction was relatively organic. The next year, the show attempted the introduction of two more females less organically, and it was . . . not as good.

Fandom attitudes have changed in the decade since Ruby and Bela were introduced to the series. Full disclosure, I wasn't watching live at that point and I've only heard tales of fan reactions to the two being vocally negative. There's a perception, now, that this was a sexist pushback in part motivated by female fans' own internalized misogyny and the fact that no one wanted anyone on the show who had the remote possibility of being a long-term love interest for Sam or Dean.

I think these points are valid, but I also think that Ruby and Bela just weren't well-written characters. They failed because they fell into sexist femme fatale tropes. The writers tried too hard to make them "strong" and just ended up making them mean and wooden. The performances too weren't the best the series has seen, either. (I will note that Katie Cassidy, who played Ruby, and Lauren Cohan, who played Bela, have both grown tremendously as actresses on *Arrow* and *The Walking Dead*, respectively.) Ruby became much more interesting in season 4, but she was still the bad girl, still a woman as the personification of evil, as was Lilith. And she still, like a lot of women . . . ended up dead.

So did Pamela Barnes. And then Jo and Ellen. And Anna. And . . . well, a lot of women. Even though Ruby was instrumental to the overall narrative of season 4, she couldn't stick around. The only characters that did, like Bobby and Castiel, were white men and . . . yeah, that's not a good look.

Whether this came from the writers making their best characters dudes, or the fact that women weren't seen at the time to viably fit into the Winchesters' life long term is a question that doesn't have an easy answer. Some would say, as I've noted, that no one would want a long-term female character because she'd be seen as a love interest for someone . . . but the fact that Castiel isn't a woman hasn't stopped a large part of the fandom from seeing *him* as a love interest for Dean, even just subtextually. Maybe it's just the threat of straightness that fans reject.

The story of the first five seasons was, in many ways, a tragedy, where no one ends up happy, or alive, at the end of things. Eric Kripke, the show's creator, had a pretty definite plan, and it was all about those two boys in their car, with the rest of the universe revolving around them— men, women, and angels of indeterminate gender alike. It had serious sexist elements, but ultimately it was a still a great story about family that fans loved. A story that *women* loved for reasons we'll get into. In the coming seasons, the way women and other side characters were treated on the show would change . . . and change again.

NO ONE LIKES IT WHEN IT'S ALL ABOUT DICK

With a new showrunner and a brave new world to explore, *Supernatural* changed greatly in season 6. With a female showrunner in Sera Gamble, we might have expected a more robust role for women, but it didn't quite work out that way.

Season 6 added and upgraded many characters, like Crowley and the Campbells, to larger roles, and introduced the first truly long-term female love interest into the narrative, with Lisa. As you can tell from that last sentence, the expanded ensemble didn't translate to more diversity, beyond Lisa. We did get a female villain, with Eve, who I think was a really interesting character, and with the Campbells we had some great opportunities to explore Mary, and what life was like for hunters like Gwen. Unfortunately, season 6 is full of promising ideas that are quickly abandoned, often in favor of immediate shock and twists—Samuel Campbell, Gwen, Lisa, Eve are all dealt with almost summarily, and the ultimate villain of the season turns out to be a beloved ally, Castiel. The bigger world was just cannon fodder for the story of Sam and Dean and *only* Sam and Dean.

This trend continued into season 7, where *everyone* was taken away from Sam and Dean, including their male allies like Cas and Bobby, and females like Amy Pond, Dean's daughter Emma, and the hunter Annie were introduced for single episodes only to be killed for temporary and often frustrating brother conflict and manpain. The only real exceptions to this were the return of Meg and the introduction of Charlie Bradbury. Charlie was a rare character who was immediately accessible to fans as their avatar, but not viewed as a threat romantically. But like all the women above, she was intended as a one-off.

The disposability of women, and to be honest, of men as well, was symptomatic of the problems with Sera Gamble's brief tenure. While seasons 6 and 7 had many great episodes, the focus only on Sam and Dean, stripping away everything and everyone from them, was detrimental to the narrative and not particularly fun to watch. We got some social and political commentary, in the form of the Leviathans, and continued the self-aware, meta trends with brilliant episodes like "The French Mistake." But none of that seemed to get the show to reexamine how it treated other characters. And again, it wasn't only women.

There's a persistent feminist criticism of *Supernatural* that it kills all its female characters. Now, I've actually run the math on this and it's not really true. Men have a higher death rate in general, but that reveals what might be a problem with the show itself—not that all women die, but that *everyone* dies. Death is cheap on *Supernatural* (for Chuck's sake, *Death* himself died for shock value), as it is on a lot of television shows nowadays. An on-screen death is easy drama, an easy shock, and on a show like *Supernatural*, where the lead characters have died literally dozens of times, it's easy to undo if one wants. Individually, death might work in a single episode, but as a whole trend on the show and in the media, it loses its impact.

The best episode of season 7, in my view, is "Death's Door," which is a wonderful and touching goodbye to Bobby . . . but it's undercut by Bobby's many returns. Amy Pond's death is particularly frustrating, not just because she was another woman in a refrigerator, but because the focus of the first third of the season was on Dean and Sam's angst over the death of this random woman we never met, instead of on the recent death of Castiel, their best friend. This was insulting to viewers on several levels, the feminist one being perhaps the least egregious.

In terms of feminism, I hate to say that under a female showrunner, things did not improve at *Supernatural*. But it's okay, because after season 7, Sam hit a dog and somehow, slowly, the way the show treated women began to change.

META FAN FICTION

Season 8 is when I started watching *Supernatural* live, and it's what really got me into the show as a fan. Understandably, having binged the show between seasons 7 and 8, I was emotionally preparing for this to be a final season. But I was also excited for Cas to be back and hoping for the best. And boy, did we get it. Not just in terms of feminism, but also in terms of story, season 8 really reinvigorated the show, and laid a new foundation that remained stable and supported new stories into the final season. In contrast to the way most of season 7 condensed the world of the show, season 8 expanded it. We got the Men of Letters, we learned more about the angels and about God, and we got to see the boys at least starting to break down and become aware of their own codependency. But another way this season really redefined itself was the many and varied female characters it introduced or expanded on.

Only one of these women, Amelia, was a love interest (and she was interestingly written, but not well cast), but the rest were just plain awesome. Abaddon, Linda Tran, Charlie, Naomi, and many single-appearance women were a kind of new breed we hadn't seen on the show. They were strong and complex and just happened to be female. I think a lot of the positive change under Jeremy Carver as a showrunner can be attributed, not just to him, but also to the writers he allowed to thrive, who had clear feminist goals and ideals. Robbie Thompson is perhaps the best known of this crew, but I would also include Robert Berens and to a lesser extent Andrew Dabb, who began writing on his own under Carver, in this mix.

Robbie Thompson in particular has attained near-legendary status in the fandom for his brilliant episodes that focused on brilliant women, like Charlie, as well as meta and outside-of-the-box episodes like "Meta Fiction," "Fan Fiction," and "Baby." The things that made season 8 very good, including the more favorable treatment of women, also reinvigorated the

fandom. I know a lot of fans who call themselves feminist, or queer, or progressive who really became part of the fandom because of season 8. Some of the seeds we saw planted didn't bear fruit, and I think seasons 9 and 10 were not exactly the same level of quality, but they still gave us new women to love. Wayward women.

In season 9, we saw the return of Jody Mills as a real character, not just someone to move the plot along. We'd loved her since season 5 and it was wonderful to see her really get deep in season 9. We got the brilliant 200th episode, where female fandom, fan fiction, and queer interpretations of the show were basically blessed by the show and *God*. We also got Alex, Jody's adopted daughter. And Donna Hanscum. In season 10 we got to see these women together, and caught up with Claire Novak, the daughter of Castiel's vessel. All these new hunters and allies were amazing, strong, damaged, and complex, and the fandom understandably latched on to the idea of them as a team. Things were looking so good, and I was so proud as a feminist to call myself a fan of the show.

Then "Dark Dynasty" happened.

I don't think I've ever seen a more negative reaction to a character's death than to that of Charlie Bradbury. It was a rough time to be in the fandom as a feminist and a queer woman. And the peculiar part of the situation was that the anger fans expressed wasn't toward the characters who killed Charlie, but the writers. It was as if a real person had been murdered. The impact of fictional deaths can be real, and devastating, but it's also a writer's job to make you feel things, even sadness. But the reaction to this death wasn't about the story, it was about a queer woman whom so many identified with being pointlessly (and stupidly) killed. It played into toxic tropes like women in the refrigerator and "bury your gays" that we all hoped we were past. Fandom was vocal about their displeasure, enough so that Jeremy Carver was famously called out for it at Comic-Con that summer.

It's hard for Winchesters to learn from their mistakes; that's been evident for over a decade. And it's hard for an entire writers' room to learn and change too. But I think that after Charlie, a change really did happen, although I can't say with who or how. Season 11 was different. We met God's sister and they solved the problem with her . . . by talking.

I liked Amara, and while reducing the "connection" between Amara and Dean to something romantic and kinda creepy was dumb, the resolution of her story was satisfying. We also got more Rowena, who joined us in season 10 and quickly became a rival for Crowley as the boys' best frenemy. She also proved to be unkillable, at the time, much to everyone's pleasure. And it was at the end of season 11 that *Supernatural* addressed one of its original sins and resurrected Mary Winchester.

WAYWARD RISING

I would maintain, and no one can argue with me because I'm writing this alone, that Andrew Dabb has presided over the most feminist era of *Supernatural*. With the addition of brilliant writers like Meredith Glynn, Steve Yockey, and Davy Perez, the series received a new infusion of creativity in season 12, and most of the folks behind the scenes realized that good storytelling doesn't need to come on the backs of female suffering.

Now, in a show like *Supernatural*, women will still suffer; we know this, because *everyone* will suffer. But they suffer because they are people in a dangerous world, not because they are women. I loved the exploration and deconstruction of Mary Winchester we got in season 12. She became more than a saint or an ideal but was revealed to be a complex and flawed person with her own needs and desires. Seeing her sons confront this about their mother was truly interesting, and as the writers developed other women in exciting ways, like Rowena and our Wayward daughters and sisters, it's been a pleasure to watch things as a feminist.

When the spin-off *Wayward Sisters* was announced, it was just another sign that the powers that be had heard us, that they got it and wanted to tell feminist stories. Season 13 was even more feminist and exciting than season 12, and it was a better season for it. It was cathartic and amazing to watch Jody and Claire and Donna and Alex and Patience and Kaia take to the fore. And it was equally heartbreaking when the show wasn't picked up. However, the fact that these women will remain in the *Supernatural* universe is comforting because their stories will continue to be important. Not only are our female characters now uniformly complex, strong, and human, but they also exist for their own purposes and story now, and while they enhance the Winchester narrative, they are not defined by it. I think the biggest clue to this is our new Charlie, who returned from an alternative world and refused to let the Winchesters define her fate or use her as a substitute for something they needed. That's interesting and great to see.

AND IN THE END . . .

The show still makes mistakes (Eileen's death in season 12 was a blunder of epic proportions, with a do-over in season 15), but I do think it's trying and aware of its narrative in a way that's new. The way the show treats women has grown and evolved, and that's great. But one of the things that has attracted women and feminist women to the show from the beginning is the way the show treats men.

It has been disheartening, somewhat, to see that the seven actors who have clocked the most episodes on the show and are most identified with it are all white cis men, but I think for a show with that kind of a cast, it still does try to serve the women well nowadays. For example, in season 14, we lost Mary Winchester again and in season 15 we started off with the death of Rowena, but then we got the resurrection of Eileen and the triumph of Rowena as the Queen of Hell.

These women's deaths and stories mattered, not just for the boys, but for their own narrative arcs that matter in conjunction with the boys and the world. Perhaps the character that's seen the greatest feminist growth, though, over three showrunners is Becky Rosen. She went from a parody of fandom to the worst version of it . . . to a grown-up, competent woman who didn't need anyone to give her permission to be herself, not even God. Making Becky, a woman who represents the fandom in so many ways, a bit of a hero while making God the final villain is incredible growth for this weird, angsty, creepy, and homoerotic show.

Supernatural has always been a show about two boys, then three when Castiel joined the party. And these men are allowed to be vulnerable and complex in a way that many characters aren't. Part of that comes from the fact that they aren't saddled with heterosexual love stories too often. I believe it's attractive to the legion of female fans because this show is actively not about conventional love stories or romance. Lady love interests never work, but that doesn't mean love isn't an important force in the *Supernatural* universe. The power of other sorts of love, the love of family and friends and even enemies, is what saves the world again and again. And yeah, the homoeroticism of it all opens all sorts of venues of interpretation of the love between all the characters, but that's a whole other book.

While *Supernatural* is a show about two men who are on their surface stereotypically masculine, from the very beginning it has critiqued and undermined that toxic masculinity to reveal something deeper in these characters, and that's feminist too. Especially through Dean we've seen his masculine posturing as just that, a performance hiding deep vulnerability and even "feminine" qualities. And these things make him better, make him more interesting and relatable to a female audience. Maybe more than anything, watching the evolution of the male characters and their complex relationship with masculinity has been the most interesting part of this journey.

And it has been a *journey*. *Supernatural* is unique for many reasons, but one thing that sticks out for me is that it has a canon so vast and varied that it's almost impossible to quantify it as one thing. There is no one author, there is no single actor or story that we can point to and say, "This makes the show feminist," or the opposite, because in a show where characters have pizza with Death and adventures with Scooby-Doo, every-thing has happened . . . or can. We can't define a series that's run as long as *Supernatural* by its sexist mistakes, just like we can't define Sam or Dean or Cas or Mary by theirs. *Supernatural* has shown us that what matters is what people choose to do going forward, how they make up for mistakes. When it comes to women, *Supernatural* has done that.

I can't guess right now how *Supernatural* will end. As I write, we only have about fifteen episodes left, but I imagine a conclusion that truly probes the idea of God as an author and how that applies to all aspects of the story.

Women started the show as mere plot devices, just as Sam and Dean were simply playthings for Chuck. But like the Winchesters, the role of

women has grown into some-thing more human and nuanced that goes beyond tired clichés and plots. I think that women on the show are so much better than they were when they started out. Death is a woman. The face of real power is a woman. And that's not nothing. So, in the end, no matter what, I'm proud to be a fan of this show and, like any Wayward woman, who I am and what I love will never be some-thing I hide or apologize for.

WHAT'S UP, TIGER MOMMY?

LAUREN TOM

When my agent called with an offer from producer Jeremy Carver for a three-episode arc on *Supernatural*, I was flattered and honored. Jeremy's wife, Anna Frike, had been a writer on *Men in Trees*, a series I had done four years prior, and Jeremy apparently liked my work on that show.

But I was in a dilemma. I was already committed to appear in a friend's independent film, and was scheduled to fly to Hawaii the following week, the same time I would have to film *Supernatural*. My Catholic guilt kicked in. Usually my guilt costs me, on average, three nights of lost sleep.

But once I realized that the role of Linda Tran afforded me the opportunity to play the first badass character of my career, my decision became clear. At 5 feet tall and 99 pounds, a badass role had never presented itself to me before. Most folks remembered me as the painfully shy Lena in *The Joy Luck Club* or the perennially nice Julie in the sitcom *Friends*.

Perhaps unconsciously, I was longing to get back to the badass, independent girl I used to be when I was a small child. I grew up in Highland Park, Illinois, a quiet, affluent suburb north of Chicago. I imagine my life

must have looked idyllic from the outside. But with the triple whammy of being raised Catholic in a town that was 98 percent Jewish, being a member of the only Chinese American family in my town, and being raised in an Asian culture that valued politeness and congeniality, by the time I entered middle school I had become an extremely lonely, shy outsider without a voice.

Apparently, it wasn't always that way. From what I'm told, between ages one through eight, I was a hell-raiser who garnered the nickname "Little Tiger" from my maternal grandfather, Da-En. My mom tells me I insisted on doing all my own stunts as a toddler, allowing grown-ups to hold my hand going down the stairs, but then climbing right back up and coming down again on my own. And lunchtime was always a search-and-rescue mission for my mom, as she allowed me to walk the half mile home from school. Day after day, the school would call to tell her that I hadn't returned back to school after lunch. So she would jump in her car and start looking for me. She usually found me sitting in the dirt on a wooded path engrossed in the rocks I had found. (As a mother today, I can't imagine letting my kids walk to and from school at six years old, but those were different times, I suppose.)

Da-En and my mom would watch me orchestrate games with all the kids on my block, allocating who would play which part. The outcomes of these games always ended up with me as the winner. "Beauty Pageant" was a favorite game, where I assigned the kids I didn't like so much to represent countries I also didn't like very much.

But even with all of this bossy behavior, my grandfather still thought I was a good kid, and used to pay me a dollar for banging out songs on the piano for him as he took a nap in the Barcalounger. He and my grandmother visited our family every weekend, and that helped solidify my strong character, which surprised no one, as I came from a long line of strong women.

My grandmother, Helen, and Da-En had emigrated from China to the United States in 1918. Helen longed to go to school and get an education, but at that time, in her small village of Hoi Ping, only boys were allowed to attend school. Undeterred, she sat on the ground outside the classroom and listened to the lessons. She vowed to one day right this inequality and assigned herself this task. She and my grandfather bought a small takeout restaurant in a blue-collar community in Chicago, which they eventually built up into a sit-down restaurant called Dang Ho. They worked this business together for fifty-five years, and unbeknownst to anyone, Helen had been secretly stashing away money for her dream. In 1987, she sent that money back to Hoi Ping and had a school built where both boys *and* girls were allowed to attend. I traveled with her to China for the grand opening. It was the proudest moment of my life.

And her daughter, my mother, Nancy, was also a spitfire who was and still remains an activist and ardent supporter of Asian causes. In 2011, President Obama gave her a "Champion of Change" award at the White House, and again, I was there to witness that great honor.

So as a child, it made perfect sense that I would take up the mantle as "Little Tiger." In fact, I became a fierce protector of my friend Terri, who lived near us and had suffered a terrible tragedy. Terri had been in a plane crash when she was two, which killed her mother and sister and left her half deaf and paralyzed on the left side of her body. My mother forced me to play with her, which I wasn't too happy about at first, but I soon came to enjoy Terri's company quite a bit. She always happily let me make her be "Miss Poland" and with a ton of grace accepted the position of perennial runner-up in every pageant. We still laugh about it to this day.

But when Terri and I entered middle school together, everything seemed to change, and I began to morph into someone I didn't recognize. We were teased mercilessly by some particularly mean kids—her for being a "gimp," and me for being a "chink." I thought to myself, "Chink!?" I wasn't sure what they meant at first. I thought I was a white Jewish girl like everyone else. But when they started singing "Ching Chong Chinaman" as they pulled their eyes back into slits, I soon caught the drift. Those daily taunts cut me to the core and filled me with rage, but I couldn't find the courage to fight back or advocate for myself. But when it came to Terri, I somehow managed to yell to those bullies, "Leave her alone, you jerks!" Those words didn't stop them, of course, and no one else came to our defense. But I do remember one girl suggesting to me that if I dropped Terri as a friend, I would most likely not get bullied as badly myself. That didn't seem like the right thing to do, and it's not how my mother raised me. So I stuck by Terri and defended her always. Looking back, I see now that this was training for my role as Linda Tran—to protect my son, Kevin (played by Osric Chau), at all costs.

Miraculously, when I turned thirteen, I fell in love with dance. I poured my heart, my soul, and all that negative energy into training four hours a day. Mostly because I loved it, but also to escape the torture that was high school. Dance was my saving grace and was the portal from which I entered the entertainment field. When I was seventeen, the national tour of the Broadway show *A Chorus Line* came through Chicago. I was encouraged by some girls in my dance class to audition, as there was a part of a tiny Chinese girl in the musical who sings about being really short and looking very young. I didn't know how to act or sing, and was extremely shy, but my mother drove me to the audition anyway. I remember clutching the edge of the piano on the side of the stage, looking down, and singing in a horribly meek off-key voice, "If My Friends Could See Me Now" from *Sweet Charity*. The director asked me to move to the center of the stage and start again. Without the security of hanging on to the piano, I felt like I had no clothes on as I inched my way to center stage like a "dead man walking."

Even though I clearly couldn't act or sing, my dancing skills got me hired for the role. I am grateful to this day that I was given this chance, as it set me on the path I've been walking for the past four decades.

Over the years (and lots of therapy!), I've gradually come closer to feeling like that brave, strong little girl I once was, which was why it was so important to me to portray Linda Tran on *Supernatural*. And although I still feel like a misfit and an outsider at times, I realize now that most people probably feel that way—our situations and particular details might be different, but we, as humans, are all much more alike than different.

Perhaps that's what has bound the *Supernatural* family so close together. We are all—fans, crew, and cast—a bunch of bighearted misfits who have come together around a show that we all love. At the end of the day, we all long for that sense of belonging; we are social animals, after all. And I have nothing but gratitude for the love and support that the *Supernatural* Family has shown me through social media and meeting face to face at conventions.

Thank you for reading part of my story. I hope to hear yours someday. And with that, I will end my chapter with a wish for you. It's the same wish I hold for my kids, and that is: May you truly know that You Are Enough. That is a given. From there, find something you really love to do, get behind that, and push with all you've got. Channel any negative energy inside you into something positive that you can share and contribute to the world. And here's a quote from best-selling author Brené Brown that seems appropriate to end with: "You either walk inside your story and own it, or you stand outside your story and hustle for your worthiness."

BEING HANNAH

LEE MAJDOUB

Playing Hannah on *Supernatural* was one of the most rewarding experiences of my career; however, I panicked when I first got the role. Hannah was already an established character, wonderfully portrayed by Erica Carroll as an angel in a female vessel with a female-sounding name. Knowing this, I put a lot of pressure on myself. "How am I going to pull this off? Will the fans believe I'm Hannah? I can't mess this up!"

One of the first things I did was watch Erica's performance. I wanted to see what Erica had done, and what had been established. What experiences had Hannah had? What was the history between Hannah and Castiel? Who *was* Hannah?

I knew angels didn't identify as male or female, so I tried to stay away from any male or female pronouns for Hannah. I did refer to Hannah as "she/her" at times, and I think that came from the fact that Hannah had been in Caroline as a vessel for some time, and had learned a lot about humanity, love, emotion, and companionship through Caroline (a cisgender woman).

When it was time to portray Hannah, I simply wanted to convey love at its purest. To me, Hannah was trying their hardest to do the right thing, and they continually had a battle going on within themselves: love or duty. I really hoped that would come through in my performance. I wanted to do right by the character, by the show, and by the fans.

I remember being so nervous when my first episode aired. I was scared nobody would believe it was Hannah. It was also important for me to be able to show the softness and affection that Hannah had for Castiel from the very moment Hannah enters that vessel. Then the moment happened. Hannah entered the male vessel and looked at Castiel. And then I saw the Twitter comments. The wonderful Twitter comments. Many people said they knew it was Hannah right away. I got so many lovely messages about how much my performance meant to the fandom. I was ecstatic and so deeply moved. The fandom's love and support continued after my second episode, and I still get messages about what Hannah means to people.

What never occurred to me until the episodes aired was how much Hannah would specifically mean to the nonbinary community and to people of color. To me, Hannah was Hannah—a loving entity who wanted to learn and connect and do right. I believe that to be true for us humans as well. It doesn't matter whether you're nonbinary, gay, straight, bisexual, asexual, pansexual, black, white, Asian, etc. I believe that we are all interconnected by love. We all experience or have experienced some sort of pain and trauma. We all feel sometimes like we don't fit in. I've felt it. I still do sometimes. Love and support have always helped me. I've always hoped to work on projects and play characters that would connect with people, further conversations, and represent those who have yearned to be represented. It's been a privilege to give an additional voice to those who have felt voiceless at one time or another. I feel so blessed to have had the opportunity with Hannah.

I was able to attend a *Supernatural* convention with Erica Carroll a while after my episodes aired, and I loved it. I was a little worried about what the fan response would be, considering it had been some time since I had appeared as Hannah, but everyone was fantastic. They were so welcoming, and I was so happy we got the opportunity to take pictures and have some conversations. I was surprised by how many people spoke to me about the importance of my portrayal of Hannah and what it meant for gender ambiguity, gender fluidity, and non-binary gender. I was deeply touched by the honesty. I walked home that evening a better person, and deeply humbled and grateful that I had played a character who gave us all the ability to have those important discussions.

I was fortunate to have had that opportunity again on *Dirk Gently's Holistic Detective Agency* as well. I never imagined I would ever play a fairy-tale prince, especially because of the color of my skin. When I booked the role of Silas Dengdamor, I was blown away. Here was a gay, fairy-tale prince, who was a person of color! Again, I was being given the opportunity to play a character who could represent so many people who had never felt represented.

I am deeply grateful to have played the characters I've played, and to work on the shows I've worked on. On top of that, I've always felt so much love and support from the fans.

You have all been so amazing, and I would not be here without you. Thank you!

THE EVOLUTION OF DOUGIE-BEAR: THERE ARE NO SMALL PARTS

BRENDAN TAYLOR

I worked my ass off in set decoration, the wing of a television show or film's art department responsible for furniture, artwork, and other decorations on set, for over ten years. It's a great job; it's fun converting an empty space into a completely different one, but it's also like moving in and out of a new home every few days. Lots of packing, unpacking, and moving boxes. At first, I was full time: 70+ hours a week, Fraturday after Fraturday. (If you work in film, you're familiar with the term: when your late-night call time on Friday forces you to sleep in and your Saturday is basically a long Friday.) But I was happy to finally be earning a decent living after being a poor student for what seemed like my whole life and to step into my mom's shoes. She was a set dec buyer. A buyer is an extension of the decorator, who drives around town sourcing items that they request. She worked on many big shows in town (including, for a few seasons, one called *Supernatural!*). So I was familiar with the work involved in that department.

I love being a part of *physically* making movies. Creating the worlds that the characters live in is a lot of work. Sometimes these worlds are mundane, like a hospital or an office. And other times, otherworldly, like an alien ship, a post-apocalyptic street, a gang lair, or a creepy mansion. And I learned so much about working with my hands and about teamwork. About working long hours to get shit done, and about the process of filmmaking itself. I was a supervisor for a few years, hiring and training crew, and also an on-set dresser, whose job is to be there for every waking minute of filming, making sure our valuable furniture and other possessions were well cared for, and that every frame looked perfect. But the acting bug always had a hold on me. I would watch the actors in almost every take, and having read the script, I had my own ideas of how the scenes would play out. I could only reset a coffee spill from an actor in a scene so many times before saying to myself, "Well, I really wish I had his job. And I could do it way better."

And so began the slow separation from Mother Film, who told me what time to get up every day and where to be, who took up all my daylight hours with her demands and attention. But she fed me, educated me, and made me grow up fast. It was time to lessen my responsibilities and train in the craft I would pursue. So I hunkered down and trained hard.

There were signs along the way that I was doing the right thing. When I decided I wanted to pursue acting as a career, I went all in. I said yes to almost everything I was asked to do. I had a drive to learn, to get experience, to make up for the lost time I didn't get as a working young actor. I had a drive to realize my dream I had put off, which now seemed just within reach.

I managed to get down to two or three days a week as a set dresser. I even worked on a few episodes of *Supernatural* as a dresser, and I'd bump into my mom at work! But it wasn't always ideal. Lean times in the industry meant scraping by, especially when turning down paid work for a cattle call audition meant racking up my credit cards. I couldn't help but think, "What the fuck am I doing?" Especially when I was begging my boss to let me go to an audition at lunch and changing out of my muddy clothes and into my dad sweater wardrobe, while driving my manual transmission car across town, only for casting to be running behind . . . only to get back to work stressed, hungry, and hoping they weren't pissed at me for being gone for so long.

But working in set dec gave me some perks as a new actor. I had insider info on top-secret shows filming around town. Plus, I had spent literally thousands of hours on film sets carefully observing all the busy bees that make it happen. And of course, set sales! I got some great deals on furniture and stuff for my house when shows wrapped. But best of all, I got clothes from the costumes department. I ended up with some great suits, some cool ties . . . and I had the foresight to collect some great costume pieces to put in my Tickle Trunk for future auditions, including a small-town deputy shirt . . .

Not everyone knows that I already had had a role on *Supernatural*, in season 8. I was a demon dude, and me, my demon friend, and Abaddon (aka Alaina Huffman) had some nefarious plans. I had gotten my family to all tune in the day it aired, not to miss my fun cameo and my biggest role to date. After all, I had disappointed them before, when I was cut from my first TV appearance ever, a one-liner on a short-lived ABC dramedy.

"Is it the right episode? We watched the whole thing twice!" Sigh. It was embarrassing to know that some of my family had spent two hours watching a show they weren't familiar with, in its entirety, desperately wanting to see me, like I had promised. I was grateful for the support, but being cut again from a big deal like *Supernatural* was a heavy blow. But I carried on with auditions, training, and acting on stage. I had a theater company with some close friends, and we put on the things we wanted to see. We couldn't be cut from our own projects.

Then, 2014 was a big year for me. I got two days on the CW's *Arrow*. (Two days? Like, I get to come shoot for a day, and then shoot more on another day??) During a brief chat between camera setups, *Arrow*'s star Stephen Amell reminded me of some valuable advice I'd heard before: "There are no small parts."

Scene study class. Scene presentations. Auditions. Callbacks. Table reads. Reading plays. Putting on plays. Watching movies. Small parts in friends' short films. It was a slow, slow grind.

Later that year, I got a random referral from an actor friend to be in a contest-entry fan-made Superbowl commercial for Doritos. It wasn't a paying gig, unless we won, which was a long shot. But after a quick web search to look up the filmmakers and see some of their work, I said, "Sure, why not. Could be fun." I remember reluctantly getting up early on a Sunday morning and driving to set, a random farm an hour from my house. But once I got there, the people were friendly, the filmmakers were grateful, and my costars, a spectacled nine-year-old boy and a pig, were delightful.

Fast-forward three months: it's the fourth quarter of the 2015 Superbowl, the filmmakers are in Arizona in a private box with the nine other finalists, and I'm at their house in the 'burbs with my mom, sixty friends and family members, the crew, the cast, and the pig. The first frame of our commercial, "When Pigs Fly" comes up on our TV screen, and we're jumping up and down hysterically as we see our little commercial along with 120 million other people. It was a moment I'll never forget.

"There are no small parts."

Then I got the email: "TUESDAY AUDITION: *SUPERNATU-RAL*—TWO ROLES!" Yes! I got another shot at being on the show! And I could go for two characters in the episode! Officer Doug, however, just seemed like a good fit. He was earnest, positive, hardworking, and had a big heart. (He was also the bigger role for the episode!) But the audition was on Tuesday, the day I was shooting for an ultra-low-budget local series. And set was about an hour from casting, which meant that I couldn't make the audition in person. Usually you want to be in the room with casting, as they can give you a redirection on the spot if they want to see it differently. So I would have to put this on tape.

There are advantages to this, however. I could fine-tune my audition before they saw it. I dusted off my small-town deputy shirt, got a coach and a professional taping room, and with my coach I did take after take until it felt right. And I taped the other role as well. A few days later, I would get the best email of my career.

I've been told all my life I'm a "nice guy." "That Brendan, he's so nice." And I am glad to get this comment. At least it's not, "That Brendan, what an asshole!" But I do have mixed feelings about this. These comments might mean that I'm kind, openhearted, and thoughtful. And nonthreatening. These are good things, of course. But does it also mean that I'm seen as weak? A second choice? A pushover? A beta male? Less of a "man"?

I've struggled with this my whole life. I was a sensitive child, and I was bullied because of it. And it's only as an adult that I've been able to accept this part of myself as being a good thing, and be okay with being seen as "nice." My acting training really helped me open up and be comfortable expressing my sadness, rage, and all the other feelings that people feel. And being sensitive also means that I sense those things in others, and I can put myself in their shoes. Thankfully, this is exactly what's needed to be an actor.

Through my training, and my theater company, I've gotten to play some really awful people too. Some not-so-nice guys. But at the root of all that nastiness and anger is always pain and suffering. It doesn't justify their terrible actions, but we can all relate to those feelings, and they are at the core of this behavior. And it's fulfilling, even fun, to enter the minds of these people, and play characters that are so far from who I am.

So there's an essence about me that is "nice." That is genuine, and real. And I accept that I've gotten work because of it. I'm the funny dad or trustworthy employee in commercials, and the jovial best friend in movies-of-the-week. And so I think I'm qualified to play a small-town cop with a simple life, who just wants to do good, who's in over his head, whose heart is mending, and who just met someone special.

Doug had to be earnest and likable and on-task, but with a touch of naivety. He is almost too earnest, to the point where he doesn't see that he's not subtle. I'm thinking of the first scene where he meets Donna and the boys. He sings Donna's praises but is just a *little* too obvious about how he feels about her, and they all catch on. I still chuckle at this scene. I made sure to have an extra-long pause in there for comedic effect, and I'm so glad the editors kept it in! That's exactly my kind of humor.

The bonus about researching Doug was that I had episodes of the show to go back and watch, with Briana Buckmaster, who plays Sheriff Donna Hanscum. This was a gift, as I got to see the evolution of Donna, and why she might be treating Doug the way she did. I watched both of Briana's previous episodes several times, and I was able to see why the other characters were drawn to Donna. From there, I could imagine what their previous conversations were like, before the plot of "Plush" (my first episode) unfolded.

I think the hint of the *Fargo* accent really adds to both characters too. Not only were there hints in the writing that they speak like that but also being from Minnesota or nearby was a giveaway. I think it adds to their comic relief and of course pays homage to the film by the Coen brothers. And no offense to anyone from that area who speaks like that! It adds a grounded, friendly, salt-of-the-earth quality, and allows others to trust them. And when these characters use quirky phrases like "You betcha" and "Darn tootin'" as genuine expressions, often in place of curse words, you can't help but find it endearing.

All of these traits could make Doug seem like a pushover (sound familiar?), so I'm glad that, in the episode, Doug is not just a doormat; he actually saves Donna's life by shooting the Bunny demon. And he also shows remorse later, knowing he shot a young boy. Keep in mind, he didn't know there were supernatural forces at work. All he experienced was killing a young man who might have killed someone first. To be a police officer and go through that, and carry on with normal life, requires a very strong spirit.

At the end of the episode, we see them come together, and Donna praises Doug for his help, but she is also able to admit to her projecting her baggage on to him. And I like how Doug cuts through the BS: "You mean treatin' me like a punchin' bag? I got baggage too, Donna." This moment of vulnerability and honesty, combined with some shared humor, was the perfect basis for the start of a healthy relationship.

We then join Doug two seasons later in "Breakdown," and learn that Doug and Donna have been a couple since we last saw them. Twice in the episode he says he loves Donna, but in a way like he's expressed it before; it wasn't a first-time reveal. And it obviously hurt Donna a lot when he left, so it's safe to say this was a serious relationship.

Doug also believes Dean when he says he's related to Donna. Dean is an authority figure, and in a pinch Dean comes up with this lie, which was intended for someone else. Doug is suspicious, as he should be, but what reason would Dean have to lie? The lie is repeated again by others, including Donna. Now, one could dismiss this as Doug just being dumb, but I think it shows how earnest Doug really is. He trusts the people around him. At this moment, we learn that Donna has not revealed to Doug what her and the boys have been through in the past.

Throughout the episode, Doug is constantly deceived—about Dean being family, about who could be behind the body part auctions, etc.— only to then learn that monsters are real when he meets a vampire who overtakes and then bites him. Poor Doug instantly becomes a vampire, tries to kill his girlfriend, and is then knocked unconscious. He wakes up in a strange motel room, and within a span of a few minutes, he realizes he's no longer a vampire. On top of all this, as he's grappling with what has happened, he is asked to join the others to *fight* the monsters? I don't know about you, but that is all pretty overwhelming. Doug didn't sign up for any of that. And he certainly didn't sign up for being lied to. These are the reasons why Doug's running away was justified.

But I also see Donna's point of view. She was hanging on to a normal life. She didn't want to lose something good in her life. She deserved love and didn't want to risk losing it. So, she made the difficult decision to not tell Doug about her true past. I don't think it was mean-spirited or reckless. I think she wanted the best for Doug, by keeping him safe. But in the end, Donna had to make a tough decision.

It seems like at the end of "Breakdown," Doug's in a headspace where Donna was when we first met her. How many of you have had to end a relationship because the timing wasn't right? I know I have. Maybe Doug is stronger than he thinks he is but lacks self-esteem and is just too overwhelmed by it all. He needs some time.

As for Donna, I think it's so important to note that the writers acknowledged she didn't need a happy ending. She didn't need a man to complete her. I feel like if these episodes were written even twenty years ago, we might have seen a different outcome. Donna is strong and true to herself. And it comes at a cost. It's just real. This is what makes Sheriff Donna Hanscum such a great role model.

When we next see Donna in "Damaged Goods," she says the breakup has been hard on her, and that Doug left the police force to work in private security. I learned about this along with the rest of the SPNFamily when it aired, and it got me thinking a lot.

That night in "Breakdown," and the breakup, was so damaging that he left the job he was proud to hold and took another similar job, so he could avoid any chance that he would encounter something like that again. Now I don't know for sure, but if I were Doug (which I kinda am), I would be thinking about that day for the rest of my life. If I was truly a protector of the people, and took that job seriously, I wouldn't be able to deny that those things are out there. And that Donna is fighting them without him, and possibly in danger when she does. Remember Uncle Ben from Spiderman? He said, "With great power comes great responsibility." Doug knows what no one else knows, other than a select few characters in the show. And Doug Stover is also one of the only ones in the SPN canon still alive to talk about it.

So, I see two hard options for Doug's future. The first is that the fear and doubt have paralyzed him, and he will attempt to ignore what he went through and move on. This is a perfectly viable survival option. We only get one life, and maybe he doesn't want monsters in it. The other option is that the truth eats away at him, and he still loves Donna. He will find the courage to change his mind, to face danger, and help the hunters. Not with the express reason to win Donna back—I don't think that would happen overnight—but to help fight the forces of evil alongside the hunters, knowing what he knows, for the sake of protecting others.

These options are both valid, and I think we know which one I'm rooting for.

Remember when Dean and Doug are sitting in Baby, and Doug asks Dean for advice? Dean says, "Doug, you're a good guy. And you're gonna be there for Donna." To which Doug replies, "You betcha." I actually had permission to change that line from the director. It was written as "Of course." It just seemed more "Doug" because of the way he and Donna speak with Minnesotan flair, and that's something that links him strongly to Donna. But I also wanted the delivery of the line to indicate that he is unwavering. He is resolute in his loyalty to Donna. But he was blindsided by the situation. I would hope he comes around to his sense of loyalty. (In *Supernatural* the Movie maybe?)

I care deeply about Doug, because I see myself in him. I'm not from a small town, and I'm not a cop, but I know what it's like to have a big heart. I know what it's like to love. I know what it's like to sacrifice. I know what it's like to feel pain. And I know what it's like to feel alone.

So, I see you, Doug. I see you.

My experience on *Supernatural* had a significant impact on me. It's one of several acting projects I've been a part of that have changed me for the better. In 2018, I had the honor of working on a short film that really impacted me. It was called *A Typical Fairytale*, and it's the story of a well-to-do couple who meet, fall in love, plan a perfect life together, and have a perfect daughter. But things don't go as planned. Their daughter, who rejects the typical "girl" activities and wardrobe thrust upon her by her conservative parents, decides she doesn't want to be their daughter . . . but their son. At first, the parents are thrown by this claim, but with the help of a fairy godmother, they learn to see their child's struggle and are encouraged to accept him. In the end, they see the error of their ways, and let their love overcome their fears.

It started as a script entered in a short film contest, where it was first read in front of an audience on stage. I was chosen to read the role of the Prince/Father. The winning script would get a budget to shoot. It didn't win. But the producers and writers wanted to make it and kept me in mind. The next year, they won some prize money to make the film, and I auditioned for the role and got it. And I still remember that audition vividly. It was very emotional, and though I'm not a parent yet, I can imagine how deep a parent's love goes for their child.

This turned out to be such a wonderful project. We had an eleven-year-old transgender actor play the boy, as well as another transgender actor play the fairy godmother. We had a very identity-diverse crew as well. Until this movie, I had never had the opportunity to talk to transgender people at great length about their lives and their struggles . . . let alone a child who had figured out so early who he was. To see the love in his real mother's eyes for her son was so heartwarming.

We are all individuals, with unique experiences, one to the next. Both *Supernatural* and *A Typical Fairytale* carry that important message. There is no one right way to live this life, so who are we to judge anyone else? We all want to love and be loved, so just live and let live.

Sacrifices must be made, to live loud, proud, and Wayward AF. In fact, I had to make a big one just to be on *Supernatural*. When I got the email to confirm my availability for shooting, I had to make a hard decision because one of the shoot dates was my grandfather's memorial service in Toronto. I told my agent and as understanding as she was, she told me if I said I had to miss that shoot day, I probably wouldn't get the role. I even thought if I could somehow get the date changed, I'd take a red-eye flight, be there with my family, and then fly back immediately. But it wasn't possible. So, after enduring the first experience in my life of losing a loved one, I couldn't go and mourn with my family or with myself. On a lighter note, my grandfather would have been over the moon that I got the gig, and I could hear his voice, "Oh, please. You're gonna miss that job for *me*?" My family supported me and understood, but I still missed my grandfather's funeral. While I was ecstatic to have such a huge, important role, it was a very confusing time.

And sadly, this has happened several times since. I've thrown away plane tickets and missed significant life events far too many times: friends' weddings, stag parties, epic vacations, friends' limited-run plays in other cities, and once, even a trip across the world to explore a romantic relationship. I've even had to miss parties and gatherings with friends in town so I could stay home and run lines for an audition.

Although this job may seem glamorous on the outside, I think any actor can tell you of the sacrifices they make to keep it up. It is a ruthless industry. But the rewards can be grand. We choose this life, don't get me wrong. No one is forcing us to do it. And for many, it's just too hard. And that's understandable. A balanced life for an artist is a balancing act in itself.

But getting an acting job is a wonderful feeling. However, getting *consistent* acting jobs is the epitome of "living the dream" . . . to pay your bills and then some, doing the impossible. But the true reward is when the roles get a little bigger, and you're on set several days on a project, getting to be *part of something*. I think above anything else, in this job and in life, we all want to feel like we belong. Getting to help shape an end product, collaborating with some great people along the way, knowing that you may have affected people in a positive way because of your skills, your input, and your voice, and seeing that impact live on in something greater—it's an amazing feeling. Money is nice, but connecting with people in a meaningful way is nicer.

I am forever grateful for my bosses: the ones who saw the dream in my eyes, the ones who let me get out of the rain while they endured it and carried my load (often literally) to see me go off and chip away at this far-fetched dream. It's a combination of gratitude and guilt I carry with me every day. So if any of you just happen to be reading this: thank you.

I'm grateful for my agents, who have seen something in me and pushed to have me seen by casting, and I'm grateful for my teachers, coaches, and actor friends, who have helped me hone my craft to go and book those roles.

Thank you, Briana Buckmaster, for being the ultimate scene partner and welcoming me into your character's world. You're an inspiration both on- and off-screen, and I'm just blown away by what you've done with your life and how you've touched others since we first met in the makeup trailer years ago. You're the funniest, prettiest, strongest, badassiest lady around.

Thank you, Jensen and Jared, for including me as one of the cool kids. I don't think I've ever laughed more on a film set. You guys are so good at what you do, it's ridiculous. But at the same time, you keep it real and honest. The dramatic scenes on camera are just as palpable as the laughing fits between scenes.

And a special thank-you to the fans. You changed the course of my career and helped me realize my dream. You embraced me and what I was able to bring to your world. Thank you for embracing Doug Stover, and thank you for sharing his joy and his pain. Because in doing so, you shared mine as well.

For anyone out there who has a dream that seems out of reach, remember: "There are no small parts." Whether you're a writer, a musician, an artist, or even an entrepreneur in business, you have to start somewhere. And small parts will lead to bigger ones. They just will. And you might also find that the journey between these parts might be even more rewarding than what lies at the end of the road.

SPNFamily Forever.

Love, Brendan Taylor (aka Dougie-Bear)

MAKE YOUR OWN DESTINY

DMITRI NOVAK

Supernatural has been a force for change in many people's lives, including my own. During my time as a fan and participant in the fandom, I underwent and completed gender transition. The show, the fans, and the cast of the show supported me through the entire process.

I was particularly inspired by Castiel's character development. He constantly faced life-changing choices and had to question everything he had ever known for millennia. One of the things Castiel said, "You can make your own destiny," stood out so strongly in my mind. *If Castiel can change his destiny,* I thought, *maybe the rest of us can, too.*

But my journey wasn't easy.

When I originally started participating in the fandom, both online and at conventions, I wasn't open about being transgender. I had yet to start the medical side of my transition, so I had very few spaces where I felt that I had the opportunity to engage as my true self without any preconceived notions or pushback. It's always hard to know when or if to come out, and whether or not people will accept you once you do. But once you come out, you can't un-ring the bell. And, at the time, I desperately didn't want to ring that bell.

I realized I wasn't alone as I found and got to know many other trans fans within the SPNFamily. But as much as we loved finding each other, we often wondered how the actors from our favorite show felt about trans folks. As the impending date for my hormone replacement therapy drew near, and as the anxiety in my corner of the community persisted, I realized that I had an opportunity to share my journey and authentic self with the fandom with full transparency and honesty. If sharing my story could help just one person, it would be worth it.

So I came out.

I created a thread on Twitter, took a deep breath, and hit "Tweet."

The response was overwhelmingly supportive and positive. I encountered so many amazing people in the fandom who began being open about their transitions because they felt safer to do so. I had the opportunity to impact my cisgender allies, who learned more about transgender people. A friend said that after reading about my journey she felt like she could better help her young trans grandson. Many reached out to ask how to be the best they could be for their trans kids, siblings, relatives, friends, and the trans community at large. I was elated and brought to tears.

During this time, despite my anxiety, I eventually decided to be open about who I was with the *Supernatural* cast. And once again, I received a great deal of acceptance and support. Misha Collins especially has been an inspiration just as much as Castiel has been. He has been incredibly encouraging and supportive throughout the process and has said some things that I find as inspiring as Castiel's words, especially, "Be kind to yourself so you can be kind to the world." Giving myself the freedom to transition and become my true self was one of the greatest kindnesses I could offer myself. I have given Misha updates regularly throughout this journey, and his support and enthusiasm have meant the absolute world to me.

The fandom, too, was with me through it all. Thanks to their support and generosity, I was able to get my name legally changed, as well as pursue surgery. For both processes, the SPNFamily banded together to help make it happen.

When the political climate shifted at the end of 2016, I became terrified I wouldn't be able to afford to get my name legally changed before the process could be made more challenging. At the request of my friends, I made a crowdfunding page, and within half an hour, the fandom helped me more than meet my goal. Two months and a court date later, a judge granted my request: I was legally and officially Dmitri Novak. I celebrated online with the fandom. Each time I am called by my name, everything feels right in my bones, like I just came home after being gone for a month.

At the Nashville convention in 2017, I showed Misha my new ID that reflected my name change. I had not quite realized the impact it had until the convention in that same city in 2019, when he brought it up during his onstage panel. He regarded it as a powerful moment and went on to express how meaningful it is that this show, the fandom, and the dynamics between us as fans as well as between us and the cast can serve as guideposts in some of our lives. For me, this was an equally powerful moment; I still can't articulate what it meant to me to hear that.

When I began to save for my surgery in 2017, my friends encouraged me to create a second fundraiser. My friend Ariel spearheaded this effort. Over the course of the next two years, the SPNFamily raised a significant portion of the cost, and as a random act of kindness during Random Act's 2019 Annual Melee of Kindness, my friend Heather F. donated the remainder, fast-tracking the process. She said I had waited long enough. I was completely floored. It was happening. I went to Florida with two more dear fandom friends, Steph H. and Little Misha, who stayed with me and took care of me in the week immediately following my operation. I was terrified, but being able to pull my phone from my pocket and see the love from the SPNFamily helped me to stay brave.

Once I had put the process in motion for surgery, I decided I wanted to have a small ceremony for transforming my binder (a tank top–style compression garment that helped bind and flatten my chest). I invited several friends and people I admired or had been inspired by, including Misha, to attend the ceremony and participate in transforming my binder into beautifully decorated strips of fabric to be used as prayer flags.

Six weeks after my operation, the ceremony began with my friend Monica D. and I meeting Misha at a park during the Burbank *Supernatural* convention in 2019. I thanked my binder for allowing me to be myself and for protecting me during the time between beginning my transition and completing it. Together, Misha and I cut the binder into strips, talking while we decorated our flags. Later, I met with more friends and we decorated the remaining strips. This was a truly wonderful experience, and I will always cherish it.

I could not have gone through the process of transition without the support of the fandom . . . every hug, every kind message, and every clap on the shoulder with an "I'm proud of you." They were there as my family, both online and off. It takes a truly special group of people to come together online from across the world, meeting up at conventions and sparking friendships, and to then be willing to come to your house after surgery to help you in and out of bed, empty your surgical drains, and wake you up every four hours with hot food and your medication. For me, the SPNFamily is truly family. Even though I spent much of that recovery time unable to respond, I felt that love. With it, I felt like I could do anything. And I did.

In my experience, the legacy of this show is ultimately the strength of the fandom and the reciprocal bonds we formed with the cast. The SPNFamily created a powerhouse that kept the show going, because we loved them so much and they loved us so much, and that love contributed to them not wanting to stop and kept the show on the air for fifteen years.

Supernatural has changed what it means to be a fandom. Through all the campaigns benefiting charities, the incredibly influential GISH, the Hurricane Harvey online rescue team, the building of the Free High School in Nicaragua and the Jacmel Children's Center in Haiti, the voting drives . . . all these things have made real-world change. *Supernatural* leaves behind a fundamentally changed group of people, inspired to do good, be weird, and be kind. To be authentically ourselves, spearheading our own ventures. To be people who will persevere no matter what—the proverbial carrying on.

THE GIRL WITH THE RAINBOW CAT TATTOO

SARAH WYLDE

I have been a fan of *Supernatural* since season 1, and it has changed my life in many ways. I have met and talked to many amazing *Supernatural* fans that I will be forever grateful for. The show has been there when I felt like I was going through everything alone. But introducing me to the wonderful character Charlie Bradbury (played by Felicia Day) has had more of an impact than anything else.

I am a big Felicia Day fan and was thrilled when I saw she was going to be portraying Charlie, the fiery redhead, IT wizard, and fangirl on *Supernatural*. The further we got into her first episode ("The Girl with the Dungeons and Dragons Tattoo"), the more I felt a connection and was drawn to this powerful female character. To say that Charlie and that episode changed me sounds cliché, but it's the truth. It was all in how they introduced her . . . and who she was.

I can pinpoint the exact moment in that episode when Charlie became important to me. Charlie is about to break into Dick Roman's office, but a guard is there. Dean tells her to flirt with the guard in order to distract him. Charlie replies, "I can't. He's not my type . . . as in, he's not a girl." After that scene, I broke down in tears.

I had finally found an LGBTQ character that I could honestly relate to and feel represented by. Other shows I watched portrayed being a lesbian as the character's label versus their identity. The fact that *Supernatural* didn't do that gave me encouragement and validation. Charlie was geeky, into women . . . and she owned it. So why couldn't I? What was I afraid of?

When the episode ended, I sat there with tears streaming

down my face, lost in thought. I realized how tired I was. Tired of hiding who I was, tired of lying to everyone, including myself. By introducing Charlie, *Supernatural* had inadvertently given me a gift. Charlie revived my strength and courage to be able to say out loud with confidence and a smile that I, Sarah, am a lesbian.

Charlie was my spark, but by no means did everything happen overnight. It still took me a little time to feel comfortable enough with myself to come out. I was bullied a lot growing up, so at a young age I figured out that if I kept quiet and to myself no one would notice me, and I could become invisible. But in doing that, I hid myself away and got lost. I still had to come to grips with how difficult coming out to the people in my life would be. I was putting so much effort into thinking I had to explain myself to others that I lost sight of accepting and enjoying the freedom that would come with it. Of course, that led to me doing a lot of overthinking. My depression and anxiety took the reins when I tried to figure out what I was going to say and played out these multiple scenarios in my head. It always ended with me getting a headache or having a panic attack . . . fun times. But whenever I started going into this overthinking spiral, I remembered when Sam asked Charlie what

Hermione (from the *Harry Potter* books) would do, and she replied, "I'm going to kick it in the ass."

So, one day, I went into the living room where my mom was reading and asked, "Can I talk to you for a minute?"

She closed her book and looked at me, and without knowing what I was going to say, I started talking.

"You know how I have never brought a guy home to meet you?"

She nodded her head and said, "Yeah . . ."

"Well, that's because when I do bring someone home to meet you, it will be a girl."

I looked at her nervously, scared to hear what she was going to say.

"That's okay," she replied with a smile.

Everything after that was a bit of a blur, but I do remember trying not to cry and us hugging. "That's okay." Those two words meant everything. That's okay. She's right, it is okay. It doesn't change who I am. I no longer felt like I was hiding; I didn't feel invisible. I felt relieved and inspired—like I was whole.

The character of Charlie Bradbury motivated me to find my confidence and to rediscover the voice I thought was lost. Later, when I would watch the other episodes Charlie was in, I still felt drawn to her and saw connections. The longer she was with the Winchesters, the more her own self-confidence grew. She found a family with Sam and Dean, just like we have this magic that is the SPNFamily.

In season 10's "There's No Place Like Home," when Charlie is split in two—our familiar Charlie and "Dark Charlie"—she is confused and struggles, and reminded me of my own inner turmoil. Charlie's inability to apologize to her mother while sitting by her hospital bed reading *The Hobbit* one last time also hit me hard.

My father passed away before I had the chance to tell him that I was gay, although I think he knew. We had a conversation over a few beers many years back. Out of the blue he said, "You know I just want you to be happy, whether that's with a guy or girl I don't care, as long as you're happy and they treat you right." Looking back and realizing he would have been just fine with it made me wish I had told him when I had the chance.

So, yes, Charlie's quest helped me with my own. When you look at Charlie's story arc, she went from a scared girl who wanted to leave a sleepover and go home to a smart, badass hunter who felt at home battling demons and monsters. She was whole.

Now, I can't help but smile when I say I like women. I have gone to pride parades and events, and I even got a tattoo to symbolize that I am whole and in no way broken. It truly is a raw, honest, and powerful moment in your life when you come out, and it should be celebrated. To think that I owe a *Supernatural* character for giving me that aha moment is kind of awesome and makes my nerd heart smile. I hope to someday tell Felicia Day in person how much her character impacted me and my life.

I want to leave you with this final note: Whether you have come out or are still in the closet, that's okay. Listen to yourself; you know what is best for you. It is also important that if there is a possible emotional or physical safety issue, then wait until you feel safe. There are organizations and information out there if you or the people in your life have questions.

ORGANIZATIONS THAT CAN HELP

The Trevor Project
www.thetrevorproject.org
1-866-488-7386

Trans Lifeline
www.translifeline.org
(US) 1-877-565-8860
(CAN) 1-877-330-6366

National Runaway Safeline
www.1800runaway.org
1-800-786-2929

National Suicide Prevention Lifeline
www.suicidepreventionlifeline.org
1-800-273-8255

To Write Love on Her Arms
www.twloha.com/find-help/
(enter your zip code for the closest help near you)

THERE'S ALWAYS PIZZA

TODD STASHWICK

Christmas morning, 1974, a six-year-old green-eyed boy bounces down the stairs on his butt (a preferred way of descending), in his home in Chicago. He rounds the corner to find, waiting for him from St. Nick, a cadre of Mego Planet of the Apes action figures and the treehouse playset. A Christmas wish come true. You see, my family would gather at my mother's grandparents' house every Sunday to tune in to CBS for the ritual airing of the *Planet of the Apes* TV series. There I was: belly on the floor, chin on hands, drinking it in. There was pizza.

This was my first fandom. I devoured the merch, played Planet of the Apes with my cousin, drew pictures of this fantastic world. I didn't *become* a fanboy; I noticed that I *was* one. From here I moved on to *Star Trek*, wherein I devoured the merch, played Star Trek with my cousin, drew pictures of this fantastic world. Then it was all eclipsed by the "I-am-your-father" of all fandoms, *Star Wars*. I devoured the merch, played Star Wars with my cousin, drew pictures of this fantastic world. You see the pattern.

So basically, my earliest memories are those of my fandoms. These stories, characters, and lands (cynically now referred to as IPs) defined my play, and my play informed how I interacted with the world. It was this early childhood imagining and playacting that set the stage for what

I now do for a living. As I grew, my fandoms continued to dominate conversations among my peers: preteens of the early '80s, speculating, arguing, and poring over every prereleased image in *Starlog* magazine. This was who we were; this is who we are. This is how we nerd. And we nerd hard.

In the forty-plus years since I collected Planet of the Apes action figures, nothing has changed. Everything has changed. That which was considered nerd culture is now culture. Avengers are now on our soda cans. BUT what's fascinating to me about us hard-core nerds is that we like to burrow. While the greater culture sloppily ingests the blockbuster franchises, there is the deep cut, the fandoms that are quietly flowing like an underground river. These fandoms may eventually break through to the wider public, but they exist for a good long time as a private club, a secret handshake, a quiet whisper beneath the noise of culture. It is the way of the nerd to boldly go where no one has gone. Giving our eyeballs to a new story that might just excite us in a fresh way. Now, it's all Taco Bell, the same ingredients just reassembled in slightly different ways. Horror, sci-fi, fantasy . . . these stories are fueled by familiar tropes: vampires, dragons, laser swords. It's these tropes that draw us to them in the first place. We love them, or some of them, or one of them. We are always seeking a new way to devour them, and it is really fun when we find one that not many have caught on yet. We want to hold it close, and at the same time, sing its song from the mountaintop. Add to our tribe.

This was *Supernatural*, fifteen years ago.

I can say, like many, that *Supernatural* changed my life. Here's the insane part: it was just a week of my life, up in Vancouver, June 2008. Then the episode ("Monster Movie") aired, on my fortieth birthday, October 16, 2008. One episode and done, and yet there are very few jobs that have been more celebrated than my week on *Supernatural*. The job itself was some of the most fun I have ever had acting. If one were a cheeseball, they'd say I really got to sink my teeth into the role. Rarely as actors do we get a chance to play huge and scene chewing and then moments later be so small and broken and intimate. I got to work with some of the kindest, most dedicated, talented folks. It was a reunion for Jared and me. We had shot a pilot together seven years prior. I love that guy. Jensen is such a hoot and a consummate professional, even after I accidently whacked him in the face for real. From the sets, to my costume and makeup, to that scooter—it was a dream job. As a horror nerd boy, I had the honor of stepping into Lugosi's shiny black shoes. Also . . . there was pizza (no garlic).

I am continually humbled by the fact that eleven seasons later, that episode is celebrated. It resonated for some reason. My Dracula has been made into many a GIF, for cry-eye. That one little episode has taken me to cons across America and overseas. I have made friends who will be in my life forever. It is a testament to everyone involved in making such a high-quality show and also a testament to the passionate fans. The fans who have embraced this lovely blue-collar show about family and monsters. The fans have taken it from the "secret club" into a staple at Hot Topic. The fans who fill convention centers around the world, get themselves tattooed, name their children Sam and Dean, devour the merch, and draw pictures of this fantastic world. The fans who will need each other when the show finishes its last season. There will be tears.

My professional career has been a fanboy's dream. My livelihood is not just limited to acting. I also have made a comfortable living as a writer. I have written comic books, video games, television pilots, and screenplays, all of them in horror, sci-fi, and fantasy. I have been able to contribute to the mythologies that I love and also dream up new ones yet to be discovered. The fact that I have gotten to contribute to worlds that I adore, watching as much as any fan, still spins me. This life has been filled with many checks off the nerd bucket list.

We are tribal creatures who use mythology to come together and understand ourselves. The television is our campfire. Being a small part of the *Supernatural* tribe showed me a lot about fandom. I've got a unique perspective by being connected to something that folks are beyond passionate about. I get to talk to, share a drink with, or sing a song for so many people who love this show and are excited that I can provide a window into it. I get it, because I am them. Since I learned to walk, I too have always wanted to revel in my own nerderies. I still wear *Star Wars* T-shirts. I attend cons even when I'm not promoting something. I spend way too much time and money scouring eBay to find action figures from the '70s to add to my bloated collection. I'm confident in saying that I will never stop being a fan, and also confident in saying that there's always pizza . . . and I have a coupon.

UNCONVENTIONAL REFLECTION

GABRIEL TIGERMAN

(interviewed by Lynn Zubernis)

What has been your experience being part of the SPNFamily?
Beyond the fun of working on the show and the crazy party of the convention circuit, *Supernatural* has been a part of some of the most significant moments in my life.

I booked the role of Andy Gallagher the same week I met my wife. I have a UK *Supernatural* convention to thank for getting to see my wife visit the Eiffel Tower for the first time while honeymooning. And when I almost lost my wife and baby during a disastrous childbirth, and we were faced with crushing medical bills while my wife was still in a coma, it was the *Supernatural* community (the fans and my fellow actors) who stepped up to help. I truly don't know what we would have done without them and where we would be now. The *Supernatural* community will forever have a place in our hearts.

Have you identified as a fan yourself and if so, how did that impact your interactions with your own fans?

I will say that it took me some time to get used to the idea that I had "fans" in the first place. Fans are for famous people like Tom Cruise and Cary Grant (that's a topical celebrity reference, right?).

But then I thought about how I, myself, am a devoted fan of the Dodgers and *The West Wing*. And, frankly, I don't know what I'd do if I met Dodgers pitcher Clayton Kershaw or director Aaron Sorkin. Or Clayton Kershaw and Aaron Sorkin at the same time . . . and Sorkin is riding Kershaw piggyback . . . and they both say, "Hey, Gabe!" in unison. I really don't know how I'd react if that all happened.

Now, where was I . . . ? Oh, right!

I've shared with fans my deeply humiliating interaction with Michael C. Hall from *Dexter*. Let's just say it involves a bowl of soup, Invisalign retainers, and a truly unfortunately timed string of saliva.

Interactions like that have certainly helped me relate to convention goers and the gamut of emotions one feels meeting actors from your favorite show.

What was your reaction when you were first invited to be a convention guest and what did you anticipate the experience would be like?

Having only appeared in one episode of the show, I assumed there had been some kind of mistake. Perhaps a clerical error. I told my manager to tell them, "Thank you kindly, but you must want a different Gabriel Tigerman."

At the time, I had seen the documentary *Trekkies* and had heard of Comic-Con, but really I had zero idea what to expect from a *Supernatural* convention. I remember walking on stage for my first Q&A and having hundreds of fans cheering. I leaned over to Chad Lindberg, who plays Ash, and said, "It's like we're the Beatles." It still feels like that sometimes.

How has the ability to interact face to face with fans impacted you? Has anything surprised you about those interactions?

It's such a unique experience for character actors to interact with their fans. I mean, usually I'll appear on a TV show or commercial and receive some fun texts from friends or family who saw it, and that's about it. Or you get people out in public who think they know you from somewhere, but they can't quite place it. High school? Starbucks? Hot yoga? Maaaaybeee at most, someone will say, "Hey, weren't you the guy in (some random show)?"

In the early 2000s, I had a commercial campaign for Burger King (my first real acting job) and strangers would yell my catchphrase at me when I was walking down the street.

Random Guy: Hey! "I'M SPICY!"
Me: Yup, that's me!

Then you go to these weekend conventions for a show that's wildly popular and all of a sudden you're like, "Oh, this is what every day is like for Tom Cruise or Cary Grant." (Who're apparently my only celebrity references today.) And then, come Monday, you're back to reality. It's very surreal.

As far as my most surprising moment? Two words: Gabe tattoos.

What's the funniest thing that's happened to you at a convention, either onstage or with fans or backstage with the cast?
Oh, God. This is a tough one. It's like being asked your favorite movie. It's just too much pressure to get it right, and as soon as you leave you remember a million better answers. There are just so many funny/insane con experiences. So, um . . . rapid fire. First thing that comes to mind! (Apologies for all the things I forget.)

Funniest experience? Probably meeting Chad Lindberg for the first time onstage and—just as I was shaking his hand—having a flashback to having read a slash fanfic that depicted the two of us in rather . . . compromising circumstances. Backstory: I had never heard of, let alone read, any slash fan fiction. Let alone read any slash fan fiction starring MYSELF! That is, until I did *Supernatural*. I was at my parents' place when my friend from high school forwarded me a small tale he found on the internet that described my character . . . uh . . . how shall I put it? . . . "servicing" Chad's character from the show. I was stunned and emitted a sound aloud that could maybe be written as, "AAAAGHLBBBWHAAA—???" At which point my mom walked in the room and said, "Whatcha reading? Can I see?"

Off the top of my head, other highlights include:

1. Being confronted by a fan completely covered in cotton balls after I revealed that I have a bizarre phobia of cotton balls. She is a MONSTER!
2. Backstage whiskey.
3. Crashing panels with Kim Rhodes (Sheriff Jody Mills) and Briana Buckmaster (Sheriff Donna Hanscum).
4. Q&As with Chad and Jeffrey Vincent Parise (Asmodeus).
5. Shirtless Matt Cohen (Young John Winchester).

6. Bringing friends to see what conventions/Friday night karaoke parties are like and it BLOWING THEIR MINDS.
7. Mad Libs . . . After Dark!
8. The many retellings of the World's Largest Groundhog/5- and 6-Legged Steers story.
9. "Oh, we're just doing this here?" (I cannot/will not elaborate.)

What do you think *Supernatural's* legacy will be when all is said and done?

Hopefully this doesn't sound too cheesy, but I think the legacy will be the incredibly loving, giving, fun, and supportive *Supernatural* community that has been formed. I've never seen anything quite like it. It's really something, and I think it will live on long past the show's finale.

A WOMAN OF LETTERS

ALLISON BROESDER

graduated from college in 2006—on the cusp of what was going to become the Great Recession. I earned a bachelor's degree in creative writing from a small Midwest university—practical, right? Afterwards, I wasn't sure what I was going to do with it or for a career, and so I drifted the summer after graduation. I landed—not surprisingly in hindsight—into retail. That was supposed to be a temporary gig while I looked for something in my field or decided on graduate school or something. Anything but working in a retail store! But Black Friday and Christmas came and went and came and went and came and went again (and one more time. Yikes!). And then the Great Recession hit and it was hold on to what you've got and ride the wave.

So, what does any of that have to do with *Supernatural*? You'll see.

In 2010, something wonderful happened to me. I decided to take a "stay-cation" and attend my alma mater's latest incarnation of a writer's festival. I had longed to return to my college days, exploring the beauty of language and the meanings lurking underneath. I wanted to retreat for a bit into a better time of my life—one that had a clear purpose and reason and goal. So, I stayed home for the week, getting up early enough to attend the day's panels and other readings. While I would get ready or prepare for my stint back in college for the week, I discovered something: *Supernatural*.

I believe that if it hadn't been for this "stay-cation," I would have never found this show—and therefore, it would have never had a chance to change my life on such a fundamental level.

The story about these two brothers sucked me in almost immediately, making me wonder who Sam and Dean (or as I called them then, Floppy-Haired Boy and Pouty-Lipped Boy) were and what their search for their father meant. I loved how complex and real the story felt for a show that dealt with demons and ghosts. I lived for the humor and the emotional moments—and something I had thought lost broke inside, free once more. Creativity started back again after a dormancy. Retail isn't exactly the most motivating environment for a creative writer—or creative anything—and so for a few years I hadn't done anything but work and nap and work some more. *Supernatural* stirred my blood and sucked me into its dark and beautiful world in a matter of a week's time. The reruns on TNT allowed me to become invested in a show that had been on for a number of years by then—and I eagerly got caught up.

It wasn't until I began to dip my toes into the fandom, however, that the show started to change my life. *Supernatural* has this uncanny ability to make us pay attention and watch the story closely for all sorts of reasons. It has layers of meaning, emotional connections, and a heartbeat about family at its center. That heartbeat is also ever present in the fandom that surrounds it. Originally, I had been cautious and nervous about joining this fandom, considering that my other previous fandoms had soured through considerable backbiting and other issues—but I had been much younger then. Maybe I was ready now. I dipped my toes in, looking at fanfic first. My creativity surged based on the sheer skill this fandom had.

I stumbled across a review site—the Winchester Family Business—and started to dip my toes in more. I commented on other pieces about episodes, leaving novel-length analyses. I hadn't really done any real "review" or commentary on text since college. I didn't even know if I could still do it—if the skill after all these years had atrophied. I found, however, that I indeed could write these reaction papers that I had done repeatedly through my college career for novels, short stories, and other classmates' works. I found that it brought color to my world. Before *Supernatural*, my world had become so gray and colorless—a monotony of same thing, different day. So, I kept reading the reviews posted, piecing together the things I noticed in the episode and what the reviewer said, and regained my voice.

By that summer, I had cobbled together my first piece for the Winchester Family Business—a deep look at Soulless Sam, a character that fascinated me for all of his implications about sociopaths, humanity, and the meaning of family bonds and love. I submitted it to the website owner, Alice Jester, in hopes that I'd at least get one piece published on her site. I hadn't thought about writing more than that, figuring that so many others had already cornered that market. The essay was academic on so many levels and not necessarily the light fare some might want from a website, after all. To my surprise, my writing really took off.

People enjoyed my work. They liked what I had to say. I felt encouraged and kept going.

And at the same time, half of a novel started brewing in my mind, and I started working on it in earnest. *Supernatural* had given me writing back. But it wasn't done changing my life by a mile.

That change occurred when I started to attend conventions. The exhilaration of meeting the cast drew me to my first one—but what kept me going back again and again were the friends I had made in the fandom. These people became more than screen names. They became sisters and brothers—and for an only child, it was a new experience! I found myself welcomed and celebrated for who I was, and I also found that my views had impacted others just as theirs had impacted me. A community had formed around this little show that could, and in so doing, it had accepted me fully into its ranks.

Our fandom isn't perfect. There's some of the negative energy that permeates any community, but at its heart, the fandom is truly an SPNFamily and we do rally together and support good work. My fandom inspires me to reach beyond myself—just as the show did when I first discovered its beautiful take on our complex world. I became an activist for causes that came from cast and crew alike. I supported *Supernatural* Assistant

Director Kevin Parks as he honored Kim Manners (one of the show's original producers and directors) in his cancer rides. I supported Misha Collins and his efforts to promote kindness through Random Acts. I jumped on board, totally, for Jared Padalecki when he launched the Always Keep Fighting campaign. I supported Mark Sheppard (who played Crowley) and his efforts to stamp out type 1 diabetes, reviving another skill I hadn't used in years: embroidery. I rallied behind the fandom for all their efforts to answer cries for help in the wake of storms like Hurricane Sandy. I may not have had much money to share, but I gave what I could and promoted and did my part.

I didn't know it at the time, but *Supernatural* was changing me yet again. We don't need to hash out the 2016 election here—or go into detail about how I feel about the results—but I feel like *Supernatural* and the SPNFamily prepared me to be ready in its aftermath. I had become active in so many wonderful causes because of my fandom and my show—and now it translated into the real world in more ways than one. Not only would it help me champion such causes as internet freedom, public media, and civil rights, but it would also lead me to finding my real career path—even if I'm not quite where I want to be just yet.

In season 8, *Supernatural* introduced the Men of Letters (not to be confused with the British version we see in season 12). The notion that the world of *Supernatural* didn't just have hunters who went about "saving people, hunting things, the family business" but also wanted to study that world, catalog it, and assist through librarianship triggered something deep inside. I have always loved to read and to write (hence my degree!). The world of storytelling and language has had me in its grip since I learned to read at the age of five. (For the record, while Metatron turned out to be a real asshat in many ways, I identified with his intense need to read everything and devote time to stories. It would be a dream of mine to spend millennia reading and writing as many stories as possible. Metatron did just that after leaving heaven behind. He created the best witness protection program ever. Until the Winchesters burst into his life, he spent all his time exploring the depths of our literary merits. It is why he tells Castiel, "Now do you understand that the universe is made up of stories, not atoms," in the episode "Meta Fiction." To him, story is humanity's pinnacle achievement, and I find myself in utter agreement with the former Scribe of God. I've played with words, stories, and books my whole life. At one point, I had thought about running my own bookstore. I had been so blind to the notion that I should aspire to do and be more.

Supernatural prodded me in the right direction at the right time. It reminded me that not everything has to be a literal "business." The Men of Letters and their beautiful library in the bunker changed everything for me. Here was a treasure trove of information—some that would have been very helpful to the brothers much, much earlier. Sure, Sam and Dean used libraries in the earlier seasons to great effect. It was part of their formula in many ways: hit up the public library for the local details about an area's history and the case—look up some lore and other pertinent details—and use their brains to make their brawn count. Sam and Dean have always used their knowledge base and research abilities to do their job. On some level, their use of the public library connected to me because it reminded me of writing research papers in college—using bits of information to form a new whole.

The Men of Letters who opened the bunker originally described it as a "last beacon of hope." I feel, on many levels, that libraries and librarians are exactly that. The access to knowledge, education, and community can change everything. It can build a better world. It can bridge divides. It can illuminate our path. It can expand our world beyond the one we've always known. Libraries allow us to explore any and every subject, to learn and to grow, and to understand one another through the beauty of language and story. Nonfiction and fiction alike give us windows into other people's lives, other cultures, other ways of being. The bunker and the Men of Letters through Henry Winchester did just that for Sam and Dean—and for me.

That was the introduction; it was Charlie Bradbury (played by Felicia Day) who sealed my fate. Sam describes her as the "smartest person in the room." Since her introduction in season 7, I related to her character on many levels—wanting to emulate some of the qualities that writer Robbie Thompson imbued her with: loyalty, a love of geek culture, a great ability to love, and a deep sense of justice. Charlie represents the person I feel is trapped inside me, and seeing her represented on screen truly meant everything. In her effort to help Dorothy and piece together the mystery surrounding the Wicked Witch, she made the comment, "Hey, these guys may have been sexist, but like all librarians, they were wicked smart, too." She's right. Librarians, those I've had the honor to work with and meet, are wicked smart. They may not know everything about a single subject, but they know a little bit about everything—enough to send someone on the right path. They're able to figure out how to navigate the endless fire hose of knowledge and information we now live with on a daily basis—and organize it.

In that moment, hearing Charlie describe librarians as being wicked smart and vital? I felt a ping go off in my brain. I started volunteering at my local public library, learning the very basics of shelving and shelf reading and the little tasks that needed to be done so our librarians could do other things in the service of their patrons. I wanted to be counted among that select group of "wicked smart"—like Charlie. She had been dubbed a Woman of Letters by Sam, and suddenly I saw my world open before me, just waiting for me. I had drifted for so long, finding my voice in writing about this show and building relationships in the SPNFamily—but this gave me a purpose for my life and what career I should have.

I want to make a difference in this world. I think it's a fundamental desire that we all share in this life. We want it to mean something. We want to do something that matters. We want to leave a real and lasting mark on the world that will outlive our mortal lives. I hadn't really known what I was searching for. I hadn't the first notion of where to start.

Supernatural showed me the way. *Supernatural* took my hand when I needed it the most and said in its unique way, "Come with me if you want to live"—and there's another geek reference to add to the list! This show showed me that life, while challenging, doesn't have to be dreary or difficult with no purpose. It doesn't have to be a string of losses or endless drudgery for big corporate profits. It can be to bring good into the world.

Sam Winchester reminded me of that fact in season 12, when he said, "Well, I mean . . . guys like us, we're not exactly the type of people they write about in history books, you know? But the people we saved, they're our legacy. And they'll remember us and then I guess . . . we'll eventually fade away, too. That's fine, because we left the world better than we found it, you know."

WE LEFT THE WORLD BETTER THAN WE FOUND IT.

And that's the magic of *Supernatural* summed up. In the last three years, volunteering at my library has turned into a part-time job. I also started volunteering for a local literacy group that helps immigrants and refugees (or anyone who wants to learn) build on their English and math skills so they can become citizens. I've also focused my efforts on eliminating some debts so that I can eventually go on to get a master's degree in library science.

Each time I go to work at the library, I feel accomplished. Even when I am doing the smallest or most mundane task, I feel as if I'm facing down monsters and demons, just like Sam and Dean. Sure, mine aren't literal or killing people, but they exist. I feel as if I'm battling back ignorance and misunderstanding. When I am helping a patron at my library with even the smallest of questions, I know I'm making a real difference in their life. It may not be tangible or fit in on a neat statistician's sheet, but it has lasting impact. I have the same experience when I tutor. Whether I'm working with someone on a complex article about a civic right or duty, or working on basic grammar, I feel the real growth of knowledge. I know I'm contributing to a brighter future for someone working hard to make their way here in a new country. Most of all, I feel as if I'm building a better and stronger community—one that doesn't have to shun our differences but rather chooses to embrace them.

Because of *Supernatural,* I plan on making sure I leave the world better than when I found it.

Because of *Supernatural,* I will become a Woman of Letters someday.

If that's not a show and a fandom changing lives, I don't know what is.

In the spring of 2019, my retail career came to an abrupt end. The store I worked at for nearly fourteen years met a grisly end at the hands of a private equity company. In the wake of that, I found myself in a more rewarding position at a group home. While working as a direct support person, I will also be attending graduate school at the University of Wisconsin, Milwaukee for a master's degree in library sciences with an emphasis on public librarianship.

Supernatural was also in transition. At the same time that my store went belly-up, the cast and crew decided that season 15 would be the last. It hit an emotional nerve, reminding us that nothing lasts forever and the only true constant is change. Regardless, *Supernatural* changed my life and the lives of those it touched both on and off set. It will continue to do so long after the last time we see the boys on screen in the spring of 2020. *Supernatural* has a legacy: it is in all of us. The good that we do. We *are Supernatural.* We are SPNFamily. We are the fruits of its changing force for good.

The show may end, but the fandom can continue to be its legacy. After all, family still don't end with blood.

FIND YOUR LIGHT

JULIE MCNIVEN

To say I'm grateful for *Supernatural* is an understatement. I had no idea what I was getting into when I was cast as Anna Milton. I had no idea that my time on that show would still be some of my favorite days on any set, ever. I had no idea that for five or six years after filming I would still be traveling the United States and the world, going to cons and meeting the enthusiastic and incredibly loyal fandom. And nothing prepared me for the friends I would make, the singing I would do, or the belly laughs that I'd have.

Playing Anna—one of my first big roles—was a huge learning experience for me. I was given the role of a meek, terrified, wide-eyed young woman—and then trusted by the incredible writers and producers to become a badass angel who would risk everything to save the world. To be honest, that sort of trust and opportunity is rare in this industry, and it's something I am constantly striving for in my work to this day. It's so very easy to be seen one way and one way only by casting/producers, and it's incredibly difficult to break out of that box and expand their ideas about you. So many of my auditions since playing Anna have been scenes where I would play a woman crying about a lost/dying partner/child. And I'm good at these characters. Vulnerability seeps out of me. That's part of who

I am, and I'm not trying to hide it. But I am much more than that, and I always hope for roles that will allow me to express that.

With Anna, I had Jensen, Jared, Genevieve, and Misha on set guiding me (whether they knew it or not) through one of my first big roles. I really couldn't have asked for a better group. Basically, I laughed ten hours a day and did some super-serious, save-the-world acting in between the laughter.

The people who surround you when you're a relatively inexperienced actor have a great impact on that experience and on the actor you end up becoming. One of the first things you learn as an actor is to "find your light"—to make sure you're standing somewhere that's lit by stage lighting. But on set, as a relatively new screen actor with microphones being shoved down my shirt, going over my lines in my head at 2 a.m. in the freezing cold, finding my light slipped my mind. During the scene where Dean and Anna are in Bobby's junkyard leaning on the car talking about chocolate cake and sex, as people do, Jensen reminded me, kindly, to find my light. Now this is something I don't have to think about. It's part of an actor's dance that happens naturally. But, during a set-up, if I find myself in a shadow, Jensen pops into my head and reminds me.

One of the strangest things for me as an actor is when I have to be half naked and intimate with someone I barely know . . . in front of a crew of mostly men. *Supernatural* wasn't my first sex scene, but I came into it wary because of an experience on another show where I was unaware that certain angles of my semi-nude body were captured. Similar to how Anna grew and learned to own her power, I needed to own mine as well. In this business, there's a tendency to not want to make a fuss about anything . . . to be helpful, quiet, and no trouble at all. Perhaps I was naive with my previous sex scene . . . or perhaps I just wanted to be seen as easy to work with. But really, I wasn't owning my space or my body.

This time, I wanted to make sure I had more control of what was going to be seen. I expressed this to Jensen, and he made sure I could see exactly what each shot looked like, and he covered me up quickly between takes. Besides the bizarreness of the director's voice coming through the walkie-talkie in the car, literally talking Jensen and me through the scene like a soft-core porn flick, everything else was just as weird as one would expect it would be. But together we got through it. In the end, I was pleased that I had Jensen's support, and that I took control of what parts of my body would be seen. My experience on *Supernatural* helped me do that—find that sense of control and ownership. Just like Anna did.

I have adored my entire experience with *Supernatural*, from my time on set to the cons. I will admit, though, that it took a few cons to get comfortable, and truly, it was the fandom that helped me with this adjustment. I have never met a more welcoming, inclusive, lovely group of magical beings. I was nervous at first and had no idea what to expect when

I stepped on stage at my first con. But the *Supernatural* Family welcomed me with open arms. When I spoke to some of the fans during signing or photos, they would share how they related to Anna. I love hearing fans' stories of how Anna inspired them. I think, for some, what they related to most was her personal growth. We all feel small and scared at some point in our lives, just like Anna did, and when we discover our strength and allow it to shine, we become who we want to be.

When Anna found her strength, she was finally able to get rid of the voices in her head and stand by her comrades and fight. Okay, so yes, she momentarily killed Sam. But she did this because she believed it would save the world. Yes, she was wrong and ultimately paid the price with her life (thanks, Michael), but she did what she thought was best. Maybe she was rash in making this decision alone. Had she listened to Castiel, her friend of two thousand years, would she be ash on the floor of an abandoned house stuck in 1978? Maybe the lesson here is that even though you've become an empowered badass, you should still listen to your friends. Yes, even after they've locked you in heaven's jail.

(Speaking of Cas and Michael, I have a bone to pick with them. Or rather, Anna does. I personally am totally cool with being stuck in the past [sarcasm] and staying a pile of ash for all eternity [more sarcasm]. Or wait . . . is Anna stuck in the Empty? We may never know.)

There's another way in which *Supernatural* has changed my life. I can't express how happy I am to have become friends with the cast members. I know I can reach out to any of the SPN ladies (not discounting the men here, but the SPN ladies are something special) when I need advice or I am feeling low, or when I'm stuck across town and want to kill a few hours. This was the best unexpected side effect of being cast on this show, and I am forever grateful to be a part of the SPNFamily. There is nothing more important than having magical women in your life that you can trust to show your entire true self to—the good, the bad, the ugly, the badass. How lucky I am that *Supernatural* has given me that . . . and so much more.

I have such wonderful memories of meeting the fans and seeing how the fandom itself grew from fans to family. Thank you so much for helping me find—and own—my light!

MIRRORS, REFLECTIONS, AND NEW DIRECTIONS

GAIL Z. MARTIN

For over a decade, I've written epic fantasy and urban fantasy books. I started out published by a large British publisher and a big New York City house, and that grew to include a variety of small and mid-size presses, plus independent publishing. Ghost stories, creepy urban legends, monsters, magic, supernatural threats, and the people who fight them . . . that's what I write. But somehow, I didn't find *Supernatural* until 2016.

I came late to the *Supernatural* party, only "discovering" the show when it was already halfway through season 11. I binge-watched all eleven seasons in time for the premiere of season 12, and began live-tweeting new episodes. I made friends on Twitter, and ended up getting to meet Lynn, the editor of this volume of essays, via Fangasm, and also met the folks at the The Winchester Family Business blog, for whom I've written a couple of guest blog posts.

The hiatus before season 12 was intolerable, so I did something I hadn't done in decades—dove into reading fan fiction. I got my start, back in high school, writing fan fiction to amuse my friends, and it not only taught me a lot about writing, but it also convinced me I could entertain people with my stories. Then I got busy with work and family, got my publishing break, and wandered away from my fan fiction roots. So I was thrilled to discover the vibrant transformative works to be enjoyed in the *Supernatural* fandom, and went down the rabbit hole, reading several hundred stories in a matter of months.

Then I took a turn in another direction and discovered the *Supernatural* slash stories (stories that pair either two male or two female characters romantically). I read several hundred of those, came up for air, and wondered what the non-fandom, published male/male romances looked like. So I read a couple hundred of those. At which point, I decided this was too much fun to miss out on, so I launched my Morgan Brice pen name, and added "bestselling urban fantasy male/male paranormal romance" to my writing career—a whole new subgenre and audience—and it all started because of *Supernatural*. I joke that as both Gail and Morgan, I've always written worlds where Sam and Dean could walk in and feel right at home.

Supernatural gave me back the sheer joy of fangirling, something I'd lost in the flurry of deadlines and adulting. It rekindled my passion for storytelling and gave me the courage to step out into new territory. I found my SPNFamily and developed new friendships and an essential connection to a wonderful new group of people. So of course, I also started attending *Supernatural* conventions, where my bonds to this fandom family grew even stronger. And through that, I started the *Supernatural* TFWNC Facebook group, which is now a fun, vibrant community with lots always going on. If you follow me on social media, you'll see that I tweet and post a lot about the show, because it's become a central part of my life.

Supernatural is actually not the first television show to change my life: *Star Trek* (the original series) was. I grew up during the Cold War, with parents who believed we were all about to die in an imminent attack by the USSR, and in a church that believed the End of Days was upon us and we were all going to either be Raptured or die in Armageddon. (I have since strongly disavowed both views, but when you're a kid, you believe what the people you trust tell you is real.) I did not have any reason to expect that I would live long enough to grow up. Then I discovered *Star Trek*, and for the first time, I experienced not just an expectation that we could have a better future, but that we could have a future *at all*. I was obsessed with this show that held out a vision that people of all races, cultures, and planetary origins could work together in friendship and harmony. The show gave me hope, where there had been none before. *Star Trek* was definitely one of my first steps toward becoming a professional fantasy writer, and it introduced me to fandom.

Many years later, I found *Supernatural* at a difficult period of transition in my publishing career, when I was making the shift from being exclusively traditionally published to having more control—and risk—in independent publishing. I needed heroes, and I needed hope. After I'd fallen hard for the show, I realized that one of the things that also made it dear to my heart was that where *Star Trek* had overcome the first of my dystopian childhood fears, Sam and Dean stopped the Apocalypse, my other fundamental nightmare. A dark shadow that I didn't even know still stalked me was finally exorcised.

I believe that finding fandom saved my life. It gave me a place where I belonged, and it gave me a desire to help create a better future. Fandom became a new kind of family, one that understood and supported me in a way my birth family never could. Fandom has also been a shelter for those of us who don't always fit in out there. We're different, but we belong together. In fandom, we support each other, and protect each other, and that's certainly a core part of our SPNFamily.

This is what I love about fandom. Fandom is fierce. We've got the biggest damn BAMF heroes who stand for truth, justice, and, most importantly, the idea that humanity's better self can ultimately prevail. Our heroes are flawed and scarred. They make mistakes and they pay a price, but they do not give up, give in, or give way. They inspire us to find the hero inside of ourselves.

What drew me to fandom in general, and to *Supernatural* in particular, were stories that shared a deep belief in honor, loyalty, friendship, integrity, courage, family (both family by blood and family by choice), and, in spite of apocalypses and dystopias, a conviction that we will survive if we keep faith with each other and refuse to leave anyone behind.

The year after Jared Padalecki's Always Keep Fighting
(AKF) campaign came out, I'd
seen a panel at a genre convention talking about depression and
mental health that had stand-
ing-room-only attendance, went
overtime, and had people so hungry to keep the discussion going
that they met up later online. I
had been very inspired by AKF
because I have always wrestled
with depression and anxiety. I
realized that while I didn't know
any actors, I did know a whole
bunch of authors, and I was also

aware that so many of us had dealt with some kind of depression or other
mental health issues, either ourselves or in our personal circles. Those
experiences not only shaped our own lives, but also the characters we
wrote about and the stories we told.

So I reached out to my author friends, the people whose books create the genres, and Hold On To The Light was born, with its roots sol-
idly in the legacy of AKF. #HoldOnToTheLight is a blog campaign with
posts by authors from around the world in an effort to stand in solidarity
with fans and to raise awareness around treatment for depression, suicide
prevention, domestic violence intervention, PTSD initiatives, bullying
prevention, and other mental health–related issues. We believe fandom
should be supportive, welcoming, and inclusive, in the long tradition of
fandom taking care of its own. We encourage readers and fans to seek
the help they or their loved ones need without shame or embarrassment.
#HoldOnToTheLight is now an ongoing campaign with nearly 200 posts
and authors, ranging from mega bestsellers to mid-listers to debut writers, talking with amazing candor about coping with the situations they
have faced, holding out hope for a better tomorrow, and letting readers
know that they aren't alone.

One of the other things that I love about *Supernatural*, and that I think is part of the show's phenomenal success and legacy, is the fact that while our heroes are "the guys who save the world," we have also seen those badass heroes cry, show fear, express doubts, and be vulnerable. Their ability to show emotion doesn't take away from their heroics or their masculinity. In a culture that gives us many unhealthy signals about bottling up feelings and not showing "weakness" (especially for men), seeing the Winchesters express their emotions and acknowledge vulnerability is hugely important.

I once had an editor try to pressure me into removing all the "feelings" scenes in an epic fantasy book (when the hero grieved the loss of his home and people dear to him). The editor didn't think it was necessary to include that. To me, it was essential to show that while the hero was a warrior, it didn't keep him from feeling love, loss, or trauma, or craving the connection of family and loyal friends. (Many of the heroes I write live with PTSD.) Fifteen seasons of Winchester angst has made me feel very vindicated for leaving those scenes in the book!

One thing I've learned from four decades of being active in fandom is that TV shows and book series may end, but the love that binds fans of those stories together never stops. I truly believe that after *Supernatural*'s fifteenth season comes to a close, the fandom and the SPNFamily will continue to burn bright and stay strong, for as long as we cherish the stories; bring new fans into the fold; and share our love of the characters, the actors, and the series with each other. Good stories last, and great stories become legends. The *Supernatural* legend will live forever.

SPOILER: THIS IS A CHAPTER ABOUT *SUPERNATURAL*

DAVY PEREZ

S itting in my office overlooking the Warner Bros.'s studio lot, in this moment in time, fifteen years is over one-third of my lifetime. Back in 2005 I was broke, and in many ways, broken. Recently out of a relationship, fired from my job, and drowning under a pile of debt that was going to get a lot worse before it got better . . . that was me. It was also the year I decided to take my creative career more seriously. The same year that a series called *Supernatural* made its debut. I remember seeing the promos and thinking, "That looks like a show I would like—if I had time to watch television." Let's flash-forward to now, hand wave past some intense years of artistic struggle, you know, all the interesting parts full of scrappy trials . . . and get to where, after working many jobs, and selling many things, I was finally beyond the (very) rough patches. I found myself with more time to watch things. I also forced myself to write some things, too. My career caught some breaks, I met some amazing advocates, and eventually in 2016, my life path collided with the show that completely changed my life.

Here is an excerpt from a blog post I wrote way back, before my first day on the job:

> *The next step begins Monday, and I am excited to the umpteenth degree. I am going from writing about our real-world monstrosities to a show about brothers who fight monsters in the real world. Horror and sci-fi are the two things that brought me to the written word in the first place. It's in my blood. I'm literally born on Halloween. To tap into this other side of my creative self and plunge headfirst into a different kind of show feels like the first day of school all over again. Considering I was kicked out of four high schools, that might not be the best analogy . . . but I think you can see my drift. Right now, from the way I see things, it is all gravy. To have the privilege to do what you love as a career, it is a huge blessing, and I am forever grateful to anyone involved with me being able to do that. It's all a dream come true. To make things even more fantastic, I could not have asked for a better second job in television: Supernatural.*

And now here's some truth. I'm about to solve a mystery for the fandom that I've heard whispers about for some time now. This revelation might make some people feel vindicated, or it might perhaps make some of the newly initiated among you feel even more welcome here. YES! When I showed up on that first day of work, I had only watched twenty-five episodes of the series. I admitted this once in an early Q&A about my experiences on the show. A writer who creates stories for a living was given the mighty responsibility of joining a show in its twelfth season and had not watched its entire run. Did this mean I didn't understand the characters? What demon deal must I have made to get this job in the first place? How could this brown kid who's been an outcast his entire life possibly know anything at all about two brothers with broken lives who are slaying personal demons while simultaneously fighting physical monsters?

Dean Winchester was likely kicked out of more schools than me, but I know a little bit about unconventional childhoods. Sam has a laundry list longer than mine on how badly his father wrecked his worldview, but again, there's a well I draw from. I came to this show excited to write things that would scare people but also to explore some new roads. I was interested in these characters who were transitioning from being two boys on the road into being two men with a legacy. Because that's where I was in my own life. I was moving on from a time of struggle into a more seasoned adulthood. Have I watched more than twenty-five episodes since that first day? That is obviously a rhetorical question.

It was not long after diving into a life of Saving People and Hunting Things that I was to experience the single-most life-changing event I've encountered to date. The night before leaving for my very first San Diego Comic-Con, my wife and I took a home pregnancy test. It was "just to rule it out" before a week of networking (day drinking). But there was nothing to rule out. Three identical tests later and we were pretty sure this was it. That little blue line was not going away. We were going to be parents. It was the first year of our marriage, and already we were being blessed with a new member of the family. We sat on the couch of our tiny apartment in silent awe. Since that night, much of my identity has become bifurcated: life before my son and now my life with him. The timing is so closely wrapped up with my arrival on the show that the two have become heavily associated: life before *Supernatural* and now my life after.

Supernatural took a struggling, broken writer and gave him a home and a family. Literally, this show is responsible for employing me consistently enough so that I was able to purchase a home for my wife and son, and our Chihuahua, Pablo. In a figurative sense, the SPNFamily embraced me even before I wrote anything. There were so many messages, follows, threads from fans; my social media blew up. In the sea of opinions that started to crash down, most of it was positive support and excitement for all of the new writers in season 12. It was overwhelming, but also thrilling to see so many people engaged with hearing our stories. And so much has happened for me in the four years since.

I arrived to the show as a "baby writer." This term has nothing to do with age. It just means you are an entry level, or just above entry level, minion. Unless you come from privilege, have independent wealth, or had some sort of rock-solid first career before joining the writing ranks, most baby writers live paycheck to paycheck. That was very much the situation I was in. I had spent the money from my first gig paying off debt. The money from my second year as a writer was spent celebrating the union in marriage to my wife, Amanda. It's a wedding people still talk about. It's a day she and I still reminisce about, reliving moments that always end in genuine smiles. So, yes, definitely a worthy investment. But when I met executive producer and showrunner Andrew Dabb, I hadn't worked for six months and was starting to sweat a little. My résumé displayed the two episodes of television I had written to date, and that was it. It made me very unsure of what the future held. My writing sample and the meeting, along with my passion for all things weird and strange, landed me the gig. But there was something else that helped nudge me over the finish line—the *Supernatural* Family.

When I learned of the opportunity, I had ten days to prepare for the meeting with Andrew. I had watched the show, but as I already admitted, I had not been a consistent fan. What the hell was I going to do? Wikis are great for getting you the facts, but there are so many episodes, so many years to comb over, where could I turn to for emotional context? You. I turned to the fans. I read blog posts from multiple sites, old and new. Some will never leave my scarred mind, but most were just genuine passions and curiosities. I took a brief turn at the fanfic and quickly realized that was your space, not mine. I headed back to the places where you talked about just how much this world means to you. Not only did this help me feel ready to talk *Supernatural*, but it also multiplied my desire to be a part of this! So your passion and my questionable talent are to blame for me getting this job.

Flash-forward again now to the present. When those final end credits roll, I will have been a direct part of writing more television than fingers on my hands. The future is always going to be uncertain, but now I have a vision for how to approach the next horizon. The blind corners on the road aren't so scary anymore. Somewhere in these last few years, among the long days breaking stories locked up in my private bunker, I found something. Two guys staring at me with their angel best friend—that plucky kid they adopted—the demons surrounding them, and all the women in their lives who try to save them as much as the guys don't believe they need it . . . somewhere in that sea of faces staring me down I heard, "And then what happens, Davy?" That is the place where I found my voice.

Supernatural will leave behind a legacy that will resonate for generations. My own family, both personal and professional, has grown from it. If I haven't name-dropped anyone specific from the show that is because there are too many to list. It's all of them. Everyone here has taught me something I will carry with me from this day forward. When I took the job, I thought I was going to come here and secretly evolve Sam and Dean into more fleshed-out, nontoxic versions of a man. I was not prepared for them to do the same to me. And I am forever grateful for the transformation.

I don't know if it is denial or just a genuine confidence of how this show will live on, but something about the approaching last episode doesn't really feel like the end. And maybe that's just it right there. If family don't end with blood, then *Supernatural* don't end with the finale. The SPNFamily will always be around, and the Winchesters will always be waiting for you in all the stories, both canon and online. In fact, I'm going to fire up my friendly streaming service right now and watch the pilot. Or no, maybe I'll cue up an episode from season 5, or be an egomaniac and watch something I wrote with tentacles in it. Whatever I end up clicking on, it's gonna be great to finally watch that twenty-sixth episode. So which one is Sam? Wait, what's Negan doing there in a robe? Damn, that is a sweet-ass car, though . . .

BRINGING THE ALPHA VAMPIRE TO LIFE (AND DEATH)

RICK WORTHY

What made being on *Supernatural* memorable for me? There's a story behind the answer.

The short violin version is that *Supernatural* came along when I had not worked for exactly twelve months. This was back in 2009 and 2010, and it had been twelve months of auditions and meetings with people saying, "We like you, but . . ." Twelve months of the Hollywood bullshit, and I had not been able to book anything. A year of hitting the pavement, as they say. Suddenly, after years and years of working, I was unable to land a job. I said to myself, *Well, maybe it's time to get out, maybe I'll throw in the towel. Maybe this time God is trying to tell me that I should bow out and do something else.*

Those thoughts were hitting me very strongly when my agent called. She and I were very close, and still are to this day, so she knew that I was near to the end of the acting road. I remember telling her that if nothing

happens soon, that's it for me. She said to hold on. "Let me see what I can find." She called back within twenty-four hours and said there's a great role for the world's first vampire on *Supernatural*, and I said okay, I'll do it. I'll go in and give it my very best, but if I don't book it, that's it.

So my agent sent me over the material, which was a good nine pages of solid dialogue and scenes. Often in these cases, they want to make sure they've got the right person, so they pretty much give you everything that's in the script. Then they want you to do that in the room with five or six or seven people as the audition. When I read the script, I thought it was a great role. I had also read for the role of Crowley previously, which not many people know, and for another couple of roles, including an angel. The *Supernatural* producers knew who I was, and I was on their radar, so I thought, *Well, at least they still think of me.* I also knew that Sera Gamble, an old friend of mine, was now producer and showrunner. So I was determined to go in and rock and roll and give it my best, because whoever got the role would be lucky to get it.

I walked into the audition and the first person I saw was Sera, whom I hadn't seen in years. I tried to keep my cool because you don't want to walk in and just start hugging and handshaking everyone. You want to maintain a degree of calm, cool, and professional and show them that you're ready to do the audition. But I saw Sera and I just couldn't contain myself. I said, "OMG, it's so good to see you! Can I just give you a hug?" She said yes, and then I sat down and did the audition. There's that third eye in the back of your head sometimes that says: *You know what? That felt pretty good.* That's how I felt when I finished the audition. I left the room and thought, *Well, I left it all in the room,* as actors say.

A couple of days went by, and I got a phone call from my agent saying that I was headed to Vancouver to play the Alpha Vampire on *Supernatural!* I was beyond elated. I was so excited and had so many ideas about how I wanted to play the character, but because I hadn't worked on *Supernatural*, I didn't know what the vibe was and how it would be when I got to set. As I've told Jared and Jensen, that show has spoiled me so much, because they were so nice to me. *Everyone* was so nice to me, including the director, Guy Bee. It was his decision to cast me; it was apparently between me and another actor, and he chose me. We have now become very close friends, and I love him like a brother. Together we shaped the level of terror that the Alpha Vampire possesses. I brought a lot to the role already with my own ideas, and then Guy slightly pointed me in the right direction, saying to lean in a little bit that way, and he was right. It is easily one of my top-five favorite roles that I've had in my career.

I loved the role so much that I was thrilled to come back two years later to do another episode. The first episode for the Alpha Vampire was "Family Matters" in season 5. I came back in season 7 to do "There Will Be Blood." Coincidentally, that's the title of one of my favorite movies of all time starring Daniel Day-Lewis and Paul Dano. I love that movie and I loved that it was the title for my episode of *Supernatural.* I also loved that episode, because it was such a powerful showdown between the Alpha Vampire—who does have a name, by the way, which I do know—and

Sam and Dean Winchester. It's a classic sort of mafia confrontation, an ultimate poker face showdown between everyone in the room who comes to the Alpha Vampire's home. I love every interaction that the Alpha Vampire has with Sam and Dean. I'm very proud of that episode.

At the end of that episode, we broke the fourth wall when I said, "See you next season." But that never came to be. I had to move on to the next thing and put *Supernatural* out of my mind—which I was never able to completely do. I was always thinking about it because I loved the role and the character so much. But I went on to do *The Vampire Diaries*, playing the father of Bonnie, played by the lovely and talented Kat Graham. That meant that I was in Atlanta filming another show for the CW, and I thought, *Well, they're probably never going to bring me back to* Supernatural *anyway*. I loved *The Vampire Diaries*, too. It was a great experience, and I loved working with Kat so much that I call her my TV daughter. After *The Vampire Diaries*, I was cast in the new Syfy show, *The Magicians*. Five years went by, and I was in Vancouver after finishing filming season 3 of *The Magicians*, and I'm chilling out with my dog, Buddy, and we're going to the park or to Petco or somewhere and my agent calls and says, "Don't go anywhere in January." I asked why not. She said literally three days after New Year's that I was going to be shooting an episode for season 12 of *Supernatural*.

I said, "Bullshit!"

My agent responded, "I'm sending you the script right now."

She emailed me the script and I was like, *YES! I'm coming back!* I knew it was going to be for the Alpha Vampire's death, and I didn't have a problem with that—I just wanted it to be good. A really high-stakes and well-earned death. And I think it was. I love, love, love "The Raid." I think it's probably my favorite episode, because I had five years to live with the Alpha Vampire in my head, and I was always thinking about him. He's even appeared in my dreams a couple of times, just sort of walking by. I remember thinking, *I'm not done with this guy yet; he still has more to say.*

When my agent emailed me the script, I was so excited that I just sat there and read it in my car—and I absolutely loved it. I loved that it was Sam who outsmarted the Alpha Vampire, and that it was Sam who puts the killing bullet in his head. I thought it was brilliant. I was hoping that Guy Bee would direct it, because he had directed the other two episodes

I was in, and it felt like me and Guy, that was our creation together. But Johnny MacCarthy directed it, and he did a really nice job.

I'm often asked several questions about the Alpha Vampire. One is not so much a question, but people want to tell me how they feel about the character. Complete strangers have come up to me and said, "I hate that they killed you off on *Supernatural*. I wanted you to be the Big Bad for the season." I always reply, "Hey, it's out of my hands, but at least he died the way I wanted him to die—with honor." That leads to the next question, which is: "What did the Alpha Vampire want?"

Everyone has very passionate feelings about the show and the characters, and this is my own interpretation of what the Alpha Vampire wants. He wants someone to beat him. He wants an honorable death, because he's essentially been walking around for at least 200,000 years unbeatable. Literally no one—living or dead—had been able to best him. He is the king of the monsters—untouchable. You can't beat him physically, but he can be outsmarted. And I think that's really what he was looking for— someone who could think a move or two ahead of him like it was a game of chess. Someone who could outsmart him and make a winning move. And that was Sam Winchester. It had to be.

I love the thing that Sam does with the bullet as they distract the Alpha Vampire at the Men of Letters command center. Sam puts the killing bullet inside the Colt.

The Alpha Vampire says, "There are only five creatures on this earth that gun cannot kill—and I'm one of them."

It's a huge power play between the two of them, and it's like, who's bluffing and who isn't?

And then Sam says: "Are you sure?"

I'm getting chills right now remembering the scene. I love that it's filmed in slow motion. Sam pulls the trigger and that bullet comes out, so slowly, directly toward the Alpha Vampire's forehead. And there's that little smile on the Alpha Vampire's face, and he says to Sam, "Clever, clever boy."

And then BAM!—that bullet comes out and it goes right through the Alpha Vampire's head. He doesn't dodge the bullet (although people have said that he could have), but maybe he didn't want to. The bullet goes right through his head, and there's that little smile. If I were to write what he was thinking right then, it would have been, "Well done, Sam, well done."

And then BOOM!—he's gone.

An honorable death.

This character, and this show, have meant a lot to me. We have the best fandom, literally, in the entire world. You can go anywhere in the world and if you see someone wearing a *Supernatural* shirt or you go to a convention anywhere, you find instant family and friends. I absolutely love that. I've been to Italy, Germany, London, Australia, so many places—for conventions or maybe just walking through the airport—and I see someone with a *Supernatural* shirt on or someone recognizes me from the show, and you exchange Instagram accounts and you've made a new friend. It's the most incredible, most dysfunctional family in the whole world, and I'm really happy and proud to be a part of it.

ALWAYS KEEP FIGHTING

ALANA KING

've loved stories for as long as I can remember. There's just something about diving into another world that fascinates me. Stories have motivated me and driven me to try new things outside of my comfort zone that I never would have attempted otherwise. When I was seven years old, I signed up for a taekwondo class because I wanted to be like Kim Possible. I stuck with it to the point where I earned my second-degree black belt. When I was nine years old, I lugged *Harry Potter* books to school in my backpack, and whenever I felt nervous, I took one out and started to read. I got in trouble for reading in class quite a bit, but I developed an intense love for reading because of those books. When I was twelve years old, I picked up a video camera and tried to make a movie with my friends based on *The Hunger Games*. I failed miserably, but it led me to discover my passion for filmmaking. And when I was eighteen, my love for *Supernatural* drove me to take a trip to Pittsburgh for a convention that would forever change my life.

When I first started watching *Supernatural*, I had just finished my junior year of high school. It was, arguably, one of the most difficult years of my life for many reasons—both personal and academic. I was stuck in an extremely toxic friendship, though I didn't know it at the time, and was unable to reach out or ask others for help with the situation. I isolated myself from my loved ones, buried myself in schoolwork, and almost completely cut myself off creatively from making videos—an outlet that I desperately needed. It all became too much, and I was miserable. That summer, I wanted to find a story to lose myself in completely. So when my cousins suggested *Supernatural*, I shrugged and said I'd give it a shot. To be completely honest, I'd heard of the show before but had never been interested in starting it. I've never done well with the horror genre, so I'd just brushed *Supernatural* off as "probably too scary for me." Oh, how wrong I was!

The first season was a little scary, I'll give it that. But it became apparent to me, even after watching the pilot episode, that it was much more than a "jump scare horror" type of show. Needless to say, I binged all ten seasons that were out at the time in less than a month. I lived and breathed *Supernatural* that summer. When I went back to high school for my senior year in the fall, *Supernatural* was up and running again with new episodes. Thursday nights became my favorite time of the week, and no matter how much work I had to do, I would always carve out an hour to watch the episodes when they aired. My senior year was as rough as my junior year, especially at the beginning. Behaviors from the previous year followed me, friendships fell apart, and my senior class endured several tragic losses right before graduation. But *Supernatural* helped me get through it. Whenever I needed an escape, I watched an episode of the show and lost myself in it. Seeing the characters deal with their struggles gave me the strength to take on my own.

When high school finally ended, I was relieved to be free of a setting that had become increasingly difficult for me. In the fall, I would head to Chicago to study film and television, something I had dreamed of doing for years. I had a feeling that my college experience would be ten times better than my high school one, even if it would present new challenges. But before I made that big move, I had something equally life-changing ahead of me: my first *Supernatural* convention. For my high school graduation gift, combined with my eighteenth birthday present, I asked my parents if they would let me go to the Pittsburgh *Supernatural* convention that would be happening a month after I graduated. Having a chance to meet the cast in person and to hear them speak about the show would be a dream come true. This was the first time a *Supernatural* convention had ever come close to where I lived, and I was not about to miss it. My parents didn't understand my love for the show that well yet, but because they're so supportive, they said yes. A month later, I found myself heading to Pittsburgh with my cousin (and my parents, aunt, and uncle, who drove us—thanks, guys!).

I wasn't sure what to expect from my first *Supernatural* convention. I had been to general Comic-Cons before, but I had never been to a convention for one specific TV show. That weekend, my mind was blown. Everyone at the convention was so welcoming and lovely. The cast members were all amazing, the panels were incredibly fun, and talking to other fans was easy because we all already had one thing in common: our appreciation for this incredible television show. As someone who has a hard time connecting with other people in social settings, I was surprised how easy it was to talk to everyone at the convention. I left Pittsburgh at the end of that weekend with even more love for *Supernatural* and a desire to be more involved in the fan community that I had just discovered.

Two months after the Pittsburgh convention, I moved to Chicago for college. Freshman year was full of confusion and uncertainty. Moving away from the small Ohio town I'd grown up in to a big city like Chicago was a huge change, and I was intimidated by the daunting tasks of making friends and establishing a new life there. I was on my own, and I didn't know how to cope with that in the beginning. I made mistakes, put my faith in some of the wrong people, and had my heart broken. The biggest thing that helped me through it all was creating videos for my YouTube channel. Up until that point, I had only posted videos sporadically and they were all about books. I never took YouTube seriously. But after attending the *Supernatural* convention in Pittsburgh, I decided to change up my content a little and try to produce videos more consistently. I didn't want to limit myself in terms of what I could talk about in my videos, so I started making *Supernatural*-themed content. At first it was just one video a week. I would upload a *Supernatural* reaction and review every Thursday night, sitting down to edit the videos immediately after a new episode aired so I could get them out as fast as possible. This caused my channel to grow a little and paved the way for other *Supernatural*-themed videos.

For the entirety of my freshman year of college, I worked tirelessly on my YouTube channel and saved up my money to go to the Chicago *Supernatural* convention in the summer of 2017. Unfortunately, the second semester of that year was harder than the first. Someone I had become close with broke my trust in a huge way, which left me riddled with anxiety. On top of that, I was dealing with homesickness, and the stress of balancing YouTube work with a full-time college course load was beginning to weigh on me. I started to spend more time alone, trying to figure out how to piece my life back together. It was during these months that I began to think I might have a more serious problem on my hands, but I had no idea what was going on. The truth is: I've been struggling with rather severe generalized and social anxiety my entire life. It's held me back from doing some of the things I love and achieving goals I'd set for myself. It's made me close myself off from potential friendships and relationships. It's affected me physically. It's made me incredibly vulnerable to judgment, pressure, and hate. But I never knew what it was, because I was never properly educated or diagnosed.

One of my biggest criticisms when it comes to my schools is that none of them ever prioritized positive mental health education. They lacked the proper resources to help students who were struggling, and did not educate us on the topic whatsoever. My first source of information about mental health came from Jared Padalecki's Always Keep Fighting (AFK) campaign. From the moment I started watching *Supernatural*, I supported the campaign and worked to learn more about what it represented. AKF means a lot to me because some of my family and friends have struggled with different forms of mental illnesses, like anxiety, depression, and PTSD. I've also lost peers and family members to suicide. I knew that mental illnesses existed, I just didn't have the proper information to realize that I was dealing with one.

After my freshman year of college, I moved back home to Ohio for the summer. I was not doing well mentally at all. My anxiety built up so much that it took all of my energy just to get out of bed in the morning. Sometimes I didn't. I needed help, but I still couldn't bring myself to admit it; I couldn't believe that I was struggling with a mental illness. My life was technically great, despite some of the crappy personal things I'd

gone through that year. So I was
fine, right? No, very wrong.

One night, at 2 a.m., I was sitting on the floor of my bathroom
crying. There was a book I had left
on the sink earlier that day while
I was cleaning called *Family Don't
End with Blood*, the collection of
stories from the *Supernatural* cast
and fans about how the show had
impacted and changed their lives.
I knew Jared had written a chapter for the book and thought that
reading it might help me feel better. So I picked it up, sat on the

floor again, flipped to his chapter, and began to read. That action changed
my life. I found myself relating to a lot of the things he described about his
own struggles with mental health. It made me feel less alone and helped me
realize that mental illness could affect anyone, even me.

The next morning, I told my mom how I was feeling. We made an
appointment with my doctor. I was diagnosed. I started seeing a therapist.
I educated myself. I got help. Jared Padalecki helped me help myself, and
I will never be able to thank him enough for that.

Almost three years have passed since I was at that low point, and looking back, I'm grateful to have had *Supernatural* with me through such big
changes in my life. Graduating from high school, moving to college, coming to terms with the importance of getting the help I need . . . *Supernatural* has consistently been there for me when everything else was changing
around me. I still struggle with anxiety every day, but finding ways to cope
with that has been absolutely crucial to where I am now. In the past three
years, I have made over 250 videos about the show. I have been to more
than fifteen *Supernatural* conventions, traveled the country, met so many
people from all over the world, made more friends than I could have ever
imagined, built a platform on YouTube, found my voice. I started fighting
for what I believe in, came to terms with my anxiety, helped some of my

favorite charities, and worked with some of the most incredible people. All of that was because of *Supernatural*, and the inspiration from Jared's Always Keep Fighting campaign.

Supernatural will air its final episode the day after I graduate from college, in the spring of 2020. In the pilot episode of the show, we see Sam Winchester about to graduate from college, preparing for what comes next and not knowing what lies ahead. In a way, I guess things will come full circle for me. When *Supernatural* comes to a close, it will be time for me to go into the unknown, graduating from college and preparing to take the next step into adulthood. Hopefully I won't have to stop the apocalypse or take a swan dive into hell, but hey, stuff happens. Nevertheless, *Supernatural* will be on the air to hold my hand through one more big step in my life, and then we'll send each other off on our separate ways. I'm terrified of that future without it, but for now, I'm taking the time to be grateful for this show and all that it has given me. *Supernatural* is special, and I feel so lucky to be a small part of such an amazing family.

STATE OF SLAY

CARRIE GENZEL

A s a young girl, I was full of fear, anxiety, and self-doubt. I always felt less than, different from the other kids. I had friends, but everything always seemed easier for them than it did for me. I felt awkward and dreaded going to school. I remember my chest tightening as my daily walk brought me closer to school, and I wished I could fast-forward time to bypass the day and be back home to hide in my room. I had a very active imagination, and I lived very much in my head, creating different worlds and fantasies that seemed so much better than the world I lived in. I hated myself and spoke to myself harshly for not being good enough in my eyes, and not fitting in, even though, from the outside, I seemed to be doing just that. I was good at being a chameleon, blending in with whatever crowd I happened to be around at school. I put on the act of who I thought they wanted me to be so they wouldn't ask me any questions.

I found my escape in high school when I discovered the drama club. Those were my people. Many of them were, like me, introverted, but we would come alive on stage. I mean, I figured I was acting every day anyway, pretending to be who I thought everyone wanted me to be, so why not go all the way and actually play a full-fledged character? That stage was the only place I felt comfortable. It was like flying, it gave me such a high; it still does. But, at some point, the play comes to an end, and I continued to struggle in my personal life.

I struggled with depression, an eating disorder, obsessive-compulsive disorder, and suicidal thoughts, all the while continuing friendships and moving through life. I never let anyone know any of what was really going on. I thought no one else wanted to hear it, or they would think I was weird, or a freak, or—the worst of all—crazy. So I kept my mouth shut and suffered in silence. I continued on like that for most of my life, and even when things were going really well, I never let myself truly enjoy it because I thought the other shoe would drop, and I waited for the bad to happen. And, if it did, it validated my belief that I didn't deserve good things, and that, really, I wasn't good enough.

To quiet my head, I started self-medicating. I tried many things— shopping, food, relationships, alcohol—but the voices continued to yell and scream at me, telling me no one would care if I was gone. Those voices, because I wasn't sharing with anyone else, became my truth, and as my mental health worsened, the only option seemed to be to end my own life. All of this was going on even as I was working in film and TV. People would often say to me how lucky I was and that I was living an incredible life. I would laugh at them, because I knew I would later go home and continue to plan my own suicide.

I got lucky. Someone came into my life who shared his story with me. I was shocked, because I knew what his life was like today, but I had no idea about his past. It was an inspiring story, but I was so shut down emotionally that it didn't really penetrate my force field of darkness. That didn't happen until months later, when, for whatever reason, on a lonely, rainy night, I remembered that story. I remembered the what-it-was-like part, and it resonated with me. I recognized myself in that story for the first time, and I got really scared because I knew I had stopped caring about myself. I had started doing stupid things, tempting fate, and being reckless, and I realized that it would be really easy for me to take an action that I couldn't reverse. I broke down in my living room and asked for help. To whom, I don't know. I just remember saying out loud, "I can't do this anymore, I need help." I drank a lot that night with the mission of passing out so I wouldn't leave my apartment and harm myself.

When I woke up the next day, I heard a voice say, "You're done." Without even questioning it, I called my friend who had shared his story with me and I told him everything and that I needed help. That call was the beginning of my life. It was the first time I had been honest about who I was and how I had been living, and as scary as that was, it felt amazing to let that big secret out and stop its hold and power over me. I outed myself to everyone I knew, telling them everything. And the outpouring of love was incredible.

That was fourteen years ago, and I have worked hard every day to be a woman I can be proud of, to be who I thought I could be but was too afraid to let go and let her out. One of the things that I have found so inspiring about the SPNFamily is the sense of community and the way it celebrates everyone for who they are.

After appearing on *Supernatural* as Lynda Bloome in "Bugs" that first season, far enough back when there wasn't social media like there is today, I had no idea what was in store for me when I was invited back to shoot another episode ten years later for "Just My Imagination." I knew while we were filming it that it was a special episode, but I had no idea that I was going to receive the tsunami of love that I did the night the episode aired. I couldn't even keep up with all of the messages and posts. Looking back, it makes sense that the episode is such a fan favorite. I felt there was something special about it after reading the script the first time, and it felt special while we shot the episode with Dick Speight, Jr. at the helm. The episode had everything that the fandom was going to love: of course, the camaraderie of the boys, but it also had humor and a lot of heart, and something I think a lot of those who appreciate the show can relate to—having that imaginary friend, or voice, that always saw the best in us and cheered us on, even when we didn't believe it. I related to those scenes with Sully (played by Nate Torrence) and Sam, and remembered that I had drowned out my own positive voices many years in the past and was grateful to have found them again. The episode represents our childhoods for many of us, when we weren't as afraid to use our imagination and, even if there was some darkness, we had that special friend who was there to save the day.

Since that episode first aired, I feel like I've been adopted by the coolest family out there. You all are the most loving, inclusive, powerful people I've ever had the pleasure of being adopted by. I've seen what you all can do when you collectively come together to make something happen, whether it's voting the show onto the cover of *Entertainment Weekly*, beating out newer "higher-rated" shows; raising money for a charity that supports a cause that touches an SPN cast member; or showing up for someone who has lost a loved one or has found themselves in a tough financial spot. I've seen you, many times, surround one of your own in support when they are in need, and I've been blessed with so many new friends I wouldn't have met otherwise—this book's editor, Lynn Zubernis, being one of them.

I launched a blog almost three years ago called *State of Slay*™, SLAY being an acronym in this case for Self Love/Appreciate You. My blog is meant to be a community of support and inspiration for those who have overcome their own demons and struggles, or who are still battling them. In it, I share my journey from the darkness, and what I do to stay balanced and positive today. Once again, the SPNFamily has come together to support and participate in what I have to say, because really, my personal message is the same as the message you all share: We are all in this together, no matter where we come from, no matter what is going on, we are all the same and no one gets left behind. We all stand together because together we are stronger. Together, we can walk through anything. Together we stand as one.

One of the things I had to learn on my journey was to trust and form relationships with women. I didn't trust most women, and so it was suggested early on in my recovery to join a support group of just women. That terrified me, but I knew I had to overcome my fear and jump in. That group of ten women made me feel safe to be me, and I learned who

I was. They didn't judge me; they just shared their truth with me, and I with them. My distrust of women had started young, through family history, and continued throughout my life until I sought help. Much of that distrust came from a lack of communication while I was growing up, not understanding what was going on and why, and not understanding someone else's illness and struggles and why behaviors seemed erratic, leaving me to fill in the blanks and believe that what was going on was my fault. That set the stage for me not trusting all women, because I had been hurt as a child by a female figure in my life. Finding the ability to let go of my past and learn to trust a group of women was very healing to me, and formed the foundation on which I now place all my female friendships.

The women of *Supernatural* are just like these women who I first put my trust in. You all operate from the same place—a place of love, a place of support, and a place of honesty in your own journeys and struggles. I have had the pleasure of sitting down with many of you and sharing my truth, and you have done the same with me. Connections have been made—deep connections. This fandom far exceeds just sharing a common interest in a television show; this fandom shares their lives with one another. The fandom lifts each other up. It shares a heart, which is magical, and I feel so incredibly honored to be welcomed in the way I have been. Your outpouring of love has picked me up so many times. You inspire me, impress me, and make me laugh. You all make my heart shine. We are women, many of us, who have come from troubled pasts. We are women who have or are still working to overcome those obstacles to be our best selves. And we are women who, together, radiate love and joy, and give out some of the best hugs I've ever had in my life. Don't get me wrong—there are a lot of kickass SPN dudes as well—but the women have really come together to find a voice and use that voice for good.

A lot of times for us actors we go to set and it's just a job. A job we enjoy and are grateful for, but you do that job and then go home and resume your life. When you become a part of the *Supernatural* cast, you get adopted into a family. It's the craziest, most colorful family that exists out there, but one with the biggest heart. It has been a pleasure to share my heart with you, and I will continue to do so.

Shine on. SLAY on. Carry on.

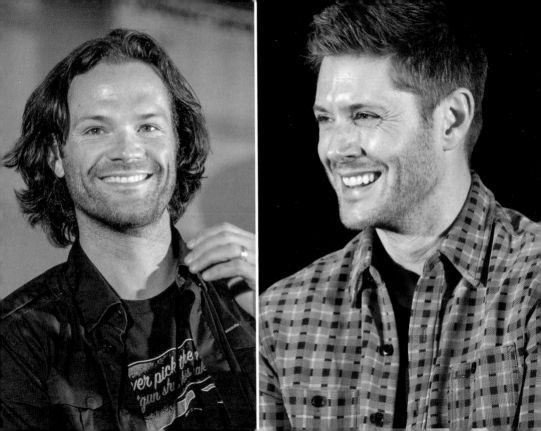

WAYWARD AND THE WAY I WANT TO BE

DAWN GRAY

Deep breath in. Remember, you can do this. Let it out slowly; step up to the mic. You don't have to tap it, but you do.

Sitting in front of a keyboard, ready to let all that's in you out . . . it's kind of like stepping up to the mic and making your own public announcement. There's some big secret that no one knows about you, and here you are putting it on paper.

So, here's my book, or a fragment of what it might be if someone picked it up off the shelf. The title of this chapter: "Wayward and the Way I Want to Be." Catchy, right? As awesome as that might be, it's also scary AF. See, most of you who know me know me as a researcher, a traveler, a writer, and now a screenwriter. But that's not who I am. That is who I let the world see. But now, it's time to tell a different story, one about a girl and a show and that one little line.

"As long as everyone wears a condom, we'll be fine."

Wasn't the one you thought it would be, was it? No, this part of the story isn't about the boys and the way that *Supernatural* changed my life the day Dean came strolling into town to look for Sam because "Dad's on a hunting trip." Nope, this one is about the women who kicked me in the ass and made me think . . . made me realize that I could do just about anything.

We thought she was going to be just another one of those characters who came and went, but she came, and like the hardass she was, she stayed. In season 5, "Dead Men Don't Wear Plaid," Sheriff Jody Mills, played by Kim Rhodes, made me feel like I could live through the worst and still come out on top. She had been through so much. She had the heartbreak and the pain, but she moved with confidence . . . even when Crowley was trying to . . . well, I'm still not sure what he was trying to pull because his game was WAY off. From that point on, I think I found a hero.

In 2010, when Kim came onto the screen, I was just starting to break out of a place I never thought I would get away from. I had been divorced for four years at that point, single for two, and I hadn't been able to leave my house in just about that same amount of time. You see, I was diagnosed with agoraphobia. Shocking, I know, especially for those who know me.

My hands shake as I type this.

The fear of panic attacks that put me out of work just after my youngest turned three, in 2007, kept me locked down. I wasn't able to go to the store alone or even get gas in my car. I never left my yard except to bring the kids to school, and even then, I still had my youngest so there was a buffer, but that was just not acceptable.

Funny enough, I remember sitting down in front of my TV and watching this woman drive up in a cop car, get out, and approach the boys . . . and that was it. I was hooked on Sheriff Jody Mills. The more I learned about her, the more I decided that I needed to take her lead. Being inside all the time, it was just me and my characters (I had already written several novels by then).

I was getting out. I was getting away . . . because if Jody Mills could do it, so could I.

Wow, writing this is harder than I thought.

I still didn't tell anyone what was going on. My mother was the only one who knew what I was struggling with because she had gone through the same thing when my siblings and I were younger. I remember leaving the grocery store with her so many times after she panicked, leaving behind an entire carriage of food.

I didn't want to live that way. I didn't want my kids to see me NOT be strong. So I decided to do the most outrageous thing in the world. I took my ex to court. I petitioned the judge to let me leave Massachusetts with my kids, and I moved 258 miles away to the town in Vermont where I had spent a small portion of my childhood.

I was a woman, alone with three small children, and I would be damned if I wasn't going to be the next Jody Mills and get myself out of my head!

And I did just that . . . a little bit at a time. I went to school for medical assisting . . . that didn't work out so well. I went to counseling, which also didn't work so well because I had developed coping strategies by then that put the doctors to shame. That is, until I met one person who didn't want to medicate or "shrink" me. She wanted to help me.

Every week, she gave me a new game plan, something else to try that got me out of my habits. She even said, "Think like Jody. Think about what she would do as a sheriff to solve the issue. Don't just avoid it like an unsolved case."

Holy hell! She was a *Supernatural* fan. The line stuck.

For the next three years, I did what I thought Jody would do. I went out and solved the case of "walking around town," "going to the store without a plan," "attending the craft show that would never end," and before I knew it, there were people in my life who were helping me, too. They knew, they got it, and they understood. WOW! I never imagined I would find my Donna Hanscum and she would be exactly like the blonde version! I also became an EMT-Basic. I worked as an administrative assistant, and I was on a morning news broadcast and several local television shows for my novels.

Before I knew what hit me, I was moving again. My middle child was diagnosed with autism spectrum disorder (ASD) and our town had nothing to offer him. So it was back to the state I had run away from.

And, back to Start.

It took me a year after moving to leave my house again. The kids were older, and they were able to go to the bus alone. They were good. I was

not. I needed to do something fast. I was losing again. So, what would Jody do? Enter the case of "the medical assistant."

That's right, I went back to school. Yep, and here I was at square one again.

It took nine months of straight As, showing my kids what I could do, and NOT missing a single day. That felt good, but when I finally got a job at one of the area's largest hospital's outpatient clinics, it all went downhill. I lost weight. It was a chore to get in the car to leave for work, and three months in, I resigned. In the course of the next few months, my panic attacks caused me to lose sixty pounds and slip into my own little *Supernatural* universe to survive.

I was living life here, but my reality was Sam and Dean. Until the SPNFamily on Twitter showed me, yet again, that I was stronger than my monsters.

Jared's battle with his own mental health was an opening. My new family was my backbone, and once again those words came back to me.

What would Jody Mills do?

Well, forget that! She would kick it in the ass!

So, I did. I started writing screenplays, and I collaborated with another writer to make a movie. We got all the way to just about production schedule and it tanked, but that was okay because I was so ready for the next step.

In my ventures, I met a man who would help me accomplish my dreams. Reno was an acting coach, a director, and a producer, and my life seemed to come full circle because you would never guess what show he worked on: *The Suite Life of Zack and Cody.*

The guy worked with KIM RHODES! Tell me that's not a sign.

In all of this sudden mayhem, I started going to conventions, testing my own limits, and getting back into life and just a little bit out of my own reality, which was still Sam and Dean. You can only have those voices in your head for so long before they become something of a staple.

The Wayward movement gave me something else to believe in. Family. This family, while at times intense, can be the most amazing and supportive lot you'll ever encounter. They help me every day to get through.

And every day they show me just how much being part of *Supernatural* can change your life.

In 2018, we shot the trailer for my own TV series. The support from the fandom on helping to raise funds for it has been amazing, and we had hoped in the next six months, episode 1 would be a reality. As things go in the industry, the pilot was put on hold and while things for that series haven't taken off, three more have been put on the table.

Late 2019 brought about the release of the Arcane series of books, and hopefully another adventure into production for a web series. It seems my life is on a *hurry up and wait* setting sometimes, but I wouldn't change it for the world.

There is just one thing I have left to do, besides hug every single one of you should we ever meet. That would be to tell Kim how much she's kept me going without even knowing she was doing it. To tell her how much her portrayal of the strong, never-give-up, Wayward sister has helped me kick myself in the ass so many times. It's amazing that I've been to so many cons and never had the opportunity, so here it is right now: Kim, should you see this, thank you! From the bottom of my heart, thank you for everything that you've done from the time you stepped on set to this very moment. Thank you for being strong, brave, beautiful. Thank you, for being Wayward AF.

CODE ORANGE

PATTY BARBERA

Two words you don't want to hear: Code Orange.

In hospital-speak, it means "stroke."

This is a story about how the *Supernatural* fandom and a book called *Family Don't End with Blood* saved my life . . . when I learned exactly what those two words meant.

In order to tell this story, I must first tell you how I became part of the fandom. I started watching the show from the beginning. I liked that Dean listened to classic rock and heavy metal. When I saw Dean's cassette collection in his '67 Chevy Impala, I knew I would be hooked on this show. I also loved all of Sam's *Star Wars* references.

Fast-forward to 2016. My friend Jennifer is a Bon Jovi buddy (a friend I met through our mutual love of the band), and she started going to Creation Entertainment conventions for the television show *The Vampire Diaries*. They seemed like a lot of fun, so as a goof I went to a *Walker Stalker* con to meet the main characters from another show I loved, *The Walking Dead*, and of course to bring a Flat Jennifer (a paddle with a flattened version of my friend printed on it) to our next *Vampire Diaries* con photo op to poke fun at my friend. I met the actors, and they were so nice that I decided to try another one. I went on the Creation site and saw that they had *Supernatural* conventions. I'd had no idea! I was so excited that I would be meeting the stars of that show that I booked the closest convention and went solo to Washington, D.C., for my first *Supernatural* con. I ended up having an amazing time and, over a two-year span, I went to seven cons.

Charity is big with the *Supernatural* fandom, and I try to support as many of the actors' charities as I can afford because they do so much good that it's hard not to participate and support these amazing actors. In this fandom, I found that we have many talented members. One in particular is an author of several books about the show, including *Fangasm: Supernatural Fangirls* and *Family Don't End with Blood.* I bought those two books at the *Supernatural* con in New Jersey in 2017.

I read both books in less than a day. One story from *Family Don't End with Blood* that stood out for me was "Stroke of Luck" by Rob Benedict, who plays Chuck Shurley, also known as God (he also fronts the band Louden Swain). He shared his experience of surviving a serious stroke he suffered at a convention. His friends, the other actors, helped save his life. I had basic knowledge of the effects of a stroke because my grandmother and a few of my friends had suffered them, but I never knew what the signs of a stroke were until I read Rob's chapter, in which he wrote about "not

being himself" the day he experienced his stroke. And later in the day, he had difficulty putting words into speech. He also shared the signs of a stroke on Facebook. These two bits of information would be tremendously helpful to me in the next few months.

On February 7, 2018, my life would change forever. As I got ready for bed, my hand started to go numb. I thought it was no big deal. I tried slapping it, but it would not "wake up." The numbness slowly moved up my arm. Then I felt a pain in the back of my head, and my whole right side went numb. The right side of my face became droopy. It was like what had happened to Rob! I quickly realized I was having a stroke. I screamed for my husband and told him what was happening. He raced me to the hospital. While in the car, I couldn't speak without slurring my words and my tongue felt fat. Was I going to die? I was terrified.

My husband got us to the hospital in record time, parked in the emergency room entrance, got a wheelchair, and rolled me in. He told the admitting nurses what was happening to me, and the nurses rushed me into the hospital as a Code Orange. I was very fortunate that my hospital had a brand-new stroke unit, and they proceeded to take a CT scan of my brain and samples of blood from my arm. I felt nothing as they did this, which scared me even more. Thankfully, the CT scan showed a very small clot that blood thinners would rectify. The next day, the clot was gone and I started seeing improvements right away. I had feeling in my legs and my right arm, but my arm was still weak. My diagnosis was clear: I had suffered a transient ischemic attack (TIA), a mini-stroke.

A TIA presents with symptoms of a stroke that tend to go away in a short period of time. They last for up to 30 minutes and cause dizziness, weakness, vision problems, and difficulty speaking. There is a high risk of having a major stroke or other serious complication in the near future if the TIA is not effectively treated. In one study, the risk of a major stroke was fifty times greater, and 20 percent of those were fatal. A TIA is an especially serious risk if the person is over sixty and/or has diabetes, the TIA lasts more than ten minutes, and if the TIA causes weakness and speech problems. If any of these symptoms happen to you, you should get medical attention immediately to reduce the risk of a future stroke.

I did get treatment right away, and so I ended up getting all the feeling back on my right side. I was able to talk without slurring my words, and within days I could walk and move my arms and legs. My doctor gave me the results from my tests several days later. My MRI showed that this mini-stroke was not my first. In fact, they found damage from a previous stroke that I never knew had occurred, which means this one was even more dangerous and the results could have been very different.

My story has a happy ending, but I know that I probably would have ignored those first symptoms and gone to bed, most likely damaging my brain, if it hadn't been for Rob's story in *Family Don't End with Blood*. I'm happy to say that I'm back to my old self with minimal damage. Many people have been changed in some way by *Supernatural*, but in my case, this amazing television show literally saved my life.

THE MAGIC OF THE MULLET

CHAD LINDBERG

I recently attended a *Supernatural* convention in Jacksonville, Florida, and a little girl came onstage dressed as Dr. Badass, my character from the show. It was unlike anything I had ever seen. I'd seen people dress as my character before, but to see this young girl and know that she related to Ash was amazing. Knowing that Ash resonates with so many people is wonderful to me.

I think it's because Ash is fun. He's charismatic and he's comic relief that is sometimes very needed on the show. Before Ash, we hadn't seen a character come along with a mullet where the mullet electrifies rather than gets made fun of! The mullet did so much of the work, but I think fans connected with the character because he's quirky, and thank goodness people responded to that. He's also not stereotypical in the sense of the masculinity that is presented on the show. That was appealing to fans, because *Supernatural* is so inclusive, encompassing every sort of human being possible. It's hard to find another show that has that magic about it. Sometimes you don't know what's going to work and what's going to connect with people, but Ash did.

I am disappointed that they didn't explore the Roadhouse further on the show. I think, looking back, that they probably should have. So many people want to see the old characters in some capacity. Back then, they thought about making us regulars (Ash, Ellen, and Jo), but they were still trying to find their footing at the time, and then it took off and became what it became.

The experience of being on the show itself was extraordinary. A special moment that stands out occurred during season 5, when I had to shotgun a beer and didn't know how. (It's on the blooper reel if you want to see it.) I had brought my sister to the set with me that day, because she loves *Supernatural* and of course she loves Jensen. I mean, who doesn't love Jensen? So I said to him, "I don't know how to shotgun a beer. It's not my thing." And he responds—read this in a deep Jensen-type voice—"*Well, what you wanna do is, you wanna come over here and . . .*" And he tries to show me how to cut into the beer, where you hold it, and where you chug

it from. He's showing me and I'm learning and then I look over at my sister and she's just trying so hard to keep it together, because she's standing right next to Jensen Ackles! That's priceless stuff.

So he shows me how to do the beer thing. The beers on set are terrible. They smell like sulfur, and of course they're nonalcoholic. As I chug the beer for the scene, the bad beer is flowing out the side of the can and all over my mullet and onto the floor. I have no idea what's going on, so I just keep doing my lines. Then I look over and I see Jared and Jensen with tears in their eyes as they try to keep it together. Once I realized what I was doing, I decided to push it further, just going with it, and then Jensen yelled, "Cut!"

Everybody was laughing—Jensen and Jared, the crew, the cast, my sister. And I forget who it was, but someone came up to me afterward and said, "Thanks, we needed that today." It had been a lot of work and things were kind of tense on set, and that broke the tension. And going back to what I said at the start, I think that's what Ash brought to everyone. It was like, we need to laugh, and this guy's silly. Both for the people watching the show and for the people making the show. I could put on the mullet and people would go apeshit on set, especially in season 5.

People who watch *Supernatural* are often curious about the paranormal work I do in addition to acting. I tell them that *Supernatural* is as far out as it gets as far as a television show, but it's all based in some sort of truth, in the myths and the legends. That's what the show's creator, Eric Kripke, wanted. And a lot of those things are real, but strangely enough, working on the show had nothing to do with me going into the paranormal. It was just one of those coincidences that happens to be cool. Shortly before I got cast on *Supernatural*, I decided to explore paranormal work after watching *Ghost Adventures*. This was before social media, but I reached out to the *Ghost Adventures* folks and they graciously had me on their show. From there, I started my "career" or my own path in the paranormal. It kinda turned into the real Sam and Dean, in a sense. And so of course, then I got cast on *Supernatural!*

Now I go out and find ghosts—or more likely, they find me—and I take people out on ghost hunts. I hope that they walk away having had fun and that we can have some conversations between the living and the dead. We go to various locations, and I always say that we're going to visit people, and they don't have to do anything or say anything if they don't want to. We're going to visit *their* place. I usually feel confident that I can walk in somewhere and get "someone" to say hi, though. We're all just floating on this crazy planet trying to figure out what's going on, and we need things like *Supernatural* and the paranormal to anchor ourselves to. Sometimes we need some validation, like, "All right, there really are things out there I can't explain."

When I'm filming something, I never have any clue what impact my work will have or how it will be perceived. When we shot the show, it had not yet become the phenomenon that it is today. Then it literally took off and became a global phenomenon, something none of the original cast saw coming. Because of this show, I've been able to travel the world for conventions and see some of the most insane places on earth. Paris, Brazil, Germany, London, the list goes on. All because of my time on *Supernatural*. The show has turned me into a world traveler.

I think one of the reasons *Supernatural* became such a phenomenon is because it's a show about family, something we can all relate to. In addition, I think everyone finds the supernatural and the paranormal interesting. We all have a fascination with myths and legends, and that was part of Eric Kripke's vision. And then, you've got Jared and Jensen, who literally have this amazing chemistry. All that mixed together made magic, and people responded to it, and it made them feel incredibly good. The show and the fandom made viewers feel included; it made them feel like they could be themselves. As the show has gone on, the conventions have turned into very safe places for people, where they can come and be themselves and be loved and feel love. There's really nothing like it in the world.

I don't like to say "fans"; it really is the "SPNFamily." They have been there for me for my good times and they have been there through my really hard times. They've helped me get through some very difficult family situations. They've shown up, and I know I can count on them. It's rare that I don't get emotional talking about the SPNFamily, because it really does go deep. I can't properly put words to the love that I receive online, and especially in person at conventions. It's something that's true magic and true love. I feel lucky to be a part of something like that.

When it comes to the legacy that the show will leave behind, let me say that first, I don't think *Supernatural* will ever die; it will always be around. People are going to continue to want their *Supernatural,* and the conventions will hopefully continue forever because we all need a place to come together. I go to the conventions to see my friends—people I didn't necessarily work with on the show but who have become great friends of mine. *Supernatural* has changed people. It has changed anyone who has watched and cares about the show. And that is its legacy: those people will go forward as different and more confident people.

I will go forward as a different person too. I'm so thankful for the relationships I've been able to forge with this show, this cast, and this fandom. It's unlike anything else, and I'm forever grateful.

THIS IS ME

MICHAEL BANH

When *Supernatural* first came into my life, I had no idea it would have such an influence on me.

When I was young, I did not have a lot of self-confidence. I struggled with my self-esteem and always looked to my family, friends, and peers to decide what I should like, how I should act, and who I should be. Nothing made me happier than to be accepted in their eyes, because I wanted to be the person everyone liked. If everyone was proud of me, then I should be proud of myself. I felt confident when others put their trust in my abilities to succeed in any given situation. I never wanted to fail anyone because failing meant that I had disappointed those who believed in me; that thought was ingrained into me. I tried not to allow it to over-power my actions or mind-set, but I accepted that truth and told myself it was okay to live my life with that idea.

I tried to excel in every possible way when I was growing up. I strove for a perfect track record in my academics, hobbies, and behavior. I had a very outstanding high school career and felt prepared for college. I chose to major in engineering because my family thought I would shine in such a challenging field. It made sense to me because I had a strong love for math and science and felt engineering was a combination of both subjects. I was confident that I'd selected the perfect field of study and was excited to start this new adventure. I had an amazing support system of friends (shout-out to my best friends, Sydney and Miki) and wonderful love from my mom, sister, and stepdad. I was ready to show everyone what I could achieve.

It was February of 2012, and I was beginning my transition to my new life as a college freshman. My new best friend, Miki, introduced me to Tumblr as her favorite social media platform and method of procrastination. She inspired me to create my own Tumblr blog so we could follow each other and share the posts we found there. I would casually open the website to see what was there from time to time, but over a couple of weeks, I began to immerse myself in the dashboard where I would like, re-blog, follow, scroll, and repeat. Suddenly, my dashboard was inundated with posts of a television show I did not recognize. I tried to ignore them, but the posts became persistent enough to the point where it was a daily occurrence. All I could gather after a few days of seeing these posts was that it was a sci-fi/horror show about two brothers, and it was obvious that this show had a large presence on Tumblr and a passionate fan base. It finally caught my interest after a few weeks, and I caved. I had to see why this show was so popular.

That show was *Supernatural*.

Supernatural was in its seventh season when I first watched the pilot one lazy Sunday afternoon, and thankfully, seasons 1 through 6 were already on Netflix. It took a while to stick, but I slowly got into the rhythm of watching one episode each day after my classes. When I got back to my dorm room, I would turn off the lights, hop onto my bed with my laptop, and watch what was in store for Sam and Dean. When I finished with homework or studying (or maybe procrastinating, let's be honest here), *Supernatural* became my escape from reality and the stress of school and life. Over time, one episode became a few episodes, and I was eager to leave my last class of the day so I could binge as many episodes as I could in one night.

As I became more consumed, though, I began to wonder why I kept watching the show. I have never liked horror shows or movies. Things like gore, suspense, and jump scares stress me out. However, for some reason, I carried on watching episodes like "Bloody Mary," "Skin," and "The Benders" without questioning it. I did not understand it at first. I just assumed it was a television show that would entertain me for forty-five minutes every night. Over time, I began to understand that I was not watching it for the horror aspect. The supernatural beings, lore, and history were still interesting to me, but in the end, I was watching it for Sam and Dean Winchester. It was Sam and Dean's story and how they interacted with the supernatural world that captivated me.

I became invested in the special bond between them—watching their connection grow as they delved deeper into the supernatural. I enjoyed learning more about the brothers' personalities, the backstory of how they grew up, and how they both complemented and contrasted each other. I loved watching them work together to assemble the clues of their current case, and it made me feel like I was solving the mystery with them.

A month after discovering the show, I could already tell I was turning from a casual viewer into an obsessed fan. *Supernatural* became the main talking point for me, my favorite style of clothing, a daydream fantasy, my phone background, an attitude, and a way of life. My room eventually turned into a shrine for *Supernatural*. I had posters of Sam and Dean hanging on my wall alongside *Supernatural* shirts hanging on hooks, DVDs and Blu-Rays framed perfectly alongside textbooks, and any *Supernatural* merchandise I could find online displayed on every surface in my room. My obsession affected my daily life to the point that when I took an exam, I imagined Sam and Dean over my shoulder silently cheering me on, feeling that they believed in me.

This love spurred me into creating a new Tumblr blog, now named @jaredandjensen so I wouldn't spam my new college friends with my sudden love for *Supernatural*. This is where I learned how to make GIF files; I've posted 2,000+ *Supernatural* edits to date. I am grateful to say I have 180,000+ followers who love the show just as much as I do. Thanks to this blog, I was also able to find a wonderful online community of new friends. These friends not only shared a mutual love and excitement for the show and were willing to talk to me about Sam and Dean, but they also felt like another family I could talk to about what was happening in my day-to-day life. I am so thankful to all my fandom friends, and I know these friendships will last a lifetime. *Supernatural* was my happy place, but it somehow became much more than a television show to me.

Supernatural came into my life at a very interesting time. When I first started watching the show, I felt like I had a strong handle on my life. I was doing well in my classes and had a new group of friends to help me deal with the ups and downs of college life. I did not need any strong revelations to change my life. At the time, *Supernatural* was just the show that gave me joy and became my go-to method of de-stressing, whether it was rewatching old episodes, making new GIF files, or talking to my friends about the most recent episode.

While college primarily holds happy memories for me, it challenged me not only academically, but emotionally as well. There were moments when I felt like I did not know what to do or that I was wasting my life away and just going through the motions of trying to accomplish something to get it over with. I watched those around me figuring out their future lives while I was still struggling to figure out what to do at that very moment. It got difficult, especially during my senior year, when I started experiencing long bouts of sadness. I started having trouble in my classes, and as a person who achieved straight As in high school, it was difficult to accept anything else in college. When I failed my first physics class, my morale took a hit. I felt so guilty and upset about failing, but I never vocalized how I was feeling because I did not want anyone to worry about me or to burden them with my problems. I also tried applying to multiple engineering internships and positions throughout my undergraduate years, but I came up empty-handed. I eventually just stopped searching because it felt pointless and I did not want to face rejection again, as previous attempts already made me feel discouraged. I did not want my family to know that I had let them down. If anyone ever asked how I was doing, I gave them a generic "I'm okay," rather than be truthful. I did not know how to deal with this sadness at first, but because of *Supernatural*, I learned how.

I did not have any prominent male role models when I was growing up until I met Sam and Dean. As a man, I greatly identified with Sam and Dean and their struggles from when they were young boys to adult men. There were a lot of expectations for me to be strong and brave because anything otherwise would make me look weak. I was told being successful meant being the best, where achievements were measured in awards, high

GPAs, and bragging rights. Anything else meant you were failing. I also had a father who was tough on me, so I felt very critical about myself and never learned how to manage my feelings. However, through *Supernatural*, I could see Sam and Dean as multifaceted, complex characters who go beyond the social constructs of what men are supposed to be.

Both Sam and Dean are strong when they need to be, but they can be vulnerable at times too. They can be merciless when battling the monster of the week, but be gentle with grieving victims and kids. The brothers showed me there is so much more to people than how skilled they are, and that it's okay to make mistakes and learn from them. They are nothing but kindhearted, selfless, and brave because they only hope to make the world a better and safer place for everyone. They take risks without knowing the outcome to save someone or one another; they bring peace and comfort to those who are hurting, and they try to be courageous in the face of danger. I wanted to be just like Sam and Dean. However, one of the most important lessons I learned from them was how to express myself.

In the early seasons of the show, Sam and Dean struggled to open up emotionally, especially with each other. In later seasons, however, you can see Sam and Dean admitting to not being okay, and that was something I needed to hear. Whenever Sam and Dean talked about their emotions, it was almost like I was talking about my own with them. I was relating to what they were experiencing. There were times when they were stressed with the impending doom of the current season, and it felt like it was all too much for them. I saw myself in their shoes and felt the same way. We did not share the same problems—a world in chaos versus final exams—but the words they spoke mirrored what I was thinking. I was able to express myself through these characters, and it was like going to therapy without having to speak a word.

As I neared graduation, I felt an immense pressure to succeed. School was demanding more of me, and the pressure of post-college life started weighing on me. I was working two research positions while taking a full course load. I did not understand how anyone could handle so much at once, and it felt like I was messing everything up. I continued to struggle with the school material I was learning and felt conflicted about whether I even made the right choice to pursue engineering. Did I not study

I DO BELIEVE IN US.

enough? Was I smart enough? The self-inflicted pressure stirred up a lot of self-doubt. Everyone around me was prevailing and finding new ventures, so why wasn't I? I had worked so hard to get here. I was supposed to make everyone proud, but in my mind, I was falling short.

By the end of my senior year, I began openly questioning what had led me to this point. What was I doing here? What do I want? Who am I? I felt like my life had no meaning. I talked to my friends and family, and they told me they were proud of me and impressed with what I had accomplished. They gave me words of encouragement, but it never reached my ears.

It was the darkest time of my life, but even then, I looked to Sam and Dean to bring me happiness and support, like they always did. I still had Sam and Dean, and I thought about everything they had gone through. They faced the biggest threats like Azazel, Lucifer, Michael, Amara, and Chuck, but every wound, battle, and breakdown only made them stronger. They showed me that even when times were tough, everything could work out in the end. It was inspiring to see people face their demons (sometimes literally) and still get out of bed every day without knowing whether they were going to succeed or fail.

One of my favorite moments in the show was in the season 8 finale when Sam goes through the final Trial to close the Gates of Hell. When Dean tells him that the final Trial means the ultimate sacrifice—Sam's life—Sam does not question it. Sam confesses that his greatest sin is the number of times he let Dean down. He says he cannot let him down again, but Dean convinces him that together, they will figure it out, just like they always do.

Sam and Dean continually go through the challenge of feeling hopeless, and their battle against hopelessness is reflected throughout the show. There are moments where both brothers have lost all confidence and feel like the world around them is falling apart, both literally and metaphorically, but they continue to fight and eventually learn to be proud of what they have accomplished. During the season 9 finale, Dean recognizes his and Sam's achievements by saying he is proud of them both. It is scenes like these that highlight not only how Sam and Dean acknowledge their successes, but also how they accept themselves for who they are. In season 14, specifically in the 300th episode, "Lebanon," the show focuses on this idea. Sam asks Dean whether he wishes that everything in this lifetime had never happened and they had just lived normal lives. But Dean says he is good with who he is and who Sam is because their lives are their own.

'CAUSE OUR LIVES — THEY'RE OURS.

Even though I stumbled a few times, I overcame every obstacle and obtained my bachelor's degree. I realized that I was so hyper-focused on trying to excel in school that I forgot my love for math and science that made me interested in engineering in the first place. I learned that my achievements should stem from within myself and what I am passionate about rather than the satisfaction of others. I was finally able to restart my search for job opportunities with new ambition, and I found success at a job in research and development and am planning on working towards my master's degree.

It took some time, but I eventually realized self-confidence and self-expression were the most important things I could learn from *Supernatural*. I never stopped to ask myself whether I was proud of myself rather than think of those who would be proud of me, but it was because of *Supernatural* that I learned how to do that. *Supernatural* taught me how to believe in myself. It was *Supernatural* that was there for me when I needed it most. Thanks to the show, I have realized that I am happy with who I am, and I feel confident saying that.

This is me, and I am finally able to say that I am so proud of what I have accomplished.

SOLDIERS' STORIES

TARA GREY COSTE

While I was on medical leave in the fall of 2017, Netflix suggested I watch a show called *Supernatural*. Largely confined to bedrest, I watched and I watched and I watched pretty much nonstop for six weeks, and when it was done, I turned to my very patient husband and said, "I think I need to watch that again. There's something important here."

As a leadership professor who studies how ancient belief systems guide modern behavior, the show's content was dead-on in my wheelhouse. But that wasn't it (or it wasn't all of it). I had been searching for a tool to help a particular segment of my students, the increasing numbers of soldiers streaming into the university through the GI Bill. These students had unique needs and special struggles, and they needed a vehicle to help them transition into a world that didn't always fit them well.

Supernatural and the lessons it teaches about heroism and bravery are powerful, and I was pretty sure the show would resonate with the veterans I wanted to create a safe space for. I wasn't wrong. As I started digging through the many academic articles and books written about *Supernatural* and the years of interviews and convention footage, I became ever more convinced that I had found what I was looking for. Not only did the show's story lines speak to me, but the real-life work of the cast and the extended SPNFamily shone with a special light that was truly inspirational.

But I had to test my thinking with its intended audience. Over the course of the next year, I bounced my ideas off a number of students, men and women who were working hard to figure out how to maintain the values and integrity carved into them through years of military service while adapting to a new reality that framed things quite differently. Once I felt I had collected enough information to do this project justice, I offered a course using examples from the show, its cast, and its fandom to explore concepts of heroism, authenticity, and service.

I am delighted to say that it worked! As one student said, "Studying the dynamic of the characters as they hunt demons and ghosts while saving the world from the apocalypse, I found great comfort in sharing the struggles with these two brothers. I battle with PTSD every day and experiencing the hardships with Dean and Sam helped me cope with my personal struggles and find strength to always keep fighting."

While I anticipated this type of reaction from the soldiers interacting with the material in the course, I did not anticipate the depth of the raw, human connections students in the course would develop with each other. One nonveteran stated, "The growth that I had in being exposed to the veterans' perspectives on support and transitions from a tribe/warrior lifestyle to trying to assimilate to 'normal civilian life' had a great impact on me. . . . The tie-in to the show and the experiences of the brothers constantly living in that on-edge state, ready for the next life-or-death battle, really showed me the strain that these vets have been under and how different it is from the life that has moved on from them while they are away fighting."

As my students worked through what Sam and Dean were experiencing, and what soldiers everywhere experience, they worked through a lot of their own challenges, using examples of divorce, death, and other trauma to illuminate human struggles and the power of the human spirit to overcome seemingly insurmountable obstacles. And they began to meet outside of class to extend the support system in areas where they needed a bit of extra backup. Because their discussions were so real and so honest, they formed strong connections with one another.

From the foundation of the show's stories, we moved on to the examples of the cast and their leadership in the development of the SPNFamily. Although many in the class were new to this world and got to experience it with fresh eyes, even the superfans found a new appreciation for the singular nature of this phenomenon. As one said, "I knew the impact that *Supernatural* had on my life, but I was not aware of its impact on so many others. The depth and reach of this show has been remarkable. Through this class, I heard inspirational stories from others and saw the immensely positive effects not only from the show but its cast, crew, and fandom. This class gave me a new perspective on something that I loved and valued and showed me important examples of modern-day leaders."

Although the show's leads are relatively humble in acknowledging their leadership roles, it is clear that they were quite deliberate in the tone they have established on set and for the fandom. Their love and appreciation of the SPNFamily are obvious. And it is this authentic and charismatic guidance that has given authorization for the myriad benefits that have arisen as the power of the SPNFamily collectively.

Of particular importance is their embrace of difference and how we are all simply trying to do the best we can with what we are given. Because the cast is so open about their imperfections, others are free to come to peace with their own challenges and to embrace what makes them unique. In class, this was especially powerful for those who had often found themselves marginalized. They came to understand that it is okay to be who they are and that their tribe, people who share their passions and values, is out there somewhere. One of these students shared the following: "I learned that we need our people to be able to move forward, be motivated to succeed, and more. The show . . . showed that I was weird . . . but that was okay, because we all have a bit of weirdness in us."

With acceptance, people come out of the shadows. They seek out ways to connect with each other and to be connected to something larger than themselves. It was this empowerment that drew me to the SPNFamily, to catalog and celebrate what had been done and figure out ways to use these exemplars to enable the potential of the populations I work with.

Inspired by the example the SPNFamily had set, I asked each student to spend a month doing acts of kindness in their communities, to seek out spaces where even a small act could make a huge difference in someone's life. What they did and what they discovered was really beautiful. One drove a disabled man seven hours to his home so that he did not have to navigate a much longer trip on public transportation. One discovered that his elderly neighbor had not been able to manage after her basement flooded, so he cleaned everything up for her. One helped her daughter create a kindness project at school so that she and her classmates could serve their community.

For soldiers especially, returning to civilian life comes at a price. Combat veterans have spent a long time under constant stress and return home tightly wound. Many who have troubles reintegrating experience a lack of purpose, feeling unneeded in a reality that has continued on without them. It is important for them to be reminded of the positive impact they already have on the people around them and to realize how much more they could be doing. It is important for us all.

In leadership studies, we teach that a fundamental skill everyone should develop is a robust awareness of self and self in relation to others. As we explored the virtues of *Supernatural* and the stories of its characters, cast, and extended family, we exposed many things about ourselves:

our strengths, our vulnerabilities, and our dreams. As we peeled away the layers of armor that life had laid upon us, we could become our true selves and, in this revelation, come to appreciate how truly powerful we all can be.

After the semester ended, one student described it this way: "The bond in our class ever so subtly grew not only from our connections with Sam and Dean but how Sam and Dean helped connect us with each other. The shared experience and exploration of leadership within the context of the *Supernatural* series fostered an interplay between fiction and reality that eventually transcended our every expectation. In fact, it challenged us, provoked us, empowered us, and in ways healed us."

LIFE-CHANGING: *SUPERNATURAL* AND THE SPNFAMILY

JOHN TAHMOH PENIKETT

Playing the character of Gadreel was a significant chapter in my career as an actor. Little did I know, though, at the time I'd booked the role, just how important a chapter it would become in my life—how I was entering a fandom so very special that one is often referred to as part of the SPNFamily. It's an appropriate name, as I soon learned that few other fandoms share the same passion and consistency. I knew little about the character of Ezekiel going into the audition, other than he was an angel. I even found out afterward that the sides for the audition (a portion of a script used for the audition process) were Castiel's lines from a previous episode.

The audition went well enough that I ended up booking the role and was told the arc was for a couple of episodes. But it was important for me to know that Ezekiel was not who he said he was; my angel was just pretending to be Ezekiel! Again, not a lot to go on, but good enough to work

with. My actor brain was off to the races. Was he a good guy or a bad guy, in the writers' view? What was this angel's motivation, his true intentions in this episode I'd been given? Was he an angel aware of the complexities of the modern world, or an angel of old from the Bible, beholden to a different time and rules? Questions, so many questions! Ones that are rarely answered for us actors. It was time to make choices.

Most trained actors love to do the work of preparing for a role. This is not something we're usually given much time to do, and even when there is enough time, we rely on any information we've been given about the character and then mix that with our own choices and the backstory to bring the character to life. Preparation, in my experience, has been absolutely key to getting out of my own head and letting the character breathe. The times I've had the most anxiety before the first day playing a new character have almost always been when I feel like I haven't had the time I needed to prepare. And of course, the times I've felt the calmest, most present, and most excited to get on with that first scene are when I've done the work. Then, there are those rare times where you read a character's story and immediately connect and understand them on a kinetic level. I've had that only a few times in my career. Ezekiel (well . . . Gadreel) wasn't that for me.

I did research and read about both angels. Gadreel, the infamous protector of the Garden of Eden who happened to let the snake in, was subsequently punished and imprisoned for thousands of years. Ezekiel, on the other hand, was the opposite of Gadreel in reputation and character. And it's clear why Gadreel initially pretended to be him. I made some choices of my own but also felt like being too prepared for this guy might sabotage me somewhat. I didn't know how much the writers were going to base these angels in SPN on what I was able to ascertain about them online. I'd been given so little background on the character, so I knew that I'd probably be given some surprises regarding who the writers thought he was and the arc of where he was going. This is often the case in TV land, and you need to be prepared to scrap some of your choices on the day ("the day" being the minute you hear this new information on set and take it in the direction your bosses are asking you to go).

My first day on set filming the episode "I Think I'm Gonna Like It Here" was a prime example of the surprises producers and directors will often drop on you at the last minute. The first scene I shot was my character getting off a bus. Easy peasy. I was then preparing for a significant scene of Ezekiel being trapped by Dean in a holy circle of fire. It was an intense and important scene, one where I was actually talking to and trying to achieve some trust from Jensen's character, Dean.

Literally five minutes before we were to film the scene, the director approached me and asked, "Do you want to see what Jared has done?"

I knew that Jared and I would both be playing versions of this angel, as he inhabited each of our vessels, but I was under the impression that I was the first to play Ezekiel. Trying to calm the sudden panic that I was feeling, I replied, "What do you mean, 'what Jared has done'? He hasn't already shot scenes as this character, has he? I thought I was going first?"

The director responded, "Oh no, he's already done some scenes. So, do you want to see it? We need to get going here."

I could barely mask my sarcasm and panic as I said, "Do I want to see what the lead actor of the show has done already with the character I'm supposed to be imitating?! YES, I think that might be important to see." Really, I wished I'd had more than the three minutes to take in what Jared had done, but I did appreciate his obvious confidence in my incredible acting abilities that I could in seconds mimic him.

"Okay, then, let's go to video village and check it out."

The scene he showed me was Jared playing Ezekiel and being very specific in his movement and cadence of speech. I breathed for the first time, because as I watched Jared's performance, it was obvious that the choices he made were very much in line with the choices that I'd made. Jared was moving his body with almost ballerina-like fluidity. He'd taken on a Shakespearian cadence to the way he spoke. Two choices I'd made were to move in a specific way—something angelic was my thought— gentle and graceful, but with no doubt of the superhuman strength underneath. I'd practiced how I wanted Gadreel-as-Ezekiel to sound too, each word clear and pronounced.

Once season 9 aired and I started doing the convention circuit, many of the fans complimented me on my imitation of Jared's version of Ezekiel/Gadreel. I was flattered, but after explaining the actual sequence of events, a lot of them were surprised. Conversely, I've also heard from fans at conventions that they were impressed with Jared's impression of *me*. Goes to show you that art is truly specific to the individual experiencing it. There are always many different reactions to an actor's performance, but at the end of the day, it seemed most fans were happy with my work.

My second day on set, I was in every scene with Jensen and Jared from the beginning of the day to the end. It was to be a huge day, with very emotional scenes and writing that required me to be sharp and emotionally available. (Well, Jared was playing like he was in a coma in bed, so not so heavy for him.) On my way to work, my best friend, who's like a brother to me, called me to say that he'd just found out that one of his best and oldest friends (and also a friend of mine) had passed away. I had been completely consumed with the big day ahead of me, and when I heard the pain and disbelief in my brother's voice at his dear friend's passing, I was heartbroken that I couldn't do more than listen and offer some words of love. Needless to say, the news of our friend's death put me in a very somber, reflective state.

Isn't it always the case that when we lose someone, we stop for a moment to try and understand what it means that we won't see them again? And then we are slapped in the face with the truth of how precious and fleeting it all is—how the things in life that were stressing us out, consuming us, are instantly put in their proper place of importance, and you know you've been obsessing over trivial matters? I had been worried about this first real day of work and how I would do. I had become obsessed about running my lines; I was going in circles about everything that could go wrong and not focusing instead on everything that might go right. This news reminded me, like a well-placed left hook, to keep my hands up, man (my hands being my wits and presence of mind to see what is both important and within my control).

That day of intense work was everything I could have hoped it would be, but it was also filled with reflection and a heavy heart. I felt gratitude for many things I hadn't acknowledged at the end of that day, and sadness at the passing of a talented, driven young man whose star was just about to shine.

Not long after this episode aired, I got my first glimpse of the *Supernatural* community via Twitter. I'd only just started on Twitter, years late to the game. But as I stumbled along, I saw the huge number of people communicating about Gadreel and the show. Now to digress a little, I cut my teeth on an important, critically acclaimed show early in my career. That show (*Battlestar Galactica*) had found legions of loyal fans even though we'd missed social media by a few years. Sure, there were chat rooms discussing our show, but nothing that compared to the sheer size and reach of social media. So, as much as I thought I knew, I truly didn't understand the potential of this new way of communicating with the world. Social media has allowed fandoms of shows like *Supernatural* the ability to reach out to thousands, if not millions, instantly.

And then there's streaming. Being able to watch *Supernatural* on Netflix led to a renaissance with a new generation of fans—ones whose parents would not have let them watch it when they were younger. They binged the show, and then, being the generation that they are, obsessively communicated about it online. This turned *Supernatural* from a long-running series with a consistent, but not huge, audience to an ever-growing heavyweight that showed no signs of stopping in its rebirth.

What I thought would be two episodes for my character turned into three. Then when I was off filming a feature in Calgary, I got the call that *Supernatural* wanted me back for another three episodes—news that I was very happy to receive. It would take me out of pilot season and allow me to play this character again . . . a character I had so much fun doing with this great group of guys and crew.

More than five years have passed since then, and only recently have I not felt like an active member of the family. I went from doing the show to interacting with the fandom via social media. Not long after, I was contracted to do the convention circuit for almost fifteen months straight, which ended up garnering more conventions with the gang overseas for the next few years. It's only been the last year that I haven't been on the circuit with them as often, and I do look forward to doing it again.

Being a part of the gang on the convention circuit was without a doubt one of the highlights of my professional career. You've all heard the stories, but needless to say, the amount of laughter and taking the piss out of each other is unforgettable. We've all seen Richard Speight on stage commanding a crowd, but the way that man can tell a story—a story many of us have heard more than once—and still make it fresh and just as funny as the first time, is awesome. I honestly feel like everybody's storytelling skills are on point when doing the circuit. If you're going to hold court, especially at a meal, you better be sharp or they will tear you a new one like you're a first-time comic bombing on stage. But as much as they give it to you, it's always done in good fun and you're forced to laugh at yourself.

I think some people forget how hard the lead cast has worked for the last fifteen years. They somehow manage to do the long hours week after week and yet get home to their spouses and kids on the weekends. They also, generously, donate one weekend per month to attend conventions, giving back to the fandom and keeping it strong and always wanting, waiting for more.

As I've mentioned, I came from a show that is one of the most critically acclaimed televisions shows of the last twenty years. For those of you who haven't seen it, *Battlestar Galactica* is a must. Those castmates of mine are family; they always will be. But, to be blessed enough in this short career that many of us have to say that I experienced a special bond with the cast of another series, one that I did for only one season, is a real blessing. With the SPN gang, I've enjoyed incredibly funny travel experiences with a group of amazing people on a show that, when all is wrapped and done, will have run strong for fifteen seasons. I played such a minuscule part of this record-running show, yet I was treated like family by the cast and fans alike. Anyone who's experienced an SPN convention has been entertained by the many different faces of guests that are staples on the circuit.

Performances aside, there are so many individual talents and characteristics that the fans look forward to with each of these guests, such as the lovely Ruth Connell, who plays Rowena, who I only recently learned is also quite the singer. Speaking of singers, there's a murderer's row of them in the gang. Rob Benedict, who plays Chuck Shurley (aka God), is the lead singer and guitarist of the fantastic band Louden Swain, which also includes guitarist Billy Moran, bassist Michael Borja, and drummer Stephen Norton, all talented musicians and beautiful human beings. Jensen, when he graces the fans, can carry a fine tune. Briana Buckmaster (Sheriff Donna Hanscum) has a great set of pipes, and I always look forward to hearing her perform. Gil McKinney (Henry Winchester), is a wonderful singer, and having done a number of conventions with him before, I found out much later how talented he is, which was an awesome surprise to me and many of his fans. And who can forget the smart and talented songbird Jason Manns, whose song "Vision" had a cameo on the Impala's short-lived iPod? For those who've never met the man, you might, at first glance, think "former linebacker," but get to know him and you quickly find that he's smart, well read, has the voice of an angel, and, to top it off, is a well-mannered Southern gentleman. As I said, all these guests bring their unique talents to the table. Watching Sebastian Roché, the charming, never-aging Frenchman who plays Balthazar, absolutely woo a crowd of screaming fans as he fluently switches among three different languages is a sight to behold.

Richard Speight, most often the master of ceremonies, is a master indeed. The man makes the job look easy on stage, like he just came out of a nice hot shower, one cup of coffee in, holding court on stage to the joy of the fans. It's hard to mention Rich without Rob Benedict. These two best friends have incredible comedic timing on stage and off.

Then there's the talented Alaina Huffman (Abaddon/Josie Sands), who's become a friend and someone I always look forward to seeing on the circuit. Matt Cohen (young John Winchester) is a gem, and an awesome dad and husband. His enthusiasm and energy are the reason he cohosts the most with Rich on the road and at conventions overseas.

There are a few people I've never really had the chance to get to know, but I'm a true fan of their work. Mark Pellegrino (Lucifer) is such a talented actor, and I've been a fan of his work since I can remember. Then there are a few who I've met outside of conventions. Samantha Smith (Mary Winchester) is another wonderful actor I hadn't seen in years, and I only recently got to see her smiling face at a convention again.

And who can forget the wonderful Felicia Day (Charlie Bradbury)? We met over ten years ago when she came on the series *Dollhouse* to work with us for a few episodes. I've been a huge fan of her work ever since. She's incredibly bright, funny, and driven. And of course I have to mention Curtis Armstrong (Metatron). I've been a fan of this man's work since I was a kid. I was delighted when I found out that I'd be working with him—and even more so once I got to know him better. He talks fondly of being a father and passionately about theater and film. He is a seasoned veteran and a generous performer who makes acting with him a breeze.

I could write chapters on all of the incredible people I've met on the *Supernatural* circuit, but I will save that for another book. I'd be remiss without mentioning the incredible fans I've met, and the staff and promoters I've had the pleasure of working for. Chris Schmelke is a sweetheart of a photographer for Creation Conventions, and he knows all the regular guests and greets them by name. Speaking of Creation Conventions, I have to mention the founders, the bosses of the show and arguably the creators of the modern convention: Gary Berman and Adam Malin. I've had the pleasure of working with a few of their excellent staff, including Stephanie Dizon, boss lady and a talented performer herself, Jen Gregory, Jen Gannon, Victoria, and Mary—all fantastic at their jobs and great to work with.

The conventions often are a perfect blend of music and fun, coupled with all the other standard convention practices of signing autographs, taking pictures, and hosting Q&As. But this fandom doesn't seem to tire of seeing the same guests and hearing many of the same stories. I think it's clear that they've all found a community, where regardless of age, race, sexual orientation, or religion, everyone is accepted and safe. When I'm at a convention, I see little fear or intolerance. Instead, I see community, acceptance, and a shared love for a show about a couple of evil-fighting brothers and their loyal angel. People spend their hard-earned money to travel for another weekend, to another SPN con, to experience largely the same thing again and again. And it's plainly clear that the thing is so damn good, that even if it's the only real vacation that these fans will get all year, they're good with that. These fans have found a tribe with people from all over the world. They've bonded over their love of *Supernatural*, and over the course of countless conventions, meals, evenings of dancing, laughter, and fun, have formed lasting friendships.

I have been doing the convention circuit for close to twenty years, and I've had countless conversations with numerous fans. Many have communicated to me that they were not extremely social growing up. Many were shy and had, or still have, social anxiety issues. But what they've found is that they feel safe and accepted at the conventions. Here is a space where other people do not judge them at all for those issues, but embrace and care for them.

There are many misconceptions about the fans, one being that they're all shy and reserved. That's true at times, but I've seen these people, especially at the SPN conventions, dance and party like it's 1999. You'd be hard-pressed to find a more outgoing and expressive group when they're on the dance floor or on stage at karaoke singing with the guests.

Alas, it is now official that the fifteenth year will be the last season. Fifteen seasons . . . such a rarity in the world of episodic television.

Supernatural will forever hold a place among only a handful of shows. I've heard fans for a number of years now dread the inevitable end of the show and what that'll mean for them and the conventions. But from what I've seen from this fandom, after all the years I've been in the business, specifically the genre business, I'd be surprised if the conventions ever stop. Maybe they won't happen with the same regularity, but with fifteen seasons and hundreds of episodes to discuss and dissect, there's little chance the *Supernatural* fandom will cease to exist in my lifetime.

Finally, for those who've seen me talk on stage, you've heard me speak at length about meditation and how it has helped me. I've always been a proponent of meditation, and I've tried to encourage people to take up the practice. I don't think I would have had the forum to speak to so many people in many different cities about meditation if it weren't for the SPN conventions. Wanting to share my passion for meditation and its healing abilities with as many people as I could, I jumped at the opportunity when my hypnotherapist, the wonderful Joanne Harris, suggested we start a meditation app. Now, we encountered many problems in our venture, but I'm incredibly touched whenever Joanne shares with me another message from someone who used our meditation site and communicated how it has helped them.

I'll always be proud of the time that when asked at a convention whether I thought meditation could help young children, I carefully answered that I thought it could. I did also remind everyone that I'm not a therapist or a psychologist, but I feel that meditation can help most anyone of every age. A year later, the person who asked that question was in one of the roundtable VIP sessions. (For those who don't know, these consist of a small table of fans, usually ten or so, who sit with a rotating cast of actors for forty-five minutes of conversation.) She asked me if I remembered her asking the question. I said I did, and then she told me she was a teacher and that she started regular meditation with her seven-year-old students, with amazing results. She shared that they all became enthusiastic about it after it became a regular practice, and even more importantly, she noticed the children becoming calmer, less prone to emotional outbursts, and, most importantly, able to resolve and deal with their conflicts better. It still makes me smile thinking about this, to know that I played a small part in it. I do hope we get to a day where meditation is taught to all children.

I'm honored to have been asked to share some of my experiences in this book for the fans. I hope I've communicated how important being a part of this show has been for me not only professionally, but also personally. I feel incredibly blessed to have been a part of this community, and I look forward to continued connections with the fans in the future on the convention circuit and through social media. Be well, my friends!

"When they say my name, perhaps I will be remembered, not as the one who let the serpent in, but as one of the few who helped give heaven a second chance."

SUPERNATURAL FAITH

JOELLE MONIQUE

When I was thirteen, I divorced God. Like every other thirteen-year-old, I dealt with a lot of new, disappointing, and difficult truths as I began the process of leaving childhood behind. My vast collection of Barbies found their way to a plastic bin in the garage. My pink room, covered in bows, transformed into a starry night. Turning the dial from Nickelodeon adventure shows to steamy, fashionable teen dramas on the WB proved a huge turning point for me. While I had barely tasted the sweetness of first love, I began to entertain the bitterness of a divorce. For those of you who've legally separated from a flesh-and-blood mortal, imagine less paperwork. Instead of leaving a dedicated partner, I left the Holy Father, the architect of my existence, the man I should trust above all creatures. I did it with the help of *Supernatural.*

My relationship with God began early. I was baptized Roman Catholic a few months into my existence. Gifted two godparents (neither of which ever felt the need to instruct me in the ways of the Lord), I was well on my way to the Kingdom of Heaven. On special occasions, funerals and weddings mostly, my family would travel to the city and visit the Southern Baptist church that my maternal great-grandfather built with his own hands. It was there I felt closest to God. In prayer, I'd ask him to connect me with my ancestors, like I was on a three-way call. The grandfather I never met, my recently parted Ma Dear, and my sweet Auntie Judy would come to me and give me advice. Under the roof my blood built, I felt invincible. I also felt like an outsider. We lived hundreds of miles from my family. In school, I was the only Black girl. The way my cousins spoke, their inside jokes, their entire demeanor, felt so far from who I was.

I also felt torn. I'd been a voracious reader since I was four, and the arguments made by Sunday school teachers for contradictory bible verses stopped holding water. Being verbally reprimanded for questioning the Lord spat in the face of my secular education. On top of this, my mother's church and my father's different church preached that only their distinct doctrine allowed admittance to heaven. Passing the crucifix in the main entrance of my home, I'd often pause to consider which theology was correct, and why God believed one of my parents didn't belong in his heavenly kingdom.

Torn, I sought a new religion. One that would incorporate the ideals of both houses of thought, without sending one of my folks to hell. My best friend invited me to her church, an Evangelical congregation, next to our school. In this church, I learned that nobody could come before the Lord. Not family, nor country, nor self-preservation came before devotion to God. Jesus dying for our sins wasn't something mumbled in prayer like in my old Roman Catholic church or honored in uplifting gospel music like the Baptist church I would later attend. It was exalted and repeated over and over again until the guilt became a tangible thing our young minds wore like armor. Soldiers in Christ became a sort of rallying cry.

For a time, it was a truly beautiful experience. Every Sunday and Wednesday, I knew where I needed to be. The church gave me responsibilities no one else would trust my thirteen-year-old self with. I could watch the children in the nursery. I helped plan a rafting expedition. My friends congregated here, adults respected me, and it quickly became a second home for nearly two years. Then I started asking questions.

As I searched for a God who could accept me, I inevitably began looking for ways I could accept myself. I knew I'd liked boys and girls since I met a girl named Carmen in first grade. But between the ages of thirteen and fourteen I began to understand what that would mean for me. Leaving the Evangelical church became my only option. Their "hate the sin, but love the sinner" rhetoric couldn't solve my desire to live my life as a gay woman. The choice was to stay closeted and be loved, or leave this second family and risk not finding a replacement.

It didn't all happen at once. I had a mental scoreboard. *Harry Potter* getting banned at the church was not in God's favor. I had loved all things supernatural ever since I discovered a book about how to entomb mummies at Borders when I was eight. Ravenous for more, the television show *Supernatural* seemed a logical next step: the hot men, the daddy issues, the struggles between heaven and hell that perfectly mirrored my troubles. Season 5 really had it all. Paris Hilton even made a guest appearance where she played herself as a laughable celebrity idiot. In fact, *Supernatural* spent a lot of time making light of its own seriousness. Sam and Dean attend a *Supernatural*-themed convention where most of the attendees are men obsessed with the homoeroticism of the series. The episode even featured a gay couple who found happiness together through the episode. The show could make me laugh at the dark things, and that's where the obsession began.

In its fifteen-year run, *Supernatural* escorted multiple fans across the horror of puberty, through trauma, over graduation, and straight into adulthood. In other words, *Supernatural* took its fans through hell and back. Sometimes, this journey happened literally—like during the season 4 finale, when Lucifer's Cage made its first appearance. Created by God to contain his most beloved son, the nearly impenetrable cage design kept the fallen angel locked away in hell for centuries. A dramatic teen, I felt I could identify.

Seasons 4 and 5 moved the show away from the typical demons and began sharing the spotlight with angels. This era, overseen by the incredible Sera Gamble, used pop culture and passion for the occult to continue connecting with the CW's growing teen audience. During these seasons, Sam and Dean Winchester accidentally jump-start the apocalypse by slaying the first demon and unlocking Lucifer's Cage.

Typically, American folklore doesn't feature the big man upstairs. Our most famous folktales come in the form of creatures. The Jersey Devil, the Beast of Busco, and Bigfoot represent unknown wilds of the untamed American landscape. These creatures also represent a form of mass hysteria. Cryptid beings share similar characteristics with the Christian beasts of burden. The good folks of New Jersey saw a hoofed bird with small wings, similar to the descriptions of a cloven-footed fallen angel who was stripped of his wings. These stories imply God exists, but never explicitly state his role in bringing such horrors to an end. But subtlety cannot be found in the *Supernatural* dictionary. For a show that takes place in a "Christian nation," as I'd heard from the pulpit many times, struggling with its relationship to the Almighty, *Supernatural* tackled the largest questions facing the country.

My most terrifying moment as an Evangelist came after a weeklong retreat when I was fourteen. Meditation, prayer, and intense physical activity took up all my waking hours. Over seven days, I learned to be a "warrior for Christ." Getting dirty, sharing your most intimate fears, and expressing your highest hopes bonds souls fast. I felt on fire when I came back. I had received the tools to be useful in the world. Like Dean Winchester, I believed God had chosen me for something important. I, too, would stamp out the devil and the evils he released on the world.

But, when I got back home, everything looked evil. Every television program contained filth. Jokes didn't feel funny anymore; they were an affront to God. I felt alone in a hostile world without God's army at my back. Simultaneously, I had to question why I didn't feel at home with my parents and my brother anymore. The cold realization was that I had put God before everyone else. But God looked more like a church; more human, and more fallible than ever before. I felt duped. Anyone who isolates you from your friends and family can't be good for you. That was the final straw. I left God and that life over the next three years. Briefly, I attended another church with new friends, but the feeling of warmth and connectedness to a higher power never returned. I had seen the control a religious body could have over an individual. I never wanted to be under a congregation's influence again.

Supernatural has never been afraid to question the idea of God. God doesn't take a back seat in *Supernatural*. He's a central figure playing his hand as he sees fit. When Sam accidentally frees Lucifer from his cage, God plucks Dean and Sam from the blast zone of Lucifer's angel essence, and places them on an airplane that's flying overhead at the same time.

Here, God is benevolent. But, looking at the situation that landed them in this mess in the first place, it's hard not to wonder why an all-powerful, all-knowing being wouldn't stop the initiation of the apocalypse. Furthermore, why would he choose a favorite son, instead of loving his creations equally? How can he promise to love for all eternity, and then turn around and condemn thousands to eternal damnation?

Sera Gamble, along with show creator Eric Kripke, worked within the strict confines of a CW-style narrative, but choosing two male leads made the show unique among the lineup of teen romances and small-town family dramas featured on the network. *Supernatural* contained the right mix of romance, adventure, and hotties to form a perfect combination to appeal to young genre lovers like me. Even more important, the show's way of breaking down the difficulties of faith with *Gilligan's Island* references didn't make me feel like I was being preached at. Instead, it felt like entering an adult conversation on terms I could understand. My disillusionment no longer felt like a hallucination. Even demon hunters, with proof of God's existence, maintained valid reasons to be angry with him.

When Dean learns God may be dead, or has just abandoned the human race and left the world to his imperfect angels, I finally saw someone hold my struggles. "Destiny, God's plan—it's all a bunch of lies, you poor, stupid son of a bitch," Dean yells at Castiel. "It's just a way for your bosses to keep you and me in line." Like Dean, the God I had been taught to love suddenly didn't exist. I felt like the world looked brand-new. Every possibility suddenly felt like probability. I could do anything, except go back. Deciding to move away from a relationship that had always felt one-sided took a matter of forty-eight hours. I didn't want to be a believer, or a warrior, or faithful. I wanted the truth.

Postapocalypse, Sam realizes he's addicted to demon blood. He took it because he thought he would be responsible for killing Lucifer when the time came. The blood made him incredibly strong. It also took a heavy toll on him and his relationship with his brother. "I don't trust me," he confided in Dean. Sam had been lying to himself for so long that confronting the truth caused him to leave hunting behind entirely. Similarly, divorcing God isolates the soul from eternal comfort. Without the All-Knowing to guide me, without an endless promise of happiness, life becomes very immediate, and it made me very angry. I thought a lot about Lucifer's Cage during that time. In there, 126 years pass in a single revolution around the sun. Residing in the deepest parts of hell, isolated from any semblance of humanity, Lucifer, and eventually Sam, were punished so severely that they would never be able to think of God the same way again.

Lucifer said God punished him because he "loved God too much." I could identify with the desire to distinguish between loving your creator and hating their creation. To Lucifer's thinking, humans stole God's light from him. Perhaps the same thing happened to me. Confession became absolution without works, leaving thousands of victims to deal with their trauma in silence. Under shouts of praise and booming gospel music were wounded tears, and almost everyone knew about it. The feigning of shock cut the deepest. Denial in the light of day made fools of entire organizations. Though the Catholic Church may be most famous for these transgressions, these sins live inside the walls of every Christian institution I've taken part in.

There's nothing not to love about God. In every religion I encountered, God presents as the personification of goodness. Leaving an entity like that behind made *me* the asshole. Some said the devil had a hold on me. Shaking that guilt took work. Watching Dad pray made me miss my relationship with the Almighty. The sense of peace God brings to troubled souls, how he listens better than any human being, the way loving him made me feel like part of a community—without him, I was truly alone for the first time.

When I finally stopped hearing his voice in my head, the silence was terrifying, but going back to a lie seemed much worse. Luckily, I too possessed a brother, Justin, who would sit with me while I figured out this new life. Whenever I felt lost, I could also turn to Sam and Dean for guidance. The best part about *Supernatural* is that no matter how dark things get, the brothers always return to one another and save their corner of the universe.

Leaving God was like moving to a big city where no one knows who you are or what you've done. Suddenly, any version of you becomes probable. Danger vibrates under the skin. I think of Dean getting lost in the fight against the angels. Tunnel vision locks him into a single mission.

My mission, five years later, with me now in my twenties and living on my own, was to try everything the church scared me away from. In full rebellion, I tried every drug, read filthy books, made friends with wildly different opinions, and explored the world. (Well, I visited two countries and avoided tourist traps, but I felt like I was making decisions about how I felt for the first time.) I moved to the gayborhood, and lived my life as an out gay woman.

Those who pray intently often describe a warm feeling when the presence of the Lord enters the room. God isn't abstract when you believe. When the institutions around him made him toxic for me and my truth, it was nevertheless a painful loss giving that feeling up. Finding a new way to believe and to walk around the world hurt. Having Sam and *Supernatural* made it easier. Having lost the love of his life, Sam shows us that grief is a process, not a moment. Over and over, he had to forgive himself for his role in Jessica's death. In watching him, I was able to forgive myself for ending my relationship with God. Now, I can wish him, and his followers, nothing but the best.

GENDER, ACTIVISM, AND SPN'S LEGACY

TANYA COOK AND KAELA JOSEPH

"When I entered the con, I felt like, 'This is my
space, these are my people; I felt safe.'"
—Interviewee on attending her first *Supernatural* Con

"I don't have a lot of money, but I have time,
and I want to use that to help others."
—Interviewee who raffles off hand-knitted work for Random Acts

I f you had told us five years ago that we, two academics, would regularly travel across the country to attend fan conventions and engage in very weird scavenger hunt behavior for charity, well, we both would have chuckled. If you had told us we'd be in year four of a multiyear research project that explores fandom-based activism, after building an academic partnership across state lines (over a tweet by Misha Collins), we would have stared at you with open disbelief. But life often takes us down paths we least expect, right when we most need to diverge from "the road so far."

From staffing mental health crisis hotlines to participating in disaster relief efforts, *Supernatural* fans have made Dean Winchester's rallying cry of "saving people" a reality. Despite critiques that the show disproportionately kills off women characters and repeatedly fails the Bechdel test (whether a work features at least two women who talk to each other about something other than a man), the fan base and its charitable efforts are largely made up of fans who identify as women. This is not a coincidence, as factors unique to *Supernatural* have created an empowering environment for women, even though women have not consistently been represented in an equitable way on-screen.

The longevity of the show and fan engagement via social media have enabled a public sphere where fans can actually lobby for more inclusive representation with respect to gender identity, racial-ethnic diversity, ability status, and LGBTQ identity. The *Supernatural* fandom has created spaces where participation in fannish activity is encouraged rather than stigmatized, in which fannish identity includes expectations of doing charitable work, feminist leadership is possible, and women feel safe and valued for their own sake. From charitable fundraising at conventions to the Wayward Daughters movement, social engagement in *Supernatural* fan spaces mirrors social movement–style activism and is arguably the most impactful and important legacy of the show. This essay explores the social activism of *Supernatural* fans with respect to expressing desire for more women-focused, intersectional representation on the show and to charitable initiatives grounded in the fandom that have led to the creation of nonprofit organizations.

KAELA'S STORY

I discovered the *Supernatural* fandom at a very precarious time in my life. I was in the later years of a graduate program in clinical psychology, applying for internships in a market where there were not enough accredited positions to go around. I stumbled upon reruns of the show one morning before a meeting with my academic advisor and was immediately hooked. Watching the show became my much-needed relaxation ritual, and conventions eventually became my grounding space over many years of professional rejection before my career took off.

Throughout my life, I've had a tendency to dive passionately into areas of interest, including sci-fi and horror franchises, but until I started watching *Supernatural*, I had never really made the leap to attending fan culture conventions—likely because I didn't know anyone else who did. Attending *Supernatural* fan conventions in my late twenties and early thirties, however, changed my life. Convention spaces became somewhere I could challenge negative beliefs about my professional setbacks (and myself in general) by communing with other women in shameless obsession over a shared love.

As a psychologist who specializes in working with gender and sexual minority (GSM) communities, I am trained to help others heal from shame by teaching them to develop a different relationship with painful self-talk, often by encouraging them to engage in communities of likeminded folks. As a researcher, I couldn't help but wonder what it was about *Supernatural* and other fan culture spaces that fostered the particular type of community that I was experiencing firsthand—a community that felt much like a family, that (mostly) unconditionally had my back, and that was incredibly active in mental health charity and activism. Then, I found Tanya, whose presentation on the *Supernatural* fandom at an academic meeting had been noticed and tweeted by Misha Collins.

TANYA'S STORY

My entry into the *Supernatural* fandom started like many others; a friend who had similar taste in pop culture recommended the show and I thought, *Okay, I'll give it a try.* I admit, I was not an instant convert. I've never been much of a horror fan, but as a lover of most things sci-fi and urban fantasy, I knew I had to give it a try. I was not instantly hooked, but by the season 1 episode "Faith," I realized I was all in. I watched nine seasons of *Supernatural* in two months despite having a full-time job and a full-time family. (We may have eaten a lot of frozen pizzas that spring, sorry fam.)

A year and a half later, I attended my first *Supernatural* convention, started cosplaying as Jody Mills, and was on the cusp of undertaking the biggest academic research project of my career.

Despite being a lifelong geek, I grew up in the 1980s in rural Wisconsin and didn't have much exposure to fan culture or conventions. But all that changed when I fell into the *Supernatural* fandom. When I started watching, I was fortunate enough to live in Denver, a large enough city to host frequent comic conventions and geek meetups, and more importantly, the INTERNET existed. In 2014, on a whim, I signed up for GISHWHES, Misha Collins's charity scavenger hunt. That experience exposed me to a side of fandom I quickly became obsessed with: the participatory, charitable, social-good-focused activities I saw fans engaged in. As a sociologist, I'm trained to notice patterns. I soon realized that while *Supernatural* was not the only fandom doing good, there were interesting and unique things happening that led me to consider how fandom-based charity work parallels what some scholars call "consensus" social movements. As Kaela mentioned, we found each other online after Misha retweeted an abstract of a talk I presented and used it to troll costar Jared Padalecki about starting a cult. So, I guess, like a lot of people who end up doing unexpected things because of this fandom, you could say this is all Misha's fault.

HARNESSING THE POWER OF FANDOM FOR SOCIAL GOOD

This turn toward social movement–style activism that we both discovered is a crucial and important piece of *Supernatural*'s legacy. Typically, we think of social movements as large, sustained efforts involving multiple organizations and stakeholders that advocate for political or social change. Classic examples include the civil rights movement, the feminist movement, and the LGBTQ rights movement. More recent examples like Black Lives Matter and the Youth Climate Strike focus their efforts on changing political structures, corporate practices, and cultures as a whole. When we talk about our work, we often receive the critical comment that fan action is not political, just charity work, or what is called a consensus movement—a type of action no reasonable person would disagree with.

All of these critiques attempt to draw boundaries that construct some as "real" activists and others as merely "online" activists, implying that online activism is lacking in value as an agent of change by its own right.[2] Evidence suggests, however, that online activism does, in fact, translate to in-person action, and can create a sense of visibility and community.[3] Historically, these critiques tend to line up with gendered devaluing of the action of women-identified people. In other words, the kinds of action and activism that women do disproportionately are socially constructed as less valuable and not true (radical) activism. The irony here is that online spaces may be particularly appealing to women and other marginalized groups precisely due to this devaluation, as online spaces are increasingly more accessible and can allow for women to recontextualize what it means to be an activist.[4] When women and other marginalized groups are excluded from public participation in politics, they join together where they do have power.

Although much of the action and efforts in the *Supernatural* fandom are focused on charity work and relief efforts, fans have shown that kindness can be revolutionary. While no one may disagree that feeding hungry children or working to prevent suicide is important, the idea of creating

2. For more in-depth analysis of how the construction of online versus "real"/in-person activism falls along gendered lines, see E. Craddock's analysis of anti-austerity activism in the UK in *Social Movement Studies*, volume 18, no. 2, 137–153.

3. For more information on the impact of online activism, see S. Harlow and D. Harp's 2012 article in *Collective Action on the Web*, volume 15, no. 2, 196–216.

4. See J. M. Keller's 2012 article in *Information, Communication & Society*, volume 15, 429–447.

an organized group of people with sustained resources and a space to dialogue about values and priorities is qualitatively different. Through their efforts to create sustained awareness about social problems, including poverty, hunger, the effects of war and genocide, and mental health issues, fans are creating a culture of engagement. This culture of engagement, *in and of itself*, can bring power to social movements, particularly the empowerment of women activists, in a landscape where women's power is otherwise restricted or challenged.

As previously discussed, when women and other marginalized groups are excluded from public participation in politics, they join together where they do have power. Prior to the internet, those spaces have been things like gender-specific volunteer groups, sewing and crafting circles, and churches. Modern fandom contains a similar potential activist space, and this is why so many charitable initiatives are morphing into social movement–style activism. Fans who may not feel connected to or empowered by "proper channels" of civic engagement tap into opportunities through their networked position in fandom. Some fans are increasingly self-defining their fan identity as one that carries participatory, behavioral expectations. In other words, thinking of myself as a *Supernatural* fan may lead me to be more inclined to try to do things that "save people." But before we focus on SPN fans' charitable action, let's take another brief moment to consider how women's participation in fandom has traditionally been understood.

WOMEN'S PARTICIPATION IN FANDOM

Until recently, science fiction, fantasy, and pop culture fans who identify as women have either been overlooked as vital contributors to fan culture or harshly judged for what the media and broader society defined as overzealous behavior.[5] Coverage of Beatlemania in the 1960s was permeated with language pathologizing women fans that is sexist at best and misogynistic

---

5. This is discussed in depth in Lynn Zubernis and Katherine Larsen's 2012 book *Fandom at the Crossroads*.

at worst, from a modern perspective.[6] Interestingly, fans of sports who identify as men and are just as zealous largely escaped the media's armchair psychoanalysis in this time period. Despite the stereotype that sci-fi fans are mostly men, it was famously women who organized one of the first and most oft-cited instances of fan activism, the letter-writing campaign to NBC that saved *Star Trek: The Original Series* from cancellation.[7] And it was also women who organized and started the first *Star Trek* conventions. Prior to the internet and social media fan sites, many women organized distribution lists of fan works and fan creative content via snail mail and later email.

Given this history of women's involvement in sci-fi fandom and fan activism, perhaps it is not that surprising that *Supernatural* would attract a large, passionate following of disproportionately women-identified fans. Many might claim that women watch the show largely to ogle the handsome male leads, but we argue that the show's main themes speak disproportionately to those who have experienced marginalization, such as those socialized as women and those who identify as LGBTQ. To paraphrase our friend Riley Santangelo of Wayward Daughters, fandom is a place that those who have experienced outsider status can come together and feel included. After all, who are bigger outsiders than Sam, Dean, and Castiel? Team Free Will chose lives of constant struggle and marginalization in order to serve humanity. The idea of giving up one's individual priorities in service to family and community is something many women can identify with. Bobby Singer's famous dictum "family don't end with blood" spoke to all of us who have found support and solidarity in created kinship and families of choice.

In addition to identifying with themes of the show, *Supernatural* fans found meaning and created relationships through in-person interactions with one another and the stars of the show at *Supernatural* conventions. *Supernatural*'s historic fifteen-season run and availability on Netflix fostered multiple generations of fans. Current fans of the show may have

---

6. See Henry Jenkins's 2013 book *Textual Poachers*, which is a seminal work on fandom culture.

7. For more information on this letter-writing campaign, see Casey Cipriani's September 20, 2016, article in *Bustle*'s online archive.

even been born after the series premiere! An uptick in fan engagement online via social media sites and the technological diffusion of smartphones from 2007 to the present also coincided with the show's run. Add to this Misha Collins's subversive and strategic use of Twitter, and you have the spark that lit the powder keg of collective, kinetic, emotional energy that has fueled fans' charitable work and civic engagement. Conventions, fan engagement online, and celebrity participation have created a fandom mobilized for social activism.

OUT OF THE FRIDGE

Despite the gap between the intended audience for *Supernatural*—the eighteen- to thirty-five-year-old male—and the actual audience of *Supernatural*, disproportionately women of all ages, the show suffered from a dearth of women characters. One of the consistent critiques of the show has been its "fridging" of women characters, a term for character deaths that are premature to a woman's character arc and serve only to further the story line of male protagonists. In season 1, both Mary Winchester and Sam's girlfriend, Jessica, are introduced with little to no character development before being killed by the Yellow-Eyed Demon to set the boys on their quests of "saving people" and "hunting things." Thus, the main women characters in the show served as little more than motivation for the boys' multiyear hunting road trip. Other early attempts to incorporate more women characters, such as Ellen and Jo in season 2, were divisive in the fandom, with fans either loving or hating them. By the time fan favorites Charlie Bradbury (played by Felicia Day) and Jody Mills (played by Kim Rhodes) were introduced, however, the fandom itself had changed in important ways.

One important variable that could help explain the different reaction to Jody and Charlie versus Ellen and Jo is the rise of social media and the ability for fans to speak directly to TPTB. When *Supernatural* first started, Facebook was in its infancy and Twitter did not exist. Misha Collins joined Twitter in 2009 and Kim Rhodes joined in 2011. By the time more well-developed characters like Charlie and Jody debuted on the show, fans could dialogue directly with their new favorites. Dialogues that started at conventions between fans and content creators/producers continued online, cementing relationship ties and ultimately leading to a large, diffuse social network. This network became a self-sustaining community among fans, eventually called the "SPNFamily."

THE POWER OF SOCIAL NETWORKS

Sociologist Mark Granovetter wrote about the power of social networks in fostering collective action and organization in 1973, long before the social media interconnectedness that is common today. Intriguingly, he claimed it was not the direct relationships between friends who knew each other well that contained the most potential, but the relationships possible by third- and fourth-order connections, a phenomenon he called "the strength of weak ties." Basically, you could call this the "I know a person who knows a person" phenomenon. Fandom-based connections provide a networked hub of individuals who can be mobilized quickly when pointed toward a common goal. Thus, when Misha Collins asked fans via Twitter to donate to UNICEF, fans raised over $30,000. This eventually led to the creation of a nonprofit organization, Random Acts, which has raised millions for various charitable initiatives to date, and is the main beneficiary of the GISH scavenger hunt.

If you think about the ways GISHers rely on their team and broader network connections to accomplish multiple seemingly impossible feats in less than a week, you can easily see Granovetter's point. In 2016, GISHers raised $215,000 to help four Syrian refugee families find more stable, permanent housing. The following years, the "Change a Life Item" called on GISHers to harness their social networks to fundraise for a dance school in South Africa, to purchase farming land in support of survivors of Rwandan genocide, and to remove unexploded ordnances (land mines) from the Vietnam War in Laos. From local food and feminine hygiene product supply drives at conventions and a grant for school-based projects to ongoing funding for the Jacmel Children's Center in Haiti and the Free School for women and girls in Nicaragua, fans are making a lasting impact in improving the lives of others and future generations through direct action and donations.

Supernatural fandom was also innovative in developing the main fundraising method for many of these charitable initiatives. Online retailer "Stands," created in 2015, partners with actors from *Supernatural* and other shows to design and sell everything from exclusive t-shirts to teddy bears. In collaboration with Wayward Daughters and subsequent Wayward merchandising campaigns, Kim Rhodes and Briana Buckmaster raised money for a nonprofit called New Leash On Life, which matches shelter dogs with incarcerated people who then train the dogs to be service animals. When many fans expressed desire for merchandise from these campaigns but did not have the means to purchase the items, Wayward Daughters and Stands initiated a donor matching campaign to help.

In addition to charitable action through Random Acts, fans have organized their own responses to urgent issues. After Hurricane Harvey in 2017, hundreds of fans joined Crowd Rescue HQ efforts. Working with the Cajun navy and first responders, a group of *Supernatural* fans called "SPN Rescue" monitored SOS posts online and helped connect people trapped by the floodwaters with rescue services. Estimates of the number of people and animals rescued through these efforts vary, but rescue totals are estimated at 29,000 people and over 600 animals. Fandom-based volunteers we spoke with approximated that they directly helped with the rescue or evacuation of 700 to 1,000 individuals. One individual we interviewed stated that 30 to 40 percent of the online volunteers were *Supernatural* fans. SPN Rescue volunteers we spoke with described ten- and twelve-hour shifts of monitoring or "scrubbing" social media for hashtags including #SOSHarvey and #SOSHouston. Many volunteers experienced personal trauma because of their efforts. One volunteer related the following: "The most difficult call I had was talking to someone while her roommate was drowning." The "strength of weak" fandom ties were used in this disaster response as well. One fan mentioned relying on the international members of the fan base and coordination via Slack chat rooms. As she put it, "I'd be logging off and [Name] (in Sweden) or [Name] (in the UK) would be ready to take over."

One of the more unique volunteer efforts by *Supernatural* fans has been the SPNFamily Crisis Support Network, a social network in the form of *Supernatural* fans trained as mental health crisis hotline responders to assist other fans in times of need. The model for this crisis line is one of peer support, not unlike peer-led crisis hotlines that exist for LGBTQ communities, such as the Trevor Project and Trans Lifeline. While the crisis support network was launched initially by actors Misha Collins and Jensen Ackles in 2016, it was largely born out of fans sharing their personal struggles with mental health in convention spaces—fans who are more likely to have been women.

THE FAMILY WE CHOOSE

So, why is peer support important? It comes down to family—in this case, chosen family. The concept of chosen family, otherwise known academically as "fictive kin," is the family that "don't end in blood," kinships outside bloodlines or marriage, the social networks we create for ourselves. The word *family* is quite literally in the name of the SPNFamily Crisis Support Network, and is a term often used throughout the fandom to describe the ties that bind us. We are, to one another, fictive kin. This becomes important for those experiencing mental health crises, particularly those from marginalized backgrounds. In research on LGBTQ populations, for example, support by family and others has been shown to mediate suicide risk, while family rejection and victimization have been shown to increase risk.[8,9] Chosen family can act as the protective factor one needs to get through periods of crisis.

We see this with other types of peer support, such as military veteran peer support programs like Vets4Vets, where research has demonstrated that increased perception of peer support decreases mental health

8. See C. Ryan et al.'s article in *Pediatrics*, volume 123, no. 1, 346–352, for more information on how family support can impact health outcomes in lesbian, gay, and bisexual young adults.
9. For more information on rates of suicide and the impact of family support on mental health, see the 2016 report by S. E. James et al. on the 2015 US Transgender Survey.

symptoms. While we don't know the full impact of the SPNFamily Crisis Support Network at this point in time, we know, at least anecdotally, that it is having the intended effect.

While the crisis support network may have gained the most press, it's not the only mental health nonprofit that has been born out of the fandom. SPN Survivors, founded by David and Karla Truxall, is another organization that promotes mental health and suicide prevention through fundraising, education, and awareness campaigns, including information on valuable resources for survivors of suicide. Members of the SPN fandom Kurt and Tricia Baker founded Attitudes in Reverse (AIR) in 2011. AIR seeks to educate young people (and the public in general) about mental health issues, reduce stigma around mental illness, and prevent suicide, co-hosting a suicide prevention conference and presenting workshops in area high schools. All three of these organizations are founded on the idea of making the invisible (struggles with mental health) visible, so that stigma can be reduced and support strengthened. When we are seen and heard by others, we can be understood, and when we are understood, we have a chance at a life worth living.

REPRESENTATION

Representation in popular media also matters, as it is a shared source of information that constructs the lenses through which we judge the world around us. Representations of women as more likely to be mentally ill and less likely to be the experts treating mental illness, despite the fact that women are more likely than men to work in mental health fields, creates harmful stereotypes about both mental health and women's work.[10] Representation also matters for how women are viewed more globally. One study by Jeremiah Garretson published in the *Journal of Politics Groups and Identities* in 2015 found that the quality and quantity of minority

---

10. For an in-depth look at this and other aspects of media and mental health, see K. Srivastava et al.'s 2018 article in *Industrial Psychiatry Journal*, volume 27, no. 1, 1–5.
For more information on the proportions of men and women in the field of psychology, see R. A. Clay's 2017 article in *Monitor on Psychology*, volume 48, no. 7.

women portrayed in television influenced attitudes of social tolerance.[11] For those who hold marginalized and minority identities, media representation can also become a source of pride and self-realization.

As previously mentioned, *Supernatural* has not been without criticism for its portrayal of women, but its largely female-identified fan base has not been silent about this. In fact, one of the most widely known social action campaigns in the fandom has been Wayward Daughters, started by fans Riley Santangelo and Betty Days. Wayward Daughters started as a conversation about women characters on the show, and how to advocate for better story lines for women and other marginalized groups. Wayward Daughters would later partner with Random Acts, as well as actors Kim Rhodes and Briana Buckmaster (who plays Sheriff Donna Hanscum), in an effort to raise funds to build the previously mentioned school for women and girls in Nicaragua. Attend a *Supernatural* convention and you will likely see many fans wearing shirts from this and other campaigns by Wayward Daughters, and you may also hear whispers of a spinoff that almost was.

In season 13, *Supernatural* aired a backdoor pilot for *Wayward Sisters*, a spinoff that would have followed women characters from the *Supernatural* universe, embodying the kind of representation that Wayward Daughters had been campaigning for. While the CW ultimately chose not to pick up the pilot, the fact that the pilot aired demonstrated how the show's fandom had evolved over fifteen years. Diverse women who wanted to see themselves represented on-screen spoke, and the showrunners listened.

Even though we didn't get the Wayward series we wanted, after Wayward Daughters, there were far more women characters in recurring roles with stronger and more developed story arcs. The return of Mary Winchester in season 12, for example, led to some interesting reflexive storytelling that brought themes and conflicts from early in the show full circle. Mary's independence and refusal to give up hunting after her return led Dean to challenge his idealized remembrances and long-buried conflicting feelings about her death. Mary in season 12 loves her sons but is also able

11. J. J. Garretson's 2015 study can be found in *Politics, Groups, and Identities*, volume 3, no. 4, 615–632.

to have her own life and her independence, a dramatic change from being killed as a plot device.

LEGACY

Over fifteen years, *Supernatural* has shown it is far more than your average genre show about handsome dudes who fight monsters. The story of two brothers in an epic battle between good and evil, who continuously (re) negotiate their family bonds with one another and those deemed honorary "Winchesters," continues to resonate with fans and likely will for years to come. The longevity of the fandom, and fans' engagement with one another and the series' stars both online and in person at conventions, has fostered a crucible of emotional energy that has led to social movement–style activism. This dialogue with fans has also led to more well-developed women characters and stronger story arcs. The main legacy of *Supernatural*, however, may be its efficaciousness in motivating people to lift each other up and try to do more to benefit their communities and the world. When it comes to saving people and continuing to fight, the SPNFamily has shown there's always a way.

FAMILY TIES

DAVID HAYDN-JONES

*(in collaboration with and derived from
an interview with Lynn Zubernis)*

O ne of the most fascinating and compelling things about being an
actor on *Supernatural* has been discovering the SPNFamily and the
global community that has
evolved and grown around the
show. I said early on in my convention Q & A panels that meeting members of the SPNFamily
(whom I have now affectionately
nicknamed "The Cousins") was
like entering a clearing in the
jungle and finding this amazing,
quirky, wonderful artistic tribe.
I continue to be amazed by the
intellectualism, the artistry, and
the enthusiasm, as well as the
support for creative works and
the role of storytelling in the

239

show. Every time I've been with a "cousin" face to face (the word "fan" purposefully avoided here), it has been an extremely warm, pleasant, and dare I say loving interaction. "Face to face" is emphasized since I believe these interactions to be the truest forms of human communion. They are the most rewarding for me. I truly enjoy making eye contact, reading body language, and listening to the nuances of intonation in the voice: a humanist's and actor's craft and trade. Online engagement via Twitter and Instagram has been more challenging. It can be a lot of work and has been a learning curve for me, albeit MOSTLY positive; however, small minorities and cabals seeking "Chuck-knows-what" have been greatly illustrative of the dark cultural trends we are navigating as a society.

I'm often asked if I'm a fan of the show. Here's where I get a little nerdy, semantic, and etymological. I have an aversion to the word *fan* due to it being the shortened derivation of *fanatic*. To me that insinuates the turning off of one's logical brain. I like to think of fans as fellow enthusiasts instead. I prefer the word *enthusiast* since *fanatic* has a religious or dogmatic connotation or, at the very least, the implication that one is accepting things at face value or without question. So when asked, I clarify that, yes, I am a big ENTHUSIAST of the show!

I have very eclectic tastes. I'm an enthusiast of many artists and art forms. For example, as a boy, I was a big *Star Wars* enthusiast, and then *Star Trek*. And no, don't ask me to choose! Both can exist in my brain and heart congruently. I guess you could say I have a reasonable amount of "Nerd cred." I say "Nerd" with a capital *N* proudly as those have always been my people. I certainly don't want to label the *Supernatural* viewers as "Nerds" (that is an individual's choice ;)). BUT I think my love and understanding of like-minded folks gives me good rapport with many in this community.

I was flattered, humbled, and nervous when I was first invited to do the *Supernatural* conventions. At the end of the day, the overriding emotion was pure excitement to go and have this profoundly unique experience that no one can quite prepare you for. Some of the other actors from the show (and others from *Battlestar Galactica* and *Stargate Atlantis*) talked to me about what to expect from con life. It was the King of Cons himself, Richard Speight, Jr. (who plays Gabriel), who gave me the best coaching and encouragement. He said, "Oh, you're a theater and comedy guy and a storyteller, you'll do just fine."

Still, I wasn't expecting the incredibly gracious and warm welcome I received. There was this moment when I truly understood the power of the show, the power of my role, and the power of television and media to affect people. My first ALL *Supernatural* convention was in San Francisco, and the audience all played kazoos at me after Louden Swain's "Medicated," which took my con premiere to a whole new level. What a wild welcome!

But the outpouring of attention and enthusiasm for my role on the show would soon be eclipsed by something far greater. The best thing to come from the SPNFamily and *Supernatural* for me was the opportunity to do some good works in the world. I want to give full credit to Misha Collins for paving the way as the innovator and leader of the community in our charitable efforts. What is so rewarding about this experience is that it's something I never would have chosen to do on my own. The Less Than Three campaign came out of the social interactions and conversations I had with people online who were following me, in a completely organic way. In fact, it came about as a misunderstanding because I was so new to social media that I didn't know that <3 was a heart. I thought, *Oh I get it, I'm being trolled. I'm being graded on the Jared and Jensen scale, who are obviously tens, so I'm less than three.* And I thought, *That's kind of harsh!* The other thing I thought (if I'm totally honest) is that it might mean they're farting at me, that maybe it's supposed to represent flatulence directed at my stupid face. Are they giving me the virtual raspberry because they don't like me? Am I not welcome here?

I expected blowback when I began playing a character like Ketch. When Ketch first came on the scene, there were some actual personal attacks directed at me on social media that I can only deduce were because of the whole character versus actor thing, the bleed if you will. It's also very possible people didn't like my acting or the way I looked. That comes with the territory of putting yourself and your work out there publicly. But I mean, these people certainly didn't know me in REAL life. That level of anonymous attack was shocking to me, though I hear it all the time with soap opera actors or others who play "villains." They get a lot of grief in their personal and online lives for the characters they play. That's a hard thing to wrap your head around, especially if you're a sensitive person, as actors often are. Like, *wait a minute, why do you hate me? I'm not that person, that's my job!* Often the biggest sweethearts are the ones who make the best villains because there's some vengeance in their own background that they want to play out . . . but I digress, that's a whole other psychological thing better serviced in therapy. ;)

So, back to the evolution of my charitable efforts. People following me on social media promptly corrected me on the <3 meaning. Case in point, a wonderful woman named Ingrid told me, "Well, that's funny because me and my partner say we 'less than three' each other." To which I replied, "That's wonderful, can we use that?" This led the community of my mates to start saying, "I less than three you," which was then abbreviated into LTTU. Eventually the community demanded, "Well, what are you going to do for YOUR charity?" I was like, "What do you mean, what am *I* gonna do? I don't have a charity." But they persisted, saying, "This fandom will get behind your charity, so what's your cause?" Well, in that moment I knew I had to try to do something deeply personal and authentic. My Nana, who had suffered for over a decade with Alzheimer's disease, and my hero Grandad, a WWII veteran and her selfless caregiver, would be the inspiration and posthumous honorees of my efforts.

Charity campaign and merchandise vendor Represent had also previously contacted me, suggesting that I do something with them, knowing that the *Supernatural* fandom was so engaged. So I created and designed the <3 = LOVE (LTTU) campaign for Alzheimer's organizations, particularly the Alzheimer's Foundation of America (AFA). I dusted off the architecture-trained design part of my brain, my passion for equal rights for all humans, and my spiritual mantra that "love is love and God and goodness are love," *et voila*! That's how the campaign came about: Through a conversation derived and inspired directly by the "FAM-DOM" (a term Matt Cohen, who played young John Winchester, so brilliantly coined). It was incredible, meaningful, and very humbling; a creative, giving-back journey that I would have never done if it were not for this community of people.

The personal relationships that I've made are the other important thing I'll take from *Supernatural*. There's real camaraderie among the cast and such kind leadership from the top (read: J2M). Everyone is great at their jobs, and there are lots of jokes, lots of joy, and of course lots of gratitude for being there at the conventions. Obviously, Adam Fergus (who plays Mick Davies) and I really cemented our friendship playing the duo we are—we've been told we're like the low-rent version of Rob and Rich on *Kings of Con*. I'll take it, haha! We have genuine chemistry. In fact, I think people can sense how much we really enjoy each other's company, so that's been wonderful. Even though we didn't have many scenes together on the show, people sometimes think that Ketch and Mick must have been friends. I think that's just the influence of our playful camaraderie on stage.

I've been asked if I think Ketch will leave a legacy behind, but right now, that's tough to say. That word *legacy* is a dodgy one for me and a concept for the audience to ultimately determine. I think it's like taste in art or wine—everyone's palate is going to be different. I think legacy is something that builds over time, over two years or five years or twenty years, so we'll eventually see what the audience is still saying (if anything) about this character. Personally, I like his journey (I'm biased of course). He went from an automaton-esque assassin to a more independent thinking, non-dogmatic individual. In *Supernatural* language, he learned how to become Team Free Will right before his dramatic demise. I love the poetry of Ketch giving his heart for the Winchesters. It's terrible and it's moving and I had so many people come up to me after Ketch's death to say that it was too soon and too sad. They wondered aloud how we, the collaborative creators, made them cry about arguably one of the most despised characters on the show.

Supernatural itself is unique in so many ways. The *Supernatural* set is a completely different place to work than most sets, and that culture always comes from the top. I know that Jared and Jensen have talked about how the wonderful producer Kim Manners sat them down in the early seasons when they were on the cusp. From what Jensen and Jared have said to me and to others publicly, the general gist and the paraphrased takeaway lesson for me was this: "We can do this ego-wise or we can do this family-wise. And if you do this family-wise, we may be able to have a nice long run. But if we start getting into the weeds and make this about ego, it's going to be a problem—so you guys decide." From my understanding, that's when the brotherhood truly cemented. J2 obviously had great chemistry already, as everyone knows, but I think that it's also true for the thirty- or forty-plus crew members and staff members who have been there since day one. The set of *Supernatural* is a family. People do not stay on television shows if they're not having a rewarding time. There are always going to be long days and hard nights and grumpiness and what have you, but at the end of the day, there's a lot of laughter and a lot of caring. I guess collegiality would be the best way to characterize the set— not a frat house, but a make-believe fun house. Welcome to the World of *Supernatural*. We're professional pretenders; welcome to the party.

Jared and Jensen immediately welcomed me as I've seen them welcome other guests so generously. And that kindness goes a long way when you're a guest going into someone else's home. To be welcomed with such open arms and with such enthusiasm makes a huge difference. I'll never forget that first day when I met Jared and Jensen. They were so generous. They wanted to know who I was as a person, where I was from. They instantly made me feel welcome.

In season 14, when I returned for that small cameo, Jared and I were at craft services late at night and he said, "It's so good to see you back here, man." We were geeking out with each other, going really academic and analyzing language and etymology and literature, doing a deep dive together. That night I asked him, "What's the secret? Why is everyone, to a person, so great on this show?" And he said, "I don't know, man. It comes from casting and the producers. We've been so lucky in fifteen seasons to have only a few problematic actors in terms of day players, and even that didn't really cause drama." That level of evenness and consistency is incredible for a television show.

I enjoyed working with Jensen so much as well. He and I got along wonderfully, and he's been so kind, collaborative, and generous to me. I loved to play around in our scenes together. There was a lot of laughter, but we also knew our roles in terms of that odd couple relationship that Dean and Ketch had.

My experience on the show has been so positive in terms of integration and collaboration. Obviously, that's the light that Jared and Jensen radiate and that they get shone back at them. It's quite extraordinary, because there are a lot of horror stories out there about toxic sets. To be fair, I should knock on wood because it's probably coming for me, because everyone has that one story, the horror show, the problems with egos. This show is not that; it's the absolute opposite. That's why a lot of actors say they're going to miss *Supernatural* so much. It's not just missing the character you play; it's also missing going to work in that environment. When you have a place like that to go act and those kinds of people to play with, that makes all the difference. In any field. I've often said that I'd rather have a shitty job where I LIKE THE PEOPLE than a great job where I can't abide the people. With *Supernatural*, you get the great job *and* the great people.

I think that the legacy that *Supernatural* leaves behind will rival a show like *Star Trek*, which has such a huge canon and lore as well as a wonderful ability to explore and retool traditional storytelling and then make it unique. I thought that was quite brilliant for *Supernatural* as well, but there's also just a record-breaking *amount* of television that the show has created. That doesn't happen in the world of television anymore. We've already seen the legacy continue in young people streaming it—a new generation of young teens absolutely gobbling it up. And then mothers and fathers and grandmothers and grandfathers—three generations are watching *Supernatural* together now because of streaming. That proves what Eric Kripke and the subsequent writers did was to really know their archetypes and hero's journey. When you then add more mythic lore and spin it on its pop culture ear, you make something that's truly tasty for an audience to devour—both young and old, female and male, non-binary and genderqueer, disabled and abled, and every self-identifying human on the wonderful spectrum that wants to be included. That's what makes the show popular—we can all find something to latch on to.

And again, we come back to family. The truly extraordinary, unique, inclusive SPNFamily.

MARATHON

ADAM FERGUS

(in collaboration with and derived from
an interview with Lynn Zubernis)

As I sit down to write this chapter, I'm wearing the shirt I wore when I ran the Seattle Marathon to raise money to combat childhood hunger. Along with Jared Padalecki, Jensen Ackles, Misha Collins, Rob Benedict (God), Jason Manns, and the SPNFamily, we raised over $250,000. The fact that I'm sitting here wearing this shirt and remembering that day makes me realize what a massive effect the people, both on the show and in the fandom, have had on my life.

Where do I start? I suppose it starts with working on *Supernatural*. I auditioned for the show on a Friday evening. It was what they call a cold audition, meaning I wasn't part of the initial group of people who were called in. But when it went to callbacks, the casting agency called me. I remember looking at the script I was given and thinking, *This is totally in my wheelhouse*—it was for a British Cockney guy. Sometimes as an actor, you're nervous in an audition because you really want the part, but for this audition, I wasn't nervous. Not because I wasn't aware of the show and didn't want to do it, but more because I figured, well, if they didn't want

me initially, I'm going to just go in and give them something different and totally blow their socks off!

And that's a lesson for any actor: the more relaxed you are, the better you can be. I did the audition, and I walked out of the room not thinking I got the job in any way, shape, or form, but that I'd given the best I could and given a good branding of the character that I'd read the night before. So I was delighted when I got the part. I was only guaranteed two episodes, but I ended up doing six. That was the beginning of what has to go down as the most enjoyable and rewarding experience of my acting life. Of course, there are other things I've done, plays that have meant a lot to me, movies where it felt monumental because I was working with Sean Penn or Harrison Ford. But the actual process and mechanics of being on set on *Supernatural* and working with that cast and crew was such an enjoyable experience. It seemed to follow on from my comfort of being so relaxed during the audition.

If you've been to conventions or watched convention videos, you might have heard my story of my first day working with Jared and Jensen.

Jared was tied to a chair in episode 2 of season 12, and I was speaking in
my Cockney accent for the first time. I'd been talking to the guys in my
normal Irish accent before shooting, and when I switched to my Cockney
accent, Jared immediately called, "Cut!" and said, "No, no, no, no, I can't
understand this guy!" Everyone busted up laughing, and I went bright
red. And then he did it again . . . and again. I had never experienced
anything like that, especially on a TV set where every minute is so valued
financially that it leaves no room for messing around. The tone that they
set that day put me in a place and in an environment where I believe I was
able to do my best work. That was the moment I realized what a special
show this was.

Sometimes actors are given latitude in changing lines or words, but
when you're doing television it's not really advisable to ad-lib. Especially
when you're a guest star, you want to toe the line and not waste everyone's
time. When we filmed the episode "Ladies Drink for Free," it was the
first time I got to read something in the script about my character's past
(being orphaned and fending for himself on the streets with a very Artful
Dodger–esque character arc). In the scene, Dean, Sam, and my character,
Mick Davies, had been drinking into the wee hours of the morning. And
the next day, Mick, because he's a seasoned drinker, gets up fresh as a
daisy while Sam and Dean are crippled over their breakfast table unable
to talk. Mick walks in and pulls a tomato juice out of the fridge—because
that's all the props people had put in the fridge. So I turned round to the
props people and asked, "Is there any orange juice or anything?" They
said no, and I said okay. Then I turned to Jensen and said, "It would be
funny if I said, 'Don't you have any vodka?' And he said, 'Oh you've gotta
do that, put that in there.'" So I did and it was a button on the end of
the scene, "Any vodka?" It really lent itself to the scene because Mick was
looking for another drink while the boys were dying at the table. And
it worked because I was so at home in the *Supernatural* Family. At that
point, I hadn't done conventions yet, but I was so comfortable among the
cast and crew and the leads of the show that I was able to voice that idea
and not feel intimidated in any way. And that was thanks to the comfort
that I was afforded by the boys and the crew. Being able to do that was
important; it made me an artist. I fight with that word as an actor, but

it really made me feel like I had some input into creating and furthering this role.

My first day in Canada, I got to the room the show provided, and there was already a note on my door from Ruth Connell (Rowena). It said, "From one Celt to another, if you ever want a cup of tea and a chat, let me know." So, right away, Ruth and I, plus Briana Buckmaster (Donna Hanscum), got together. Ruth told us, "There are these things called conventions . . ." Now, I'd heard of Comic-Con and *Star Trek* conventions, but I didn't have any idea what a *Supernatural* con would look like. Ruth urged me to get onto the circuit, as it's known, but at the beginning I wasn't keen on it. I kept thinking that it was more important for me to do a good job on the show. I didn't want to come across as that bit-player guy trying to elbow his way onto some circuit that's for the leads of the show.

Then the next day, I went on set to do my first costume fitting, and Ruth was on set shadowing Phil Sgriccia (sometimes actors shadow directors to learn what it's like to be a television director). She asked, "Are you allowed by production to be introduced to the fandom?" And I said, "Yeah, I think I am." So, right there she snapped a quick photo and put it on Twitter. And my phone just *exploded.* I remember thinking, *Okay there's something here that I'm not quite aware of . . . the fandom is HUGE.*

I did my first convention in Blackpool, England. The hilarious thing about a convention there is that Blackpool used to be a destination for holiday vacations with parks and amusements, but now it has kinda fallen apart. We were driving to the hotel where the convention was and the sign said, "Norbrook Hote." Because the *L* in "hotel" had fallen right off the wall. It was completely rundown and I thought, *Okay, this is a bit weird.* Then David Haydn-Jones (Arthur Ketch) and I got up to do our first panel. And for the first time in a long time I was able to get onstage and FEEL the love from the audience that I used to feel when I was doing theater. That "grá," as we say in Irish . . . that love for you and the thing that you've done in your small time on the show. One of the things I miss most about theater is the audience reaction and feeling that difference in applause from night to night . . . either they liked it or they didn't, or it was a good crowd or a bad crowd. That's something we live for as actors. It's also like, wow, they really love what I did, so it's like getting a gold star from a teacher for doing good work. And you don't get that so much as an actor.

I quickly got up to speed with what the cons were about, and from there we went straight to Rome to do another, and then back to filming, and then I think Chicago was my first Creation con. At that point I thought, *There's something different about all this.* A friend of mine at the time, who's a restaurateur, said to me once, "Let me get this straight—people pay for your autograph and your photo and spend hundreds if not more dollars over a weekend? I don't get it." I responded, "Well we went to that golf trip a few weeks ago. You're not very good at golf, but you still spent a couple thousand dollars on that golf trip and you got fun out of it." That was my answer then, but now I'd answer differently, because it's not really about us at these cons. It is to a certain degree, but people get so much more out of this than just us standing onstage. It's about community. When we talk about SPNFamily, it doesn't mean the actors and then the rest—it's a family. And like every other family, it has its ups and downs and problems, but it's all about seeing people who rescue you from the dark parts of life we all have. There's a certain type of person who is a *Supernatural* fan, and I think they're more awakened than the majority of the populace, because they're more in touch with their feelings. And they feel so at home, be they gay, straight, transgender, a jock, or whatever, they can walk into that room and say, "I'm comfortable with who I am right now."

I'd never really experienced that before, and it's powerful.

It reminded me of what I learned doing my very first professional play. It was a play for Dublin Gay Pride, and I was to play the lead and make out with a guy and I had to be naked on stage. I had struggled, when I first decided to be an actor, with why I wanted to be an actor. Did I want to be in this profession because I really loved acting, or was it some kind of drive to be in the limelight or be famous? But I can say with confidence now, when you're still an actor after twenty years, like I am, it's because you love the actual work. It's because acting is all you can do. When I got that role I thought, *If I can do this, I can do anything.* Because my experience so far was that I'd gone to a Catholic boys' boarding school and homosexuality was always pushed under the carpet or frowned upon or joked about (though in a very homoerotic way). But that night, for that performance, some of the biggest rugby players in Dublin (football players, you would call them in the US) came out and they sat in the front row and watched that play and at the end they all said to me, "Holy shit, dude, that was remarkable, that was great." There was no nudge-nudge or anything. I was twenty-two years old, barely out of school, and we hadn't washed all that stupidity off us at that time, so it was a real life-changing moment, an experience that has always stuck with me—that feeling I had when I saw the big 6'7" captain of the rugby team stand up and applaud. I was like, *Fuck, I didn't realize I wanted his approval*, but then it meant so much when I got it. I probably would have cared too much if he had laughed (though, mature man that I am now, I realize it would be more a reflection on him than on me). Which brings me back to conventions. When you walk out onstage, as David and I do so often together, there is a feeling of acceptance. That's what being part of the SPNFamily is all about.

I'm so grateful to the fans that I can keep reliving this and keep seeing people who enjoy my work. We talk about ego, but I think there's no harm in saying that I love meeting fans because they love talking to me about stuff I did that I'm proud of. Anyone who says otherwise is probably trying to rain on your parade.

I get asked a lot where I think Mick's story line would have gone if he had stayed on the show. I think that last speech he gave—which was cut off by a bullet in the back of the head—shows that he'd definitely be with the Winchesters. That's the path he had chosen, and it was such a beautiful little arc, such a wholesome, fully formed arc. I would have liked to stay on the show, of course, since it was the most enjoyable acting experience I've had, but I'm okay with the way it ended.

I had always thought that I'm not a network actor, that I'm too dramatic from my past as a theater actor to be on these procedural television shows. I've gone out for other network shows and only booked a couple, but when I booked *Supernatural* I thought, *Oh, I'm so wrong about network television*, because the writing is exceptional on this show. Back in the day I did a show called *Being Erica*, and the lead of that show, Erin Karpluk, asked me to help her out with an audition for *Supernatural*. So I went over to her house and read with her, and she ended up booking the part for two episodes. Then, when I told my buddy Mark Rolston (an amazing actor who's been in *Aliens, Shawshank Redemption, The Departed*, and more) that I was going to be on *Supernatural*, he said that he had played Alastair on the show. He said, "Dude, you're gonna have a blast."

And I did. And it changed my life. Back in the day, when people recognized me on the street, I would have to list like seventeen things that they might have seen me in. Now, it's always *Supernatural*. I only did six episodes, but it goes to show the strength and the reach of the series.

Shows that exist for a long period of time do so for different reasons. Maybe they have something about them, be it like *Game of Thrones*, which was an epic show forced upon us by HBO with all this big advertising and famous actors, and it's great. Then there are shows that get their audience because of their quality. That quality initially comes from the numbers 1 and 2 on the call sheet. And that speaks to what I said about Jared earlier . . . how he brought me into the community. He and Jensen both, after 300-something episodes, walk on the set, and it's like it's their first episode. They give 110 percent. They make it so special for everybody coming in. But it also speaks to why they still love doing the show. It's not just the money or the comfort of being an actor and not being out of work. Sure, that's a very enviable situation for any actor, but there's something more, something beyond seasons 7, 8, 9 . . . and still they want to stay on the show. And that has to be the writing. The writing is paramount to this show's success and longevity. All the writers on the show love writing the show, and it's cyclical because they love writing the show because the guys keep reinventing themselves, working hard to produce every single episode.

I remember one day while shooting, I was in Jensen's trailer, and Jared, Jensen, and I were having a chat, and the show came on the TV. We all watched an episode that the three of us were in while waiting to be called back to set. Jared and Jensen watch the show religiously; they critique it thoroughly because they're invested in it. And I think that's the reason it's gone so long. The boys, the directors, the producers, the writers—I'm not giving my Oscar thank-you speech here, but that's truly why the show has existed for the time that it has.

As far as the legacy of *Supernatural*, we're still in the tail end of the honeymoon period as I write this, before the show disappears. People love it as much as they always have, if not more, because they know it's ending. I don't know how they'll feel next year after the last convention is finished, but it seems to me that *Supernatural* has to go on in some capacity, whether it's a spinoff or something else that keeps the *Supernatural* dream alive. Jared is doing *Walker, Texas Ranger*, and I'm sure Jensen will be off to dizzying heights. And Misha is an entity unto himself . . . he could do anything, including be president. I'd vote for him. He's a true hero of mine, a gentleman and an absolute scholar. But I can imagine those guys in a few years wanting to reunite and do a *Supernatural* movie or something. I think anything is possible with this fandom and this group of actors and producers and writers.

I remember when Ricky Gervais did *The Office*, and after two seasons he said he was ready to finish. And I had so much admiration for that guy because he didn't bow to producers or the moneymen who wanted to bleed it out and make loads of money for the next twenty years. As an artist, that's really admirable. But since I've been part of this *Supernatural* fandom, I'm like, *Fuck, guys, why do you really have to finish?* After fifteen seasons, we could do twenty. There's nothing to say we couldn't because the writers have consistently reinvented the show with such poise and such accuracy, and that's not easy. If you told someone fifteen years ago that you're going to write a show about two guys fighting demons, werewolves, and vampires, and you asked them how long that could possibly last, they wouldn't say, "Probably fifteen years." They would more likely say, "Two, maybe three max." But for the reasons I just explained, *Supernatural* has gone this long and it could go until the boys are in wheelchairs! For *Supernatural*, it truly has been a fifteen-year marathon.

There are things in life that you always think you want to do. I want to go to the moon or I want to go to space or see the *Titanic* or whatever . . . hypothetical things. I'm a big dreamer—you kinda have to be as an actor—but I never really wanted to run a marathon other than so I could say that I ran a marathon. And I honestly didn't realize the extent of the task. I was a smoker right up until five weeks before running the Seattle Marathon. And I only gave it up when my girlfriend, Haley, knocked me on the head as I was lighting up and said, "You're about to run a marathon!"

I'm in such awe of the other guys, especially Misha, who was the driving force behind this charity run. Misha did all the work so I could just be part of this massive thing we did simply by running. I didn't train that well . . . not the actual regimented training you should do for a marathon. So I got there the morning of the run, and I was shitting myself because I was really worried about not finishing. I mean, what if Jensen, Jared, Misha, Rob, and Jason all finish and I don't? But the competitor in me kicked in. I ran the first 5 miles with Rachel Miner (Meg 2.0), each of us taking turns pushing her wheelchair, which she uses due to her multiple sclerosis. Rachel stopped at mile 5 and the rest of us ran on. We got to mile 7, the first water stop. My girlfriend came up with everyone to help out, and I said to her, "Um, my knee is already sore." She said, "You've got 19 miles to go, so keep trucking!"

Jason and Rob drifted off to complete the run on their own, and at mile 10, Jared and Jensen ran off ahead. So it was just me and Misha. Misha used to run every morning, but he was injured going into the marathon and was doing all he could just to hang on. We got to mile 19, and I swear to God, if it wasn't for the *Supernatural* fandom, we both would have walked the next 7 miles. But there were fans at almost every corner. So we'd walk for a couple of minutes and then were like, *Oh, the fans are coming up, let's go!* So we'd run and then once we started running, we didn't want to stop.

At dinner that night I had to ask the waiter for two bags of ice, which I strapped to my knees with napkins. I could barely walk.

But we raised over $250,000 for Random Acts. I say "we" in the grander sense, but I'm proud to be part of that and happy I was given the opportunity. I'm so honored to be their friend and to be a part of this show.

CONVENTIONAL WISDOM

APRIL VIAN

L et me tell you a story.

My husband introduced me to *Supernatural* five years ago. It began innocently enough, something we could watch together. I was hesitant at first, as it wasn't my typical genre. A week later I was wrapping up the first season. My love for the show was unexpected and initially embarrassing, and I had no reason to give when someone asked why I liked it.

I caught up quickly and fell into the fandom slowly. As I caught up to the current season, I began to like fan pages and started to follow the actors on social media, then I eventually found GISHWHES, the global fandom charity scavenger hunt organized by *Supernatural* actor Misha Collins. I remained a loyal fan, tuning in weekly; I supported the causes of the actors and wore the shirts and the jewelry. Friendships were made and strengthened. However, I still couldn't quite explain my fascination with this show. It was more than just the story, more than the actors, something I couldn't quite put my finger on . . . something I thought but couldn't quite say.

In 2017, I went to my first *Supernatural* convention, and I can now point to the reasons I am fascinated by the show. I have hundreds of them. With every Q&A, every photo, every song, I learned something, felt something change. Just a few days before the convention, I would've been embarrassed to say that a fan convention had altered me in any way, and I would've been scared to write. I had the opportunity to listen to some amazing people and experienced a great deal in such a short time. The lessons did not stop after the convention, and I continue to look back at that weekend for inspiration, for hope, and for friendship.

As I sit down to write this, less than two weeks afterward, the con feels like a dream, and I stare at the photos in disbelief. I don't know how long this will last. There is every possibility that by the end of the week, the routine of work and kids and dinner and chores will take over and the magic and the peace that I have felt since attending will fade. But I hope not. I sincerely hope that the lessons I learned during that time stick with me and that I will recall the words and the stories, not only of the actors and the musicians but also of the other members of the SPNFamily, and that I will be able to maintain this perspective and this feeling.

I have heard a lot about post-con depression, but that's not what I feel. I feel exhilarated and renewed, and I want to keep it. Like a lot of the *Supernatural* Family, I suffer from anxiety. Generally I shy away from big crowds and strangers; I keep physical contact limited to those who are closest to me. I don't talk to people I don't know; I get nervous in lines or even walking in front of people. I would take a failing grade before speaking in front of a class. At the con, I spent three days surrounded by large crowds of strangers, a large number of whom felt the need to hug me. I didn't shy away from it. I walked down the aisles without a second thought of how I looked or whether I would trip. I bought more photo ops and have stared at them in wonder. I don't like to be touched, especially by strangers, but there I am in the middle of a group hug with one of my best friends, along with Mark Sheppard (who played Crowley) and Misha.

My friend Jackie and I began our journey in the middle of the night, arriving at our hotel to room with two strangers already there and asleep. With no other choice, I crawled into bed with a total stranger at 1:00 in the morning and hoped for the best. This would be the first of many opportunities to conquer anxiety, to take a chance.

Bright and early Friday morning, Jackie and I were expectedly giddy with anticipation for what lay ahead. Rich Speight and Rob Benedict came out to kick off the weekend. The first song I recall hearing was "Wagon Wheel." This has been a longtime favorite in my family—one we sing at

every bonfire and get-together. At that moment I felt at home and experienced an odd connection to our host for the weekend. The next day, Rob and Jason Manns sang "Hallelujah," another favorite. At this time, I didn't understand these connections, but the understanding would come. I found myself impulsively buying a photo op with Rob. I wasn't really sure why, but I felt like I *had* to meet him. Rob was our first photo op. We made it through mostly in control and with the expected jokes and posts about hugging "God."

As the weekend progressed, I found myself talking to strangers. I dressed as a gypsy and wore more makeup than I have since high school. I spoke with celebrities like they were friends. Aside from overcoming deep-seated fears and social anxieties, I found myself being inspired to be kinder, to take better care of myself, to love myself, and to actually *be* myself. Maybe I even *found myself* during that weekend.

By Sunday, I decided I needed a Louden Swain album, and again, I acted on impulse and purchased *Saturday Night Special*. (I feel the need to reiterate here that this is all very out of the ordinary for me. I don't follow impulses like that, particularly ones that cost money.) I had kept it together, mostly, through all the photo ops, karaoke, even a casual run-in with Rachel Miner (who plays Meg). My composure cracked with my next impulsive decision to have the album signed by Rob Benedict and the rest of the band. I was able to conjure up an appropriate and clichéd response to, "Hey, how are you?" but that was it. Every question and comment I had been thinking of in line suddenly vanished when the opportunity was presented. I went back to my seat still giddy, if not a little puzzled by my reaction to an actor I had already met and had been confident I could speak to. I'm a pretty controlled person for the most part, so my unexpected reactions and decisions were way out of character for me.

The rest of Sunday went by in a blur of laughter and tears. The sadness and feeling of leaving home as we left the hotel was unexpected. We said our goodbyes and the sleeping strangers we met Thursday night had become sisters. On the way home, we played *Saturday Night Special* to keep the mood going. We listened to every song. I found that I really enjoyed Louden Swain, that the lyrics made sense to me in a way that I couldn't explain. I marveled at the brain that could write something as potent as "She Waits" and as fun as "Eskimo" . . . the words strung together in such a unique way that spoke to me so clearly.

I could go on for days about what I've learned and how I changed, but perhaps the biggest change and lesson occurred after I returned. And that is where I truly need to begin. This is where I begin to feel silly. I am no longer embarrassed by my fandom. I've met far too many amazing, educated, and talented people to be ashamed at this point. However, events that have unfolded since I have returned home have baffled me. (Before going forward, it is important to understand that I am a scientist at heart and in mind. I have always processed the world differently than others. I analyze everything and everyone; I identify the function of each behavior that I observe. I truly believe that everything happens for a reason and one of my favorite pastimes is discovering what that reason is.) I wasn't expecting the "why" in this case to be quite so big or bordering on magical.

Recounting this experience is unnerving.

Monday, I had to return to work. I wasn't ready for the weekend to be over, absolutely not ready for that feeling of acceptance and excitement to go away. I had discovered that I enjoyed feeling that carefree, taking chances and making new friends. I made a conscious decision to be more myself and to like myself. I drive a lot for work, spending hours a day in the car by myself, so I brought the CD for company in an effort to prolong my post-con buzz. Midway through my day, "She Waits" came on and I found myself sobbing in the car. This was unexpected. Was this part of the post-con crash? What was wrong with me?

I listened to it again. In that moment, I realized that Rob had put into words what I had been carrying in my heart for thirty years. The difference here was it had been my mother who left, and I was the one who waited. My parents divorced when I was six years old and my younger brother and I remained with my father. One of the reasons I related to the Winchesters was that we were all raised by a single father during a time when that was rare. From that time on, my mother was in and out of my life. I waited for phone calls, for visits, for some kind of explanation. She would be around for weeks at a time, and then without warning I would find myself waiting for her to show up for a birthday party or promised visit. Eventually I convinced myself that I wasn't waiting anymore, that I didn't really care. For years I was angry about this, but until I heard Rob's words, I had never cried about it, never admitted that I had ever been sad or disappointed about it. Rob's words reflected the sadness I had never acknowledged. This realization hit me hard as I sat in my car. For the first time I realized that I had waited, had never really stopped waiting, for my mother to return, to have a mom.

I only know as much of Rob's story as he has shared publicly at concerts, so I won't claim to know his feelings in any way, but still I related to that song. I wondered if perhaps this was why I was drawn to him over the weekend, why I impulsively bought the photo op and the album. Maybe I was just meant to find this band and hear that song.

I listened to "She Waits" over and over until I could listen without crying. I discussed the song, my experiences, my unexplained choices at the con with Jackie and my husband. I wanted desperately to share the song with my mother. My relationship with her really hadn't improved in adulthood. Our communication was sporadic and visits were sparse.

Fans light up the ballroom in support of Rob Benedict during "She Waits."

Becoming a mother myself had increased my resentment, making it more difficult to understand why she had left. While I had forgiven her, I didn't understand her. When I was in my early thirties, my mother left a longterm toxic relationship and moved to the state my brother and I resided in. For the past four years my mother had been living within a couple miles of me. We spoke often, celebrated holidays together, but we had never talked about the past, about the missing time. I had forgiven her long ago. Age, maturity, and my career in mental health had given me insight, and I hadn't knowingly harbored any anger or resentment for quite some time. Just the thought of bringing up these emotions with my mother terrified me. I had put it off, tucked it away, assuming that bringing it up would just result in unnecessary pain for both of us. Until I had heard that song, I'm not sure I had even ever acknowledged that I was still sad, that I had waited, for years, and was even still waiting, though this time to see whether she'd leave again. This realization was scary, to say the least. I'm an adult, married with children. I'm well educated with a graduate degree in psychology. It didn't seem possible that a song, a convention, a television show of all things, could set off this chain, but here I was. I spent the rest of the week listening to the album in its entirety and worked out how to begin a conversation thirty years in the making.

On the Friday after the convention, I texted my mother. I summed up my weekend and told her I had heard a song, acknowledged my part in our emotional distance, and the wall I had put between us, and asked if she wanted to talk. I shouldn't have been surprised by her swift and enthusiastic "yes." The next day, my mother came to my home for coffee and a conversation. I explained the best I could what I experienced at the convention, the chain of events that culminated with me crying in my car. I admitted that I had waited, that I had been sad. I told her how disappointed I was when I waited and she didn't show. That now I found it hard to count on her, to trust her word—that I was still waiting for her to leave again. She understood what I needed to say. She understood my experience and encouraged me to go to another convention to continue to discover myself in this way, surrounded by this newfound support of the SPNFamily.

I played her the song and we both cried. She apologized again and again. The album continued to play as we spoke. She shared with me her own history and troubles. We all have our own demons to fight and some of us are better equipped than others. My mother shared with me where she had come from, the demons that followed her into motherhood. She acknowledged that for a long time, she couldn't always beat them, but she had always loved us. We talked about my children, about going forward. At the end of it, there was a sense of peace and relief that we hadn't felt between us since I was a child. This conversation had been hanging over every interaction since she had returned to my life. Just like that, it had started mending; this deep wound I hadn't even acknowledged out loud had healed. I had a mother again.

Maybe the reason some things happen is because there is a higher power in charge and all this was part of a larger plan. Perhaps my sudden interest in Rob Benedict and Louden Swain and my impulsive purchases of photos, albums, and kazoos were meant to be, so that I could hear that song and get to this place. It took a whole television show, an entire weekend, for a song. Perhaps spending three days in an environment where I felt loved and accepted, where I could be myself for the first time ever, had relaxed me enough to the point I was finally open to this realization that had been lurking under the surface all along. Or just maybe there is a little magic in this world after all. I like to think that this was meant to happen, that this is just one lesson that I have learned and will learn from my involvement with this fandom.

As I write this, the day after meeting with my mother, it has been less than two weeks since I returned from my first con, and I have nine months and four days until my next. I look forward to what I still have to learn and discover. I can't wait to soak in the energy and love that was so prevalent throughout the convention that it managed to follow me home. I won't pretend to know any of the actors well enough to be familiar with their stories or their thoughts. But I owe Rob and the other members of Louden Swain a debt of gratitude that cannot be repaid. I truly love each song I've heard, and I will purchase more albums and more photos, and perhaps the next time, at the very least, I will be able to manage a thank-you when I go through the autograph line. I found so much inspiration in my time at the convention. I truly believe that the words of all of the actors came together to help me find a place where I had the courage and confidence to move forward.

There are some aspects of my life that will remain unchanged. I still have to go to work, and wash the dishes . . . and my children still bicker, although they now also have mastered the kazoo solo. There are still problems to fix. But the undercurrent that carries me through my days has changed. My life no longer feels permeated by anxiety and sadness, by constant feelings of inadequacy. Instead, the undercurrent is calm and supportive, even peaceful. It seems that this conversation with my mother was at the root of much of my anxiety. And from here I am free to move on further than I ever have before. It remains unbelievable to me that all of this came from a television show, and that I am part of a fandom that can create this type of environment, this type of change in an individual. The scientist in me wants to delve into this more, to see how permanent these changes are, to find other stories, to find the sense and the "why" of all of it.

I'm sure it would be fascinating research. For now, though, in the interest of a little girl who waited long enough, I'll just accept the magic.

INTERVIEW WITH THE ARCHANGEL

RICHARD SPEIGHT, JR.

(interviewed by Lynn Zubernis)

Richard Speight, Jr. joined Supernatural *way back in season 2 to play a character called the Trickster. That character was immediately popular with fans, and Speight found himself invited back to the show and then invited to* Supernatural *conventions. His character was eventually revealed to be the Archangel Gabriel, an integral part of the ongoing mythology of the show. Then, in season 11, Speight began directing* Supernatural *with the episode "Just My Imagination." He has since directed several episodes of the Netflix series* Lucifer *as well as returning to direct a total of eleven episodes of* Supernatural, *including four in the show's fifteenth and final season. I've chatted with Richard many times over the course of the show's fifteen seasons and sat down with him again to hear his unique perspective on* Supernatural*'s evolution and legacy.*

Why do you think the Trickster resonated so quickly with fans that you were invited to conventions?

I'm not sure why that character resonated with fans so quickly, but I do think there's something unique about the first five years of *Supernatural* under the Eric Kripke umbrella. In its later seasons, people came to expect fascinating and diverse guest characters, but in its infancy, in its early years, I think there was still the element of surprise in everything the show did. By no means is that to say that the show hasn't stayed fresh, but back then, the show was still finding an audience and finding its identity, so some of those early characters are the characters who were there when people first fell in love with the show and are characters people still connect with. There's sort of an "original gangster" vibe to the whole thing. It's all timing. The show was new, those characters were new, and conventions for the show were new. So it created this nexus of newness, so to speak, and through that, I think those characters, we actors who played them, and the show itself all became inextricably linked.

The show has a legacy, but the iconic characters have a legacy too, and so do you and your fellow actors. What do you think Gabriel's legacy is, and what did fans take from his unusual redemption arc?

Interestingly, I feel like the fans I encounter tend to focus on the fun side of Gabriel, while what I found interesting was the flawed side. I find it fascinating that he broke his own covenant with Loki, which was what got him into trouble to start with. Then he went after Loki's kids, which is what escalated the fight between them. So he was on the side of humans, sure, but he didn't come into the situation with clean hands. He's a complex figure. He could easily have been made a cartoon character and only been goofy or funny or just a rascal, but the writers didn't sell him short at any point. Instead, they let the character evolve and change and have depth and heart. I also think there's something about the humanity of the angels in *Supernatural* that people connect with, because even angels have flaws on this show. Even angels have concerns and worries and even angels are of questionable moral fiber, and I think that allows the audience to relate to them in a very different way than if we were portraying angels as ethereal beings of higher value.

They're certainly not stereotypical on *Supernatural!*

Exactly! But what specifically will they take away from Gabriel? I don't know. Really, that's kind of like looking at a piece of art and asking someone what they get from it. I'm not comparing Gabriel to the Mona Lisa, but you look at a canvas, and whatever you walk away with is what it is. It really doesn't matter what the painter intended. Whatever people connect with, be it the goofiness, the wackiness, the sinister side, the questionable morals, any combination of any of all that, or something completely different—whatever it is, there's no wrong answer.

Authorial intent doesn't really matter, that's true. How have *Supernatural* and the SPNFamily impacted you personally?

Certainly from a professional standpoint, it's massive. I direct television now, which has been a big leap.

I remember when you first said you wanted to do it, many years ago, long before you did it.

Yeah, because it's not easy to figure out how to do it. The thing about anything in life—acting, directing, any job—is that regardless of how clearly you can see what you want to do and focus on it, there's not always a clear path to success. You can't always see the rocks that will take you across the creek. You might have to go find your own rocks and put them in there. And finding the right rocks that will match the depth of the water and get you to the next rock is challenging. It takes time, energy, effort, guess work, and *hard* work. So I worked my tail off—wrote and directed my own short film, *America 101*, took it on the film festival circuit for a year, got accepted to and completed the Warner Bros. Director's Program, shadowed three different *Supernatural* directors . . . Still, at the end of the day, it was up to the brass behind the show (who at that point were Bob Singer, Jeremy Carver, and Phil Sgriccia —and Chad Kennedy at Warner Brothers). They gave me the professional opportunity of a lifetime when they let me direct. It wasn't exactly a quick yes from them. It took years. But when they finally felt I was ready and had earned it, they gave me a shot—and it realigned the trajectory of my career. I will always be grateful for that.

Yes, with four episodes to direct this season!

I know! It's awesome! I feel very fortunate because at no point has this been *my* show. At no point have I been a regular on *Supernatural* or under contract. I've always just been a guy who guest starred in a few episodes. But the way the show is made reflects the theme of the series itself, meaning that behind the scenes, there is a value system that parallels the values reflected on screen—the value of family. When I first showed up to direct *Supernatural*, the people who bring the show to life—the crew, Jared, Jensen, Misha, the writers and producers—treated me, a four-episode guest star, like an insider—a family member. That concept on any other show, on any other set, would be ludicrous.

I am so lucky that I was able to connect early on with some of that crew (Brad Creasser, Robin Stooshnov, and I have been friends from day one of my first episode back in season 2). But that only happened because the crew is *connectable*. Open, kind, welcoming, chill . . . Not all crews are. That speaks volumes to their collective character and, in my opinion, reveals a key ingredient to the show's longevity.

How does it feel directing this season, knowing it's the final season?
It's not too different on set, except for every now and then when it is. For example, earlier this season, we took a group photo for *Supernatural* Day, the anniversary of the day the first episode aired. It was a big group picture, with every crew and cast member on set that day in it, and afterwards, everyone—especially Jared and Jensen and the crew that had been there all along—was like, *Wow, this is the last time we'll do one of these photos*. And I realized, *Yeah, it* is *the last time.*

Directing my last episode will be emotional. Even though I knew they were announcing the final season in advance of the fans finding out, the official announcement still landed like a stone on my chest. It was like, *Ooof.* Suddenly it was real. But on set, the work is still the work, the show is still the show, the job is still the job. We're still trying to make great television.

What do you think is the legacy of the show itself, after all this time?
In spite of all the visual effects, the big fights, and the crazy characters that come and go, *Supernatural* hangs its hat on the old-world values of *family don't end with blood,* and *we stay together because we're brothers—or at least like brothers.*

Sam and Dean are brothers from a flawed family. They are each other's life raft. And the world around them—the demons, the spirits—all may be analogous to the politics and social strife of our time, but I feel like the show's timeless theme of *we stick together no matter what* resonates with people and connects them to the characters and to the show because they can relate. They *want* to relate. Everyone has been lost. Everyone has been alone. Everyone hurts. Everyone gets scared. We all just want at least one person—someone, anyone—to love us enough to stay with us when everyone else goes away. To value us more than we value ourselves. Sam and Dean are that for each other. And Castiel is key to that dynamic as well, as someone who isn't blood but who has worked their way from the outside in.

The *Supernatural* take on family ain't the Lifetime version. It's dark, it's rough, it's painful, it's broken. It may not be a perfect family, but it's *our* family. It may not be a perfect world, but it's *our* world. And I think the way Sam and Dean and Castiel choose to navigate that world and how they deal with each other along the way is inspirational to a lot of people and will continue to be an inspiration for a very long time.

I'M PROUD OF US

JENSEN ACKLES

Fifteen years is a long time to be on a television show. When Jared and I were in our twenties, we went to Vancouver thinking that we'd just put our lives on hold and press pause for maybe a season or two, and then we'd come back, press play, and life would go on.

That's not what happened.

It just never got un-paused. And I'm very thankful for that.

We were on *Supernatural* when the first iPhone came out. We were on *Supernatural* when Twitter began. It took a long time before we were confident that we'd have another season, but over the years we kept coming back and coming back as they moved us around in the lineup. Some of those slots that we ended up in were the slots they put shows in to die. But we didn't die—the fandom kept us alive. Fan support has actually increased over the years, and that's been one of the most humbling things that has happened to us. We've watched new people continuously join the fandom with the changing TV landscape of binge-watching and streaming. That's been the most shocking thing to us—that the fandom continued to grow. Looking back now, I'm proud of the work that this team has done for this long, because it *has* been a team. It takes a lot of very talented people to make television, to give viewers the best product we can make, and I'm really proud of that product. After this long on a

show, to still truly love what we do and be proud to hang my hat on that at the end of the day . . . that's what I'm going to take with me. That's one of the legacies that I'm proudest of, knowing that we all put in the effort and nobody phoned it in.

I'm also proud of the tone we've had on our set. It's one of the best compliments we can receive as a cast and crew when guest stars or guest directors say that they love the tone of the set and feel like it's a welcoming, warm environment where they can create and have a good time, and they want to come back. More times than I can count, we've had people say that this is the best set they've ever been on and one of the most fun and comfortable sets they can remember. Nobody likes to work in a toxic environment. I've been on sets like that, with everybody walking around on eggshells. So Jared and I have made an effort. We know that when we walk on that set, we're setting a tone. And I'm proud that he and I have put in the effort to make our home a place where everybody's welcome.

It's hard to express what I'm going to take away from this. Lifelong friends . . . experiences of a lifetime. I think that the people who have found *Supernatural* and become part of the fandom and found each other through the show—the SPNFamily—are probably the legacy that we're going to be proudest of. We are so fortunate to have a fandom that is so charitable and vocal. I've heard more times than I can count, "I met my best friend through the show." I love that there's such a love for each other, and for us; it's a really cool relationship to be in with a fandom. We may not have won a lot of awards or have accolades covering our mantels, but when we walked out on that stage at Comic-Con for our last panel in Hall H and heard nearly 7,000 people applaud us, that was about as big an award as we could have ever won in our lives. It was like a celebration of what we've all built together with *Supernatural*, and it was very emotional. It's not awards or reviews that determine whether a show is successful; it's the relationship with the fans. If you make yourself accessible like we have and you can interact with the fans and they can tell you their stories and why the show means something to them . . . that's success. Our fans are better than any award.

The decision to end the show was not an easy one. This world has lasted much longer than maybe we originally intended it to, and I'm very thankful for that. We made this decision with heavy hearts, but at the same time, we never wanted to stick around so long that the production started to wane. We felt like we still had tons of energy, tons of passion, and tons of love for the show, so we wanted to go out with a bang. Nobody wanted to see the show fizzle out. We wanted to do the biggest service to this show that we could by going out strong. So it was taking that leap of faith and saying, well, let's get out that paint and paint the finish line and hold our heads high because what we've accomplished is unlike any other. We wanted to do justice to this crew who has stuck with us all this time and to this family and to these characters and to the fans that have kept us going. One of the reasons why we were able to be here so long is because this was never just a job. It was an amazing opportunity that Jared and I recognized and held on to for dear life.

What will I miss about playing Dean? I'll miss his badassery. As a functioning person in society, you don't really get to do the things that Dean does. I will miss walking into a room with all the confidence in the world and lopping off a vampire's head or throwing a '67 Impala into a reverse 180. I'll miss all those cool things that we got to do. And along with the badassery, I'll miss the humility that is also peppered into these characters. I think that balance is what makes them real to us and what makes them real to the fans. You can't just have someone who's always a badass and never breaks. There has to be that balance and that vulnerability. I think being able to play those two extremes is cathartic for us as actors, and I will miss being able to do that. It has been a privilege to play a character like Dean who has inspired so many people, because any excuse to give up is not an excuse that is good enough for the Winchesters. This is who they are. They fought because they believed in what they were fighting for, and that's a part of the show that people connect with—to keep fighting the good fight, not giving up because the odds are stacked against you. *Supernatural* embodies that kind of resilience. I think Dean's legacy is that he never gives up. He keeps fighting no matter what. The show carries the message to always keep fighting for each other, and that has inspired the fandom to keep fighting too, whatever fight they are facing.

I don't think we'll ever say goodbye to these characters. They're woven into the fabric of our makeup and who we are as individuals. I think for many years we have pulled from aspects of our own personalities and our own selves to craft our characters, so it all comes from a place that is within us already. It's gonna be really tough hanging up those boots and hanging up the keys to the Impala. I've been doing this the majority of my adult life, and it's been quite a ride. This show changed our lives fifteen years ago, it's changed our lives several times since, and we will never be the same.

When I look back on *Supernatural* and what I'm proud of, it's that we got to the tell the story of Sam and Dean and how they always kept fighting against whatever odds and whatever struggles. What has made the most difference to people in real life is that the show has carried that message. We started out thinking we were making a horror show about monsters, but it became clear pretty quickly that's not what made the show important. So many fans have told me that what is special is that it's a show about two brothers who will do anything to fight for each other and to fight to save the world. Not in a way that people tell them to or according to what's written in a book, but by making their own choices about what's right and wrong and always trying to do what's right. That's the legacy of the show and that's what has made a difference.

And let's be clear. *Supernatural* will never end. The show might, but what it has built? This will never end. Besides, nothing ever stays dead on *Supernatural.*

A SPECIAL MESSAGE FROM MISHA COLLINS

Supernatural has changed all our lives.

I'm grateful for all the good things it's brought, not only to me but to the world. I hope that in the future, this fandom continues to function as a family and be a force for good even after the show is over. Even though the show will end, this family is not going anywhere. It's going to be a part of us for all of our lives.

IMAGE CREDITS

INTERIOR

Pages 2 (left, middle), 11, 13, 208, 228, 257, 265, 271, 274 by Kim Prior
Pages 2 (right), 29, 33, 100, 148, 163, 247 by Krista Martin
Pages 6, 260, 263 by Liz Madsen
Pages 7, 17, 22, 84, 85, 88, 93, 95, 97, 98, 125, 154, 155, 172, 182, 185, 203, 224 by Sherri Dahl (shr2dal)
Pages 24, 61, 146, 173, 187 by Chris Schmelke
Pages 50, 55, 56 by Tedra Ashley-Wannemuehler
Pages 73 by Rebecca Roberts
Pages 78, 105, 144, 198, 199, 200 by Mary Twist
Pages 108 by Brendan Taylor
Pages 122, 123, 275 by Monica Duff
Pages 130 by Hansi Oppenheimer Squee Projects, LLC
Pages 134, 189, 239 by Suzanne McLean

INSERT

Page 1 (top right, bottom), 13 (top) by Suzanne McLean
Page 1 (top left), 3 (bottom left, bottom right), 4 (bottom left, bottom right), 13 (bottom left, bottom right), 14 (bottom left), 16 (top) by Krista Martin

ACKNOWLEDGMENTS

Thank you to all the contributors who shared their stories and art and photos to celebrate fifteen years of a television show that has meant so much to so many of us. Both the actors who brought the show to life and the fans whose lives it has enriched wrote candidly about their own journeys with *Supernatural*. It was sometimes difficult as we all tried to cope with the reality of *Supernatural* coming to an end, but everyone wanted to put together a way to remember how special this show and this experience have been.

So much gratitude to the wonderful people at BenBella who once again partnered with me and the SPNFamily to create this book, especially Leah Wilson (who never quibbled with way too many emails in a day), as well as hardworking editor Joe Rhatigan, and the amazing Tanya Wardell, Monica Lowry, Alicia Kania, and Sarah Avinger for all their help. Special thanks to Cristine Griffin for once again creating magic with her beautiful cover art, and my partner in crime Kim Prior for pulling together all the glorious photos that brighten the book's pages (and taking lots of them). Thanks also to the Creation Entertainment folks who bring the SPNFamily together at conventions, especially Adam Malin, Gary Berman, Stephanie Dizon, Monica Gillen, Chris Schmelke, Leticia Serafin, and the unstoppable Liz and Kristen Madsen.

As always, I'm grateful that my supportive family and my professional colleagues all do their best to understand the importance of this little television show in my life and my career. A special thanks to the ones who really do "get it" and often share "it" with me, especially Kim Prior, Laurena Aker, Alana King, Mary "Max" Holston, my first partner in fandom crime Kathy Larsen, Alicia Ramos, and the OG LJ gang that has been with me from the start, and (always) Ashton Zeto. This wild ride wouldn't have been the same without you (and frankly I'm not sure I would have survived it!).

Finally, a special thank you to Jared Padalecki, Jensen Ackles, and Misha Collins, who made this show what it is and never stopped caring about the characters that mean so much to the SPNFamily that has grown up around them. And to Eric Kripke, a debt of gratitude that I'll never be able to repay for creating this little show that changed so many lives.

ABOUT THE EDITOR

Lynn Zubernis is a clinical psychologist and professor at West Chester University, and a passionate fangirl. She has researched and written about fandom for the past fifteen years, after falling head over heels in love with *Supernatural* shortly after its debut. Her first edited collection with essays from the *Supernatural* cast and fans is *Family Don't End with Blood: Cast and Fans on How Supernatural Has Changed Lives*, including Jared Padalecki's moving and very personal story of battling anxiety and depression. Along with fellow pop culture psychologist Travis Langley, Lynn also edited *Supernatural Psychology: Roads Less Traveled*. Lynn and fellow fangirl/professor Katherine Larsen have written *Fandom at the Crossroads* and edited *Fan Phenomena: Supernatural* and *Fan Culture: Theory/Practice*. Lynn and Kathy told their own story of being fangirls (and why that's awesome) in *Fangasm: Supernatural Fangirls*. Lynn has also written for *Slate*, *Supernatural Magazine*, *The Conversation*, *Frolic*, and *MovieTVTechGeeks*. She blogs at fangasmthebook.com about fandom and, of course, *Supernatural*. Follow her on social media at FangasmSPN on Twitter, Facebook, and Instagram.

The author and publisher will donate 20% of the royalties from sales of *There'll Be Peace When You Are Done* to SPN Survivors and Random Acts.

We hope that the messages in *There'll Be Peace When You Are Done*, from both cast and fans, will encourage us all to be unafraid to ask for help and to be ourselves, to carry out random acts of kindness globally and locally, and to Always Keep Fighting—and that these donations will help SPN Survivors and RA carry on their important work toward these goals.

SPN SURVIVORS is a 501(c)3 nonprofit organization dedicated to promoting mental health, wellness, and suicide prevention through education, outreach, and advocacy. **More information at SPNsurvivors.org.**

RANDOM ACTS is a registered nonprofit whose mission is to conquer the world one random act of kindness at a time. **More information at randomacts.org.**

How a Show, and the Support of Its Fandom, Changed and Saved Lives

FEATURING MORE ESSAYS AND SPECIAL MESSAGES FROM *SUPERNATURAL*'S CAST, INCLUDING:

Jared Padalecki ("Sam Winchester")

Jensen Ackles ("Dean Winchester")

Misha Collins ("Castiel")

Mark Sheppard ("Crowley")

Jim Beaver ("Bobby Singer")

Ruth Connell ("Rowena MacLeod")

Osric Chau ("Kevin Tran")

Rob Benedict ("Chuck Shurley aka God")

Kim Rhodes ("Sheriff Jody Mills")

Briana Buckmaster ("Sheriff Donna Hanscum")

Matt Cohen ("Young John Winchester")

Gil McKinney ("Henry Winchester")

Rachel Miner ("Meg Masters")

FamilyDontEndWithBlood.com

WANT MORE *SUPERNATURAL?*

IN THE HUNT

COMPLETELY UNAUTHORIZED

Unauthorized
Essays on
Supernatural

Edited by
Supernatural.TV

Tanya Huff
Dodger Winslow
Randall M. Jensen
Gregory Stevenson
Avril Hannah-Jones
Robert T. Jeschonek
Tanya Michaels
Amy Garvey

Sheryl A. Rakowski
Mary Borsellino
Jacob Clifton
Carol Poole
Emily Turner
Jamie Chambers
Heather Swain
Jules Wilkinson

Mary Fechter
Tracy S. Morris
Amy Berner
Maria Lima
Shanna Swendson
London E. Brickley